Woke-Proof Your Life

Teresa Mull

Woke-Proof Your Life

A Handbook on Escaping Modern,
Political Madness and Shielding Yourself
and Your Family by Living a More
Self-Sufficient, Fulfilling Life

CRISIS
PUBLICATIONS

Manchester, New Hampshire

To my dear parents,
thank you for woke-proofing my childhood

Contents

Introduction

*D*o *you know what "woke" means?*
I asked a lot of people this question throughout the course of writing this book. Everyone had at least some vague idea of what wokeness is, but most had trouble putting their finger on it. Wokeness, fittingly, has taken on the indefinable nature of pornography, about which Supreme Court Justice Potter Stewart said in 1964, "I know it when I see it."

In fact, Dave, a small-town restaurant owner I interview in chapter three, expressed in words what many furrowed brows and thoughtful *ummms* implied in response to my question: "I'm not sure what it is," he said, "but I know it's bad."

As this is a book about wokeness and how to conquer it, let's define what we're talking about here:

Wokeness (noun): a sociopolitical ideology characterized by the manipulation of noble goals (such as equity, inclusion, social justice, and environmental stewardship) by tyrannical, left-wing zealots for the purpose of controlling and destroying American society.

Woke (adj.): 1. alert for ways in which noble goals can be manipulated for the tyrannical control and destruction of American society.

2. having features of wokeness, i.e., radical left-wing ideologies (redistribution of wealth, racial segregation, totalitarianism); wealthy elitist architects; noble goals that serve as smokescreens for self-serving outcomes; bullying tactics (censorship, cancelation); virtue-signaling; fearmongering.

Regarding the Book's Purpose

If you're like most Americans, you've sensed society growing decidedly more divisive, hostile, and stressful since the COVID-19 outbreak.

Have you ever walked through a neighborhood, and had a single dog bark at you? Another dog barks in response, and the next thing you know, the entire street is a deafening chorus of agitated dogs barking at you for no reason. The only way to get them to stop is to throw a treat or a toy their way.

In these woke days, daily life can often feel like a lot of people are barking senselessly at you. You can get them to stop momentarily by meeting their demands — reparations or exalted status, usually — but the next time you walk through the neighborhood, they'll bark again. The best thing to do is to keep on walking and going forward, to avoid that part of town altogether.

One aim of this book is to diagnose America's ailment: how did our society get this way? Another is to offer a cure: how do we recover?

Our country's collective moral compass has been haywire for some time, but COVID offered the perfect chaotic, fear-filled storm for the devil to bring down the Shining City on the Hill that he's been chipping away at for decades.

In these pages, I seek to demonstrate how:
- The sexual revolution led to increased godlessness
- A godless society becomes a self-absorbed one
- An excess of advanced technology creates a soft, entitled, bored, and boring society

- Digital media, and social media in particular, preys upon empty, lonely, purposeless people and fuels their egocentric vices and misery
- Boredom and isolation amplified by COVID mandates led to increased screen time
- Digital platforms are ideally suited to stoke fear and division
- Screen time, fear, and division accelerated the national mental health crisis
- Wokeness is dependent on screen time and a mentally compromised society to succeed
- Wokeness is a poison more lethal than most people realize
- By boycotting the rotten woke culture, returning to God, and embracing the Judeo-Christian values and traditions that made America the greatest country in the world, we can build an impenetrable, alternative society of our own that is immune to woke forces

Rather than continue getting punched in the face by woke sucker-punches, this book's intent is to guide like-minded, traditional Americans to a separate path that is outside the reach of wokeness. When fighting is futile, we should focus on self-preservation and on cultivating a community so strong, woke attacks don't make a dent. For every woke action, we must execute an equal and opposite reaction, and sometimes, the most devastating thing you can do to the woke mob is to offer them no reaction at all.

Realize it, my brethren;—everyone who breathes, high and low, educated and ignorant, young and old, man and woman, has a mission, has a work. We are not sent into this world for nothing; we are not born at random.... God sees every one of us; He creates every soul, He lodges it in the body, one by one, for a purpose. He needs, He deigns to need, every one of us. He has an end for each of us; we are all equal in His sight,

> and we are placed in our different ranks and stations,
> not to get what we can out of them for ourselves, but
> to labor in them for Him. As Christ has His work,
> we too have ours; as He rejoiced to do His work, we
> must rejoice in ours also. (St. John Henry Newman)

On the Style

Alienation and division are two chief weapons of wokeness, and so to overcome this cultural scourge, we must band together and present a united front. I've written this book hoping to reassure normal, non-woke Americans that not only are they not "the only one," but quite the opposite: they are in excellent, vast company.

I also aspire to foster a community of like-minded people who can instruct, encourage, inspire, enjoy, and learn from one another. To this end, I maintain a casual, conversational style throughout this book, wishing to convey a sense that we're friends, chatting over a cup of coffee. Part cultural analysis, part reference book, part solution-oriented ranting, part self-help book, part happy warrior pep-talk, and part memoir (I'm in the process of woke-proofing my life, too!), I hope this work strengthens readers' convictions and provides points and perspectives helpful in persuading others to pursue a woke-proof life. If nothing else, it's always nice to have your own convictions validated by others, right?

My aim is to offer a holistic approach to woke-proofing your life by appealing to the mind (and follow-the-science types) through facts, figures, and statistics; to the heart, with personal anecdotes and first-person, "been-there-done-that" proof; and to the soul, through the reassurance of Sacred Scripture and of many holy men and women whose insights are scattered throughout like so many pearls of wisdom.

I do not purport to have discovered anything new about human nature or to present revolutionary ways by which to enhance our earthly existence and our chance of making it to Heaven. The point is to *return* to the habits that throughout human existence have never failed us. I hope to impress upon readers how far off the path of civil society we've wandered, remind people how much more pleasant and functional culture was just a few years ago, and present old knowledge and tried and true wisdom in a fresh, enticing, hope-filled way for the world-weary.

About the Interviews

I've included *lots* of insight from people much wiser, more experienced, and more virtuous than I am. That said, the theories and views expounded throughout are formed from the perspective of a traditional, conservative Catholic, and unless explicitly indicated, should be applied to me, the author, and me alone. Only three of my interviewees, that I'm aware of, are Catholic.

The beauty of the woke-proof lifestyle is that its benefits are universal; adoption of woke-proof principles provides neutral territory where everyone can lead health-enhancing, virtuous lives apart from political turmoil. And so, for instance, I did not ask my homeschooling resources what they thought of climate change, or my sociologist self-sufficiency expert her opinion of environmental, social, and governance (ESG). The point of woke-proofing your life is to *not* have to talk about these things!

What unites all of the sources in this book is a common desire to escape modern sociopolitical madness and protect your family by living a more self-sufficient, fulfilling life.

> Be one of the small number who find the way to life, and enter by the narrow gate into Heaven. Take care not to follow the majority and the common herd, so many of whom are lost. Do not be deceived; there are only two roads: one that leads to life and is narrow; the other that leads to death and is wide. There is no middle way. (St. Louis de Montfort)

1

Battle Fatigue
Are You Fed Up Yet?

My brother Geoffrey and I are best friends. We animate one another and have the most fun when we're together. Geoff is slightly older than I am, but *much* wiser, so on nights we're tempted to hang out a while longer and indulge in one more round, he will remind me: "No one ever woke up the next morning and said, 'Man, I wish I'd stayed up later last night and drunk more.'"

This maxim comes to my mind often. When I see a couple sitting across from each another at a restaurant, silently absorbed by their respective phones, I wonder, "Will they regret not interacting more with their loved one?"

When I scroll through a news feed and learn of someone's untimely death, I look away and consider guiltily, "I will die one day, possibly sooner than I expect. What am I doing wasting my precious time in this mindless way?"

When I drag myself away from the duties of my desk job for a walk with my dog in nature, I always feel my mood boosted and my spirit refreshed. I invariably ask myself, "Why didn't you do this sooner? And why don't you do this more often?"

The time I feel the pull of *"What even am I doing?"* most, though, is when I find myself mid-rant about how it isn't fair that a transgender "woman" gets to swim on the women's team, or why "fat activism" is harmful, or why Black Lives Matter's habit of torching private businesses is wrong, or why five-year-olds shouldn't be subjected to a "drag queen story hour," or some other very obvious argument that should never have to be articulated.

It is in these exasperated moments that I'm most compelled to wonder, "Why must I waste my energy on this? Why am I enabling the radical, progressive mob, which has zero interest in honest debate and has no concern whatsoever for the truth, to rob me of my valuable time, energy, and brainspace?"

> "Time is the currency of life. Spend it
> wisely." (bumper sticker on tractor trailer
> in Connecticut, September 2022)

Chances are you picked up this book because you are sick and tired of having to contend with and finance depraved political and cultural campaigns rampant in everyday life. You are not alone: A poll released in April 2021 found 58 percent of Americans "oppose any type of corporation using its power to influence any type of political, cultural, or social change across the country."[1] Only 35 percent support such behavior. Similarly, a poll released in February 2023 found, "78.8 percent [of respondents] said they were more likely to do business with a company that stayed politically neutral and tolerated viewpoints of employees and customers across the board. Just under 59 percent said they were 'much more likely.' "[2] Another poll published in October 2022 found that 64

---

[1]   Jacob Bliss, "Poll: Most Americans Oppose Woke Corporations," *Breitbart*, April 15, 2021, https://www.breitbart.com/politics/2021/04/15/poll-most-americans -oppose-woke-corporations/.
[2]   Jacob Bliss, "Poll: Most American Voters Prefer Businesses to Stay Out of Politics," *Breitbart*, February 15, 2023, https://www.breitbart.com/politics/2023/02/15/ poll-most-americans-voters-prefer-businesses-stay-out-politics/.

percent of voters blamed woke politicians for the crime surge.[3] And as of July 2021, just one-third of people identified as "woke."[4]

Clearly, the numbers are on our side. A majority of Americans maintain the same traditional principles you do, have commonsense, and long for the days when bringing up politics or religion was considered impolite. Yet, somehow, we let popular trends and the media dictate the woke narrative. Now, it's nearly a sin of omission if you don't use any excuse to spout off about which bathroom(s) a non-binary trans-demisexual who identifies as a cloud has the right to use.[5]

We've gotten way off the path of civility, and, dare I say, *normalcy.* A lot of younger folks, too, have never known a time when virtue signaling was not a prerequisite to establishing social status, getting into college, and advancing their careers.

Don't be fooled. Just because the progressive extremists are loud and well-funded doesn't mean the rest of us are outnumbered or overmatched. Millions of Americans feel the same way you do: burnt out from the 24/7 doomsday news cycles, bleary-eyed consumerism, interstate traffic jams, and omnipresent identity politics. We're up to our eyeballs in pronouns, microaggressions, robocalls, lawsuits, triggers, TikToks, and guilt trips. And we all just want a break.

We've been cowed, coerced, and canceled with labels of "homophobe," "xenophobe," "transphobe," "racist," "fat-shamer," and "white nationalist" for long enough. We know that we are decent people and that our Judeo-Christian American values are what made our country

[3] Harvard CAPS/Harris Poll, "Key Results – October," October 2022, https://harvardharrispoll.com/key-results-october-3/.

[4] Gabriela Schulte, "Poll: One-third of voters identify as 'woke,'" *The Hill,* July 16, 2021, https://thehill.com/hilltv/what-americas-thinking/563415-poll-one-third-of-voters-identify-as-woke/.

[5] Callie Beusman, "'I Look at a Cloud and I See It as Me': The People Who Identify As Objects," *Vice,* August 3, 2016, https://www.vice.com/en/article/zmbeae/i-look-at-a-cloud-and-i-see-it-as-me-the-people-who-identify-as-objects.

the best in the world — not a mark of shame to apologize for. We are nostalgic for a time before powerful progressives turned every aspect of our lives into a radical social cause. And we maintain an intuition that we still have a lot more in common than not.

Blessed are they who are persecuted for the sake of righteousness, for theirs is the kingdom of heaven. Blessed are you when they insult you and persecute you and utter every kind of evil against you [falsely] because of me. Rejoice and be glad, for your reward will be great in heaven. Thus they persecuted the prophets who were before you. (Matthew 5:10–12)

NORMAL: Non-Woke, Ordinary, Rational, Moral, American Leader

Since the name of the modern game is "self-identity", let's play along and get a jump on the label-makers. Let's identify ourselves. We are NOR-MAL: Non-Woke, Ordinary, Rational, Moral, American Leaders. We believe in right and wrong, that men and women are beautifully different, that children's innocence should be preserved for as long as possible, that all people, regardless of race, sexual orientation, or "identity," are created equal and endowed by our Creator with the unalienable right to life, liberty, and the pursuit of happiness. We believe the laws of nature exist as laws for a reason and that our world operates optimally when those laws are obeyed. We don't eye our neighbors as a likely enemy, looking for ways they (or their long-dead relatives) have unwittingly slighted us and now owe us something. We're peace-loving folk who'd rather help one another thrive than accuse and punish each other.

This book provides practical ways we, the canceled majority, can stand up for ourselves and restore America's values and culture. Remember that you were put on this earth for much more than struggling with a small group of irrational Internet bullies. When you think of what brings you the deepest fulfillment in life, the moments you treasure the most and the memories you look back on with the deepest fondness, do they involve buying a bunch of stuff, being mindlessly entertained, showing off online, or slobbing away on the couch with a box of Grubhub in one hand and a phone in the other?

Trust me: at the end of the day, you will not regret *not* spending more time engaged in a futile war with people who are unable (or unwilling) to define the word "woman" and who think a man can give birth.

If you relate to this feeling of exhaustion and alienation from society, you are in crowded (and obviously great) company. Most Americans are disenchanted with this modern life. Studies show — and a trip to, say, any nearby airport will confirm — that modern humans in general are miserable.

Anxiety, Depression, Drugs, Crime, Obesity, and Stress

In 2022, happiness levels reached "record lows."[6] The American Psychological Association reported recently that stress in the U.S. has reached "alarming levels."[7] Nearly 20 percent of American adults (50 million people) suffer from mental illness. Cases of suicidal ideation, major depression, and anxiety have spiked dramatically in recent years and continue to rise, especially among the young.[8]

---

[6] Harry Enten, "American happiness hits record lows," *CNN*, February 2, 2022, https://www.cnn.com/2022/02/02/politics/unhappiness-americans-gallup-analysis/index.html.

[7] American Psychological Association, "Inflation, war push stress to alarming levels at two-year COVID-19 anniversary," *APA*, March 10, 2022, https://www.apa.org/news/press/releases/2022/03/inflation-war-stress.

[8] World Health Organization, "COVID-19 pandemic triggers 25% increase in prevalence of anxiety and depression worldwide," *WHO*, March 2, 2022, https://

Remember how difficult it was to "fit in" as a child and teenager? Imagine those awkward, difficult teenage years now, with your every flaw or perceived misstep magnified by the pressures of social media and broadcast to the whole world. Think, too, about wanting to wear trendy clothes, listen to "cool" music, and so forth, and how these challenging aspects of growing up have been compounded by keeping up with changing woke terminology. The pressure not to say the wrong thing or insult your peers must be immense, especially as expectations change by the day.

Nearly 42 percent of Americans are obese,[9] costing us billions of dollars in health care and causing self-inflicted suffering and hundreds of thousands of premature, preventable deaths each year.[10] Drug and alcohol abuse and addiction are at record levels.[11] The number of Americans using hallucinogens has skyrocketed in recent years.[12] Violent crime is increasing.[13] About half of marriages end in divorce. In recent years, this rate has declined slightly, but only as marriage rates have also hit historic lows.[14] The U.S. Census reports the number of children living with only their mother has doubled since 1968: "About 7.6 million (11 percent)

www.who.int/news/item/02-03-2022-covid-19-pandemic-triggers-25-increase-in-prevalence-of-anxiety-and-depression-worldwide.

9   Centers for Disease Control and Prevention, "Adult Obesity Facts," *CDC*, May 17, 2022, https://www.cdc.gov/obesity/data/adult.html.

10 University of Cambridge, "Obesity linked to premature death, with greatest effect in men," *The Lancet*, July 13, 2016, https://www.cam.ac.uk/research/news/obesity-linked-to-premature-death-with-greatest-effect-in-men.

11 American Addiction Centers, "Alcohol and Drug Abuse Statistics," October 21, 2022, https://americanaddictioncenters.org/rehab-guide/addiction-statistics.

12 Columbia University Mailman School of Public Health, "New Study Estimates Over 5.5 Million U.S. Adults Use Hallucinogens," *National Institute on Drug Abuse*, August 18, 2022, https://www.publichealth.columbia.edu/public-health-now/news/new-study-estimates-over-55-million-us-adults-use-hallucinogens.

13 Richard Berk, "Is Violent Crime Increasing?" Penn Arts & Sciences Department of Criminology, https://crim.sas.upenn.edu/fact-check/violent-crime-increasing.

14 Joseph Chamie, "The end of marriage in America?" *The Hill*, August 10, 2021, https://thehill.com/opinion/finance/567107-the-end-of-marriage-in-america/.

children lived with their mother only in 1968 compared to 15.3 million (21 percent) in 2020."[15]

But the devil comes with his artful wiles, and, under the color of doing good, sets about undermining [the soul] in trivial ways, and working it in practices which, so he gives it to understand, are not wrong; little by little he darkens its understanding and weakens its will, and causes its self-love to increase in one way or another he begins to withdraw it from the love of God and persuade to indulge its own wishes. (St. Teresa of Ávila)

The mental health crisis isn't limited to young people plagued by the pressure of being hip, either. The U.S. Preventive Services Task Force now recommends that "all adults under 65 be screened at their doctor's office for anxiety."[16]

"Experts" will cite such things as inflation, war, and the aftermath of the COVID-19 outbreak as top reasons for people's despair and suffering. The COVID outbreak certainly enabled architects of evil to incite fear for the purpose of isolating, manipulating, and controlling people, and to pit people against each other with greater ease. But economic hardship, conflict, and disease have always been part of the human experience. So how is it that now, when most people in America have extremely easy access not only to basic survival needs, but also to luxuries — "80 percent

---

[15] Paul Hemez and Chanell Washington, "Number of Children Living Only With Their Mothers Has Doubled in Past 50 Years," United States Census Bureau, April 12, 2021, https://www.census.gov/library/stories/2021/04/number-of-children-living-only-with-their-mothers-has-doubled-in-past-50-years.html.

[16] Korin Miller, "Health Panel Now Calls for Anxiety Screenings for People Under 65," *Prevention*, September 21, 2022, https://www.prevention.com/health/a41314502/anxiety-screening-under-65/.

of U.S households have at least one smart TV, or smart something;"[17] "97 percent of Americans now own a cell phone of some kind"[18] — we are all much more wretched than we've ever been? What's changed so radically in just a few years' time?

Choose Your Battles

Think back just a few years ago: things were simpler. Life moved at a slower pace. Most of us remember a time when you knew your neighbors on a first-name basis, when you could send your kids to the local school on the bus (or, heck, even let them *walk* to school ... imagine!), confident that what they were learning was nothing more than reading, writing, arithmetic, the Pledge of Allegiance, and how to play baseball.

When you could sit down to take-out with your family without realizing you just donated 10 percent of your bill to transgender college athletes, carbon-neutral shoes for underprivileged, endangered newts, or some other social justice cause *du jour*. You could watch the evening news — and *just* the evening news — and hear a generally straightforward account of the day's events, untarnished by political bias and sensationalism. You could relax afterward with a television program that contained neither preachy racial messaging nor transsexual overtones and was not peppered with advertisements reminding you how sexist traditional gender roles are.[19]

---

[17] Stephen Silver, "80 Percent of U.S. Households Have At Least One Smart TV (Or Smart Something)," *National Interest,* June 10, 2021, https://nationalinterest. org/blog/techland/80-percent-us-households-have-least-one-smart-tv-or-smart-something-187418.

[18] Pew Research Center, "Mobile phone ownership over time," April 7, 2021, https://www.pewresearch.org/internet/fact-sheet/mobile/.

[19] Tim Cross, "Did Gillette's 'The Best Men Can Be' Campaign Succeed? Here's What the Data Said..." *Videoweek,* January 17, 2019, https://videoweek. com/2019/01/17/did-gillettes-the-best-men-can-be-campaign-succeed-heres-what-the-data-said/.

> I want your heart to be like this: well compact and
> closed on all sides, so that if the worries and storms
> of the world, the evil spirit, and the flesh come upon
> it, it will not be penetrated. Leave but one opening to
> your heart, that is toward heaven. (St. Padre Pio)

These days, though, nearly every element of our lives involves a socio-political fight of some sort. We're forced to pick sides of the "social and racial justice" debate when we choose our cereal (as if choosing between oats 'n honey and maple cinnamon weren't already hard enough!).[20] We must identify as or with someone or something far-left when we do the most basic, seemingly innocent things, such as watching professional sports or staying at a hotel. Even buying candy involves making a statement nowadays: so-called "queer artists" designed a special Pride Month Skittles package to encourage people to "see the rainbow."[21]

There is, of course, no escaping the lifelong spiritual warfare that is the duty of us NORMALs to engage in "from cradle to grave," but we must pick and choose our battles. It is easy to become caught up in and righteously angered over the absurdity of woke poisons, which seem to seep into more crevices with increased potency every day. But to allow these things to overshadow the overwhelming beauty and goodness of our world and to consume us completely, to the point that we're constantly agitated and distracted from nobler work, is a disservice to God and His countless gifts. We must fight, yes, bravely and unwaveringly, but we must do so strategically and in a balanced way that does not sacrifice our sense of calm joy in the face of adversity.

[20] John Carney, "Breitbart Business Digest: Kellogg's Is Dying of Wokeness," *Breitbart*, June 21, 2022, https://www.breitbart.com/economy/2022/06/21/breitbart-business-digest-kelloggs-is-dying-of-wokeness/.

[21] Dan Avery, "Pride 2022: Food and Drink Brands Giving Back to LGBTQ Causes," *CNET*, June 24, 2022, https://www.cnet.com/deals/pride-2022-snack-brands-giving-back-to-lgbt-causes/.

This approach does not mean we're compromising, giving up, burying our heads in the sand, or running away from reality; it's about returning to the ways of our fathers and building an impenetrable fortress that fosters truth, beauty, and goodness within a harmonious community that respects human dignity, promotes service, honors and celebrates creation, and fortifies true virtue.

Remember that even Jesus instructed His disciples not to waste their time on those determined not to listen: "And if the house is worthy, let your peace come upon it; but if it is not worthy, let your peace return to you. And if any one will not receive you or listen to your words, shake off the dust from your feet as you leave that house or town." (Matt. 10:13–14)

Irreconcilable Differences?

We are called to be *in* the world but not of the world (John 17). To woke-proof your life is to return to a calmer, community-minded, nature-centered, Christian way of living. Consider it a rural revival, if not actually physically, then at least in a slower-paced, country kind of mindset that maintains Christ as its focus and keeps the distractions of the world at arm's length.

The foundation of the woke-proof movement can be summed-up in two words: *simplify* and *localize*. Free from the false fears perpetrated by modern progressive culture, we can focus on what truly matters: building a life based on love of God and service to Him and to our neighbor.

The point here isn't that we, the NORMALs, need to become survivalist preppers, live off-the-grid, and learn to tan beaver pelts (though that sounds pretty cool, too). But somewhere between the Amish and the Pride Parades, there's got to be a middle ground.

The journey to woke-proofing your life will involve recognizing when debate is worthwhile and when your time would be better spent on other activities. I find it helpful to view the current sociopolitical climate as one might a flash-in-the-pan celebrity marriage. The go-to excuse for divorce in Hollywood is "irreconcilable differences," with ex-couples explaining how they arrived at the "difficult decision" to separate after their lives took them on "different paths." Though, of course, they will continue to navigate co-parenting and will lovingly remain best friends as they move forward . . . *separately.*

Oh, that American society would embrace the "dignity" and "respect" these luminaries purport to have for their former flames after concluding they no longer have anything in common with them! Let us take a cue from these enlightened, famous folk and consider how the NORMALs, who view the world as it is, can possibly work together with a set of extremists who make acting out a sex scene between gay and transgender couples a required part of their high school curriculum.[22]

Let's give celebrities credit where it's due. Sometimes, there's simply no way to reconcile with people whose views and practices are so contrary to our own. It's impossible to journey along the same path when your fellow traveler is determined to arrive at a different destination. This does not mean NORMALs need to stop, drop, and roll any time something woke comes our way (this maneuver is reserved for avoiding awkward encounters in public places), but it is certainly our duty to safeguard our senses, that we might use the precious time we are given on this earth productively.

Again, we should not write people off out of hand or impose an old-fashioned shunning on them simply because they espouse some woke ideologies. We are to judge people "by the content of their character," and proceed accordingly.

---

[22] Patrick Hauf, "Thousands of Massachusetts Parents Pull Kids From 'Woke' Sex Ed Classes," *Washington Free Beacon*, November 13, 2021, https://freebeacon. com/campus/thousands-of-massachusetts-parents-pull-kids-from-woke-sex -ed-classes/.

Wasting time is not in our creed. (Mr. Vladimir
Belcher, my high school history teacher)

Some people would rather not be bothered. They are annoyed by wokeness and do not comprehend the evil ends toward which the ideology tends. They haven't analyzed the situation deeply enough to realize that, as the saying goes, "The road to Hell is paved with good intentions" — or in the woke case, with intentions *claiming* to be good.

Other people are timid, adopting a go-along-to-get-along code of conduct so as not to ruffle feathers. Many naturally conservative-minded people are polite and kind and want to "be nice" to people, which is how we got into this woke mess in the first place. I get it, believe me; I hate confrontation more than anyone I know. But guilt is harder to reconcile with than the passing awkwardness of having to decline your neighbor's invitation to their daughter's same-sex wedding, or the momentary discomfort of asking your friend if you can meet somewhere other than the coffeeshop with the Black Lives Matter sticker on the window. Author Jon Acuff refers to this tendency as *toxic empathy*: "When someone I love is headed toward a health, financial or relational train wreck and instead of telling them the bridge is out I encourage or even celebrate the decisions that are slowly destroying them because I want them to like me."

Many other people are understandably taken in by the powerful woke rhetoric. Having not paused to consider the long-term consequences of the movement they profess to support, they "know not what they do." The woke puppet masters are cunning, using vague, fell-good terminology and capitalizing on heightened emotions to manipulate the public.

These people, with a "foundation built on sand" (Matt. 7:26), are easily swayed. They genuinely and understandably fall for the chicanery. We NORMALs have had it drilled into us from birth that we are to care for the poor, to feed the hungry, give drink to the thirsty, and welcome strangers. This certainly doesn't just mean simply in a tangible sense. So many people today are poor in spirit, hungry for love, thirsting for truth, and lonely for God's friendship. I often think of the opening lines of *The Great Gatsby*: "Just remember that all the people in this world haven't had the advantages that you've had." Not everyone has been blessed to grow up in a faith-filled household, or to be born with natural humility, or to have encountered an abundance of love and beauty from an early age. Keep this in mind, and let us have compassion on our neighbors.

It is the duty of every NORMAL to build our foundations of stone, which the winds and floods of pagan culture cannot shake (Luke 6:48). Those who fail to anchor themselves to the truth risk being carried off and lost in the confusing sea of "evolving" ideologies. Truth does not evolve. Those who argue over what is good and bad, right and wrong, have no basis for doing so if they do not believe truth is unchanging. If truth is relative, then nothing is worth debating. It is the duty of those blessed with the gift of prudence to try to share it with others — to attempt to guide the misled, foolish, and evil ones gently to the truth with compassion, reason, empathy, facts, and by example — helpfully spelled out in these pages with cases of real-life, virtuous people doing just that!

> Dismiss all anger and look into yourself a little.
> Remember that he of whom you are speaking is
> your brother, and as he is in the way of salvation,
> God can make him a saint, in spite of his present
> weakness. (St. Thomas of Villanova)

Keep in mind that many in the woke tribe are nihilists. The only "truth" they believe in is whatever ideology they can mold and reform as needed for earthly gain. These people blatantly reject the truth and will shamelessly do or say whatever it takes to earn tenure at Sarah Lawrence College, be re-elected, excuse their own depravities, satisfy an emotional flight of fancy, impress their Twitter followers, and on and on. Arguing with these people is a waste of breath. It's like playing cards with a six-year-old who knows just enough to change the rules of the game when he starts losing, but isn't clever enough to realize that you're onto his trick.

It's one thing to be a hypocrite; as none of us is perfect, we all are bound to stumble in contradiction to the beliefs we profess. What sets the class of woke hypocrites apart, though, is their ability to excuse and justify their behavior — never admitting their double standards, but arrogantly excusing and evading fault with the skill of Barry Sanders dodging linebackers (and safeties, and linemen, and…).

Let's use a quick example to illustrate my point. Recall what things were like in 2020. Businesses were shuttered and Americans were ordered to isolate at home and quarantine, to wear masks if they *had* to leave their houses and postpone weddings and miss family funerals in the name of protecting everyone from the COVID-19 virus. Then-U.S. Speaker of the House Nancy Pelosi beat the drum in how necessary it was to shut down the entire country, declaring, "what we have to do is shelter in place. That is really the answer." She said it was "really unfortunate" that protestors were disobeying lockdown orders.[23] But then, Nancy, not wearing a mask, visited a hair salon at the height of the pandemic. The salon was closed due to the COVID mandates she championed. When she got caught, Pelosi called it "a set-up" and shamelessly said, "This salon owes me an apology."[24]

A lesson for life: before you try to debate someone, first establish whether the other person believes in right and wrong, whether truth is absolute, and whether he or she practices what she preaches.

---

[23] Melissa Leon, "Nancy Pelosi says people protesting stay-at-home orders is 'really unfortunate,'" April 18, 2020, *Fox News*, https://www.foxnews.com/media/nancy-pelosi-protests-stay-at-home-orders-chris-wallace-fox-news-sunday.

[24] Seema Mehta, "Nancy Pelosi says her visit to a hair salon was a 'setup.' Stylist backs her up," *Los Angeles Times*, September 20, 2020, https://www.latimes.com/politics/story/2020-09-02/pelosi-hair-fallout-salon-mask.

Selfie-Centered and Anti-Social Media

Recall again the not-so-very-distant past: it was safe to assume that your average fellow American believed in God, the principles of an Abrahamic religion, the Ten Commandments, civic duty, and patriotism. People would debate the nitty-gritty details for creating a thriving society, but at least we stood on common ground when it came to what a successful country should look like. Generally, it was safe to assume people outside of the nuthouse believed in self-evident truths.

But then, something changed, and it's been snowballing ever since. In an ever more desperate attempt to destroy NORMALs' healthy, wholesome lifestyles, the left began using more extreme tactics and moving the goalposts to undermine our Christian society.

For example, consider how, in 2020, the *New York Times* chronicled Joe Biden's "evolution on LGBTQ rights," writing:

> Joseph R. Biden Jr. voted for the Defense of Marriage Act in 1996, blocking federal recognition of same-sex marriages. Two years earlier, he voted to cut off federal funds to schools that teach the acceptance of homosexuality. In 1973, Mr. Biden, in an off-handed response to a question, wondered if homosexuals in the military or government were potential security risks.
>
> But today, Mr. Biden, the presumptive Democratic nominee for president, has so completely identified himself with positions embraced by L.G.B.T.Q. leaders that his history on gay rights has faded into the mist. If he is elected president, said Chad Griffin, a political consultant and longtime gay rights leader, Mr. Biden, the former vice president, will be the "most pro-equality president we have ever had."[25]

---

[25] Adam Nagourney and Thomas Kaplan, "Behind Joe Biden's Evolution on L.G.B.T.Q. Rights," *The New York Times*, June 21, 2020, https://www.nytimes.com/2020/06/21/us/politics/biden-gay-rights-lgbt.html.

The same "coming around" to progressive extremism can be seen in the career of the Clintons. Bill Clinton signed the Defense of Marriage Act and the "Don't Ask, Don't Tell" legislation,[26] and Hillary changed her mind on the issue just before she launched her 2016 presidential campaign.[27] Ditto Barack Obama, and many Democrats who have shamelessly increased their support for whatever sort of policy will make them appear "tolerant" and "inclusive."[28]

Tweaking one's views on things and changing one's mind upon further learning and reflection is, of course, a mature, honest, healthy thing to do — and also the point of this book. What I'm describing here is not that. So-called conservatives and Republicans are guilty of "evolving" on issues too, but the frequency, speed, and degree to which radical, left-wing power-seekers alter their views is unmatched. Their evolution is about as mature as a six-year-old girl declaring her favorite color and about as honest (and self-serving) as telling said six-year-old girl her teddy bear can't play right now because "it's tired." As far as health goes — well, just look at the health crisis the increase of such "progressive" tendencies has wrought, and tell me if a foundation of sand (sorry, *evolution*) is a positive thing.

Remember when, in 1992, Bill Clinton called for abortion to be "safe, legal, and rare"?[29] Fast-forward to 2022, when *Roe v. Wade* was overruled,

[26] Simone Pathé, "How Democrats Came Around on Gay Rights," *Roll Call*, July 28, 2016, https://rollcall.com/2016/07/28/how-democrats-came-around-on-gay-rights/.

[27] Dan Merica, "Hillary Clinton Has a New Position on Same-Sex Marriage," *CNN*, April 23, 2015, https://www.cnn.com/2015/04/15/politics/hillary-clinton-same-sex-marriage/.

[28] Ariane de Vogue, "Obama's Evolution On Gay Marriage," *ABC News*, May 10, 2013, https://abcnews.go.com/Politics/obamas-evolution-gay-marriage/story?id=19150614.

[29] Caitlin Flanagan, "Losing the *Rare* in 'Safe, Legal, and Rare,'" *The Atlantic*, December 6, 2019, https://www.theatlantic.com/ideas/archive/2019/12/the-brilliance-of-safe-legal-and-rare/603151/.

and the year Democrats made abortion the top issue of the midterm election cycle. Vice President Kamala Harris declared the Supreme Court's decision "a direct assault on freedom — on the fundamental right of self-determination to which all Americans are entitled." Biden referred to the Court's decision as "an attack" and called "the MAGA crowd" the "most extreme political organization that has existed in American history" for cheering the decision.[30] Abortion went from being preferably "rare" to being "essential to health care."[31]

Progressives remind me of Amy Poehler's character from the cult film *Mean Girls*, who says, "I'm not like a regular mom, I'm a *cool* mom." In trying to be hip and trendy, the "cool mom" offers her daughter and her daughter's friends alcohol and encourages her teenage daughter to hook-up with her boyfriend in the family home. The cool mom's house does become the go-to hangout spot. But the cool mom's daughter is a bratty, self-centered disaster who has zero respect for her mother and only uses her for money and other material benefits. Does that sound like a dead ringer for the entitled victim class the progressives have spawned or what?

Eroding Values and Beliefs

It isn't safe to assume anything these days. In fact, assuming something about another person would be considered stereotyping, and that will land you in Dante's Sixth Circle. The fabric of beliefs that held Americans together is being unraveled by a determined group of woke string-pullers who have started at the top.

---

[30] Danielle Kurtzleben, "Here's why Democrats are making the abortion debate about more than abortion," *NPR*, May 5, 2022, https://www.npr.org/2022/05/05/1096815765/heres-why-democrats-are-making-the-abortion-debate-about-more-than-abortion.

[31] H.R.3755 — 117th Congress, "Women's Health Protection Act of 2021," September 27, 2021, https://www.congress.gov/bill/117th-congress/house-bill/3755/text.

A Gallup poll released in May 2022 found just 81 percent of Americans believe in God, which is down a whole six percentage points from 2017 and marks the lowest level since Gallup began its annual Values and Beliefs survey. Between 1944 and 2011, more than 90 percent of Americans believed in God. In the 1950s and 60s, a consistent 98 percent of respondents believed in God.[32]

> The Christian ideal has not been tried and
> found wanting. It has been found difficult;
> and left untried. (G.K. Chesterton)

More startingly is this report NPR published in September 2022: "A Pew Research Center study shows that as of 2020, about 64 percent of Americans identify as Christian. Fifty years ago, that number was 90 percent."[33]

Christianity has been the linchpin holding our society together since its founding. It is the basis for our Constitution and the rule of law and rules of engagement we take for granted. Without Christian principles, anything goes, like that transgender teacher in Canada with "size-Z prosthetic breasts."[34] This person is allowed near children (though, admittedly, she can't get *too* close to them).

Disparity in the belief in God is just one way to track the divergent mindsets of Americans, but it's a big, far-reaching one. Belief or nonbelief

[32] Jeffrey M. Jones, "Belief in God in U.S. Dips to 81%, a New Low," *Gallup*, June 17, 2022, https://news.gallup.com/poll/393737/belief-god-dips-new-low.aspx.
[33] Sarah McCammon, Michael Levitt , Kathryn Fox, "America's Christian majority is shrinking, and could dip below 50% by 2070," *NPR*, September 15, 2022, https://www.npr.org/2022/09/15/1123289466/americas-christian-majority-is-shrinking-and-could-dip-below-50-by-2070.
[34] Yaron Steinbuch, "Who is Kayla Lemieux? Meet the Canadian teacher with Z-size prosthetic breasts," *New York Post*, March 3, 2023, https://nypost.com/article/who-is-kayla-lemieux-trans-teacher-with-prosthetic-breasts/.

in God dictates the way people perceive life and live it, and what they perceive to be life's objective.

"By Their Fruits You Will Know Them"

A fundamental problem in modern life is that few people take the time to ponder their existence and its purpose, and whether their daily habits are leading them toward or away from a final product they'll be satisfied with when, on their deathbed, they reflect upon it. Thinking about "the big picture" and the four last things — death, judgment, Heaven, and Hell — is passé in a world that prioritizes convenience, pleasure, and instant gratification above all else. The contemporary ethos is that "happiness," manifested in physical and emotional pleasure, is all that matters and is an end in and of itself.

What woke culture is proving by the physical, mental, and spiritual health crises it has brought about is that pleasure-seeking, i.e., doing "what makes you happy," doesn't work. Believing that you can be happy outside of the source of all that is good, and that happiness can be obtained without discipline and sacrifice is the devil's gambit. What the woke disciples are finding out the hard way is that ignoring consequences doesn't do away with the laws of nature that God, in His infinite wisdom, has established for our benefit. You can "do what makes you happy" by eating all the lesbian M&Ms you want, having all the sexual partners your schedule can accommodate, and blaming all your unhappiness on racism, but that still isn't going to make you "happy."

The woke mob is empty and angry, and rather than practice introspection and try to improve their own outlook and circumstances, they, like Adam in the garden, turn to someone else to blame for the miseries brought about by their own disobedience.

It is a characteristic of any decaying civilization that the great masses of the people are unaware of the

25

tragedy. Humanity in a crisis is generally insensitive to the gravity of the times in which it lives. Men do not want to believe their own times are wicked, partly because they have no standards outside of themselves by which to measure their times. If there is no fixed concept of justice, how shall men know it is violated? Only those who live by faith know what is happening in the world; the great masses without faith are unconscious of the destructive processes going on, because they have lost the vision of the heights from which they have fallen. (Fulton J. Sheen)

The Death of Death

Another aspect of culture I find noteworthy, but woefully underreported, is the fading significance of death in modern society. Traditional funerals with a viewing and burial are on the decline and have been for some time.[35] People are now more likely to hold a "celebration of life" and burial service "at a later date convenient to the family." Scattering ashes or opting for an urn that is never picked up from the funeral home are common practices.[36]

What's more, the blessings of modern medicine, technology, and safety advancements mean we don't experience the reality of death that was prevalent a couple generations ago — thank God — before antibiotics, automation, and so many remarkable discoveries increased our life expectancy. Sudden, sometimes tragic death was much more common a hundred years ago, and when someone died, the community would be

[35] National Funeral Home Directors Association Statistics, April 15, 2022, https://nfda.org/news/statistics.
[36] Susan Fraser, "What Happens to Uncollected Ashes?" *In the Light Urns*, May 1, 2015, https://inthelighturns.com/funeral-information/happens-uncollected-ashes.

presented with his corpse, laid out in the parlor of the family home, where people would pay their respects and literally come face to face with death. Now, as our society distances itself from death and avoids the thought of mortality and eternity more and more, the less we consider how our behavior in the here and now affects what comes after.

We've also become so accustomed to constant comfort that minor discomforts and inconveniences vex us disproportionately (the airport is another good place to observe this fact). Discomforts are also, in general, much easier to allay than they've ever been. As our ability to "seek pleasure and avoid pain" becomes cheaper and easier, we lose an appreciation for the reward won from hardship. That suffering could be beneficial is a foreign concept in a time in which there's a treatment for every ache, pain, "crepey skin," receding hairline, pudgy thigh, and overheating knee (seriously, how are you living without the Calming Comfort Cooling Knee Pillow?). Sometimes it seems as if a huge swathe of our society is living inside an infomercial, obsessed with "self-care" and creature comforts. The more entrenched this self-absorption becomes, the more we breed a spoiled, soft, lazy, childish civilization.

> God does not put you in Hell. You put yourself there, because your hearts become so hardened, so stubborn and inclined to seek your own comfort. (Mother Angelica)

My father, a retired Penn State philosophy instructor, has a related theory: our world is so sanitized that we've forgotten our intrinsic human filth. His "outhouse theory" holds that modern man is declining because of his pride, and his collective pride has increased at the same rate as outhouses (and other, shall we say, *more natural* hygiene practices) have been abandoned. Simply using an outhouse regularly, let alone tending to it — sprinkling lime to keep the odors down and scrubbing it — was a lesson in humility, as was shoveling pig manure, using a chamber pot, enduring lice, body odor, and other inconveniences — cold baths, bumpy buggy rides, and so forth.

"Confirm Humanity"

I'll add that as our technology has advanced at warp speed, behavior that ignites the human faculties keeps being circumvented. The other day, while completing some task online, I was asked to tick a box to "Confirm Humanity." We are to the point that technology, known as "CAPTCHA," — Completely Automated Public Turing test to tell Computers and Humans Apart — is asking *us*, "Are you a robot?"

We are less engaged in our natural environment and the activities that have separated humans from beasts than we've ever been. Why get up early and toil in a garden when you can sleep in and go through the Dunkin' Donuts drive-thru later like a sheep that rolls over and instinctively starts munching grass? Why craft a wooden bench by hand out of a tree that fell in your yard when you can order a premade one online from the comfort of your La-Z-Boy? Why take a walk and admire the beautiful details adorning historic houses in the neighborhood when you can get from point A to point B in climate-controlled comfort with a robot telling you exactly where to turn for optimal speed?

Another contributing factor to society losing its humility is in our collective disconnect from the mighty forces of nature. Our ancestors considered and contended with creation constantly. They didn't have the technology to manufacture much and had to rely on the whims of the weather, the benevolence of the soil, the miracle of a homeopathic remedy, and prayer. They had to submit to the unpredictable and uncontrollable mercies of nature — and respect it. They were much more in tune with the Creator, keenly aware of His power, reliant on and humbled by His might.

Nowadays, people will sometimes speak of feeling "humbled" when they stand beside the ocean or witness a magnificent sunset. Yet they are not humbled when they buy a banana from a New England grocery store in the dead of winter, or when they absentmindedly snap a photo with their iPhone and send it to a friend living halfway across the world, or click twice and two days later receive a left-handed banjo on their doorstep from Amazon (who would do such a thing?).

People take for granted that technology is in charge. Humans can create and control much more now than they ever have, and we're forgetting who has granted us our intellect and dominion to be able to do these remarkable things. How is it possible our ancestors understood much less about the physical world and had much more limited control of things than we do, yet were less anxious than we are today? The answer is: because they had more faith than we do.

As we are increasingly separated from creation, we forget how much we rely on the one who created and governs it for our every need, and we become the nine Samaritans who did not come back and thank Jesus when He cleansed us. (Luke 17:11–19)

Our Final Purpose

Once we lose God, we lose our identity. Without God, how are we to know why we were made? What were we made to do? How are we to go about doing "it"?

Let's return to my wise dad and the ancient philosophers for some observation:

Aristotle referred to four "causes," or factors that go into the make-up of a thing, all of which need to be known to have a complete understanding of the thing. Think of Michelangelo confronting a piece of marble he's going to make into a statue. The statue will be made out of the marble, so the material out of which the thing is made Aristotle calls the "material cause"; it contributes to the being of the thing.

We think of a "cause" of something actively doing something, like Michelangelo himself making a statue. He would be what Aristotle calls "the efficient cause," the process that brought about the thing. What's he doing? He's forming that piece of marble and giving it shape, and it ends up being a marble statue of Jesus, let's say. The form that is given to the marble is the formal cause. The thing is composed of matter and form. It is matter that is formed in a certain way. But that matter had to be formed by Michelangelo, the "efficient cause."

Now, Michelangelo had in mind a purpose for that statue. And the purpose of the statue Aristotle calls the "final cause," the final purpose. You don't understand the statue fully unless you understand what it's made of, what it's a statue of, how it was brought into being by the little chippings of the instruments and so forth, and the purpose, the "final cause." The final cause is what's being lost sight of completely today. Think of marriage, for example. What's the purpose of marriage? It is to provide an environment for the upbringing of children. Now when you lose sight of that, you can call anything a "marriage." People have perverse notions of all kinds of things today, because they've divorced things from their final cause, which Aristotle calls the telos.

Most things in nature — animals, for instance, pursue their *telos*, their end or purpose, their final cause, automatically. It's built into them. But people can deviate and must have some understanding of what their final cause is.

The woke agenda, of course, is a major component in the prevailing anti-God, anti-consequences attitude that prioritizes satisfying the self as the human *telos*. This attitude has existed since Genesis, when Adam and Eve chose themselves — their desire to be like gods and for the tree that was "pleasing to the eyes" (Gen. 3:6) — over their love of God. Self-centeredness is at the root of every sin. As Fulton Sheen explained, "Wars come from egotism and selfishness. Every macrocosmic or world war has its origin in microcosmic wars going on inside millions and millions of individuals." Death to self, by contrast, is the summation of Christianity and a tenant of many other religions, which is why religion is constantly under attack by the devil and his minions.

Wokeness preys upon man's natural inclination toward selfishness, but takes it a step further. Rather than simply encouraging individuals to indulge themselves in pleasure, the woke insist that everyone else not only condone but *contribute to* the indulgence.

"Woke," according to Google Dictionary, is an adjective meaning, "alert to injustice in society, especially racism" (the term, as noted in this book's introduction, has *evolved* — there's that word again! — beyond race). While it's certainly a noble aspiration to keep oneself continually aware of the wrongdoing around you, a sample sentence Google had used for "woke" revealed the concept's wicked essence: "We need to stay angry, and stay woke."[37]

Why does "stay angry" come first? The word order implies that woke people are intent on having a feeling that the Bible tells us "tends only to evil" (Ps. 37:8) and are looking to justify it. This analysis matches perfectly with the way we see wokeness manifest itself: pathetic people, empty of God (and not even restlessly seeking him), a community, and a sense of purpose (*telos*), are angry and searching for meaning in their lives. They attempt to find it by virtue signaling with a selfie and a lecture on "toxic masculinity" for some social media likes and retweets from Internet strangers and bots. Not surprisingly, this doesn't quite do the trick, which is why, as the woke movement generates momentum, our country is more depressed, angry, and anxious than ever before.

By the anxieties and worries of this life Satan tries to dull man's heart and make a dwelling for himself there. (St. Francis of Assisi)

[37] Lang Tien, "Social justice and being woke: Making sense of modern movements," *Thirst*, November 10, 2021, https://thirst.sg/social-justice-and-being-woke-making-sense-of-modern-movements/.

"A Low Self-Opinion, Man"

The progressive left takes advantage of the vulnerable class of people they "liberated" by convincing them they are being oppressed, discriminated against, and marginalized. It's easy, once you've lured a generation away from God and His teachings, to turn people's focus inward, onto themselves, their desires, anxieties, problems, and unhappiness. To dwell on oneself is to invite misery, and this world is certainly a miserable one.

Our society seems made up of millions of iterations of the person Henry Rollins sings about in the 1992 Rollins Band song, "Low Self-Opinion." The lyrics say, "I think you got a low self-opinion, man/ You never wonder why/ All this bitterness wells up inside you/ You always victimize/ So you can criticize yourself/ And all those around you ... Get yourself a break from self-rejection/ Try some introspection/ And you just might find/ It's not so bad and anyway ... I know the self-doubt that treats you so unkind/ If you could see the you that I see/ When I see you/ You would see things differently/ I assure you."

Lacking a sense of self-worth and the dignity they inherently possess in knowing that they've been made in God's image and likeness, the woke look to the capricious world for validation. When this method inevitably fails to satisfy them, they go to greater and greater lengths — tattoos, surgeries, displays of ersatz virtue, increasingly bizarre "identities," absurd pronouns, and so forth — to gain earthly approval.

When this routine grows tiresome and proves ineffective, the woke become envious and frantic. Rather than work hard, improve themselves, or content themselves with the good things they have been granted, they initiate the blame game. They're envious of the NORMALs and the wholesome life we nurture, and so they lash out, seeking to deprive us of our peace and joy. "My unhappiness is everyone else's fault, and if you don't acknowledge that, I will punish you." The woke have moved from demanding to *mandating* that everyone not only accept them and their depravity, but that everyone participate in it along with them.

At the top, the cunning con-artists who direct the woke tragedy do so to gain power, money, and prestige. Their puppets, all those lost souls who fall for their lies, are desperate to fulfill the self-serving "rewards" the woke leaders persuade them they "deserve." Woke "problems," after all, are always "solved" by granting the "victim" more money, privileges, status, etc. (and when has it ever been enough?), and by putting down another class of person. Far from "equality," these people's objective is to certify that all NORMALs are "privileged" and therefore, *fill-in-the-blank*-ists or -phobes.

Too many people spend money they haven't earned, to buy things they don't want, to impress people that they don't like. (Will Rogers)

The Exhausting, Vigilant Headhunt

Do you ever recall seeing a woke warrior who seemed happy? Who among us, intent on a vigilant headhunt, *could* be happy? It's an exhausting, stressful, unpleasant life, as everyone you encounter is one slip of the tongue or silent slight away from becoming Enemy Number One. And as a woke warrior, you are never satisfied. You spend your days inventing reasons to accuse your innocent neighbors of "crimes" they didn't commit — "crimes" that didn't even exist until a few years ago.

This is how we NORMALs have become embroiled in a losing battle we had no part in creating, apologizing for made-up slights and offenses that have been invented by a group of people who will never be satisfied and are, in fact, not looking for true justice, but simply for power, money ("reparations"), and notoriety — anything but an apology and true contrition. When all you have is a fragile ego, you see, you will do anything to keep feeding it, refusing to acknowledge that the one thing that will satisfy it is something bigger and better than you — the one thing your ideology explicitly rejects.

"A lot of wokeness is almost like a fake religion," a very insightful friend observed to me. "You must acknowledge whatever it is that makes me so special, and if you're not actively acknowledging it, you must worship Adolf Hitler."

Another extremely astute friend of mine, who also happens to be a practicing psychologist, expressed to me this reflection:

> Woke people don't realize it, but as much as they may disavow traditional religion, they have essentially come up with their own barbaric substitute for religion. The rules, thoughts, and dogmas of this school of thought are not allowed to be questioned and must be imposed upon other people with the harshest tactics and unrelenting brutality (ironic for such a tolerant and loving bunch).
>
> It is particularly troublesome to me that there is no forgiveness allowed with this new woke "religion." If somebody happened to say the N-word in a joke when they were three years old, 30 years ago, before he encountered the wider world and became "woke," there is no chance for forgiveness. Ever laughed uncomfortably when somebody made a sexist/gay joke and didn't know how to respond? Unredeemable. Cancelation is a must — no quarter, no exceptions.
>
> It is sad to me that in an ideal world, human beings maturing through a healthy life development would experience the cycle of transgression, repentance, and forgiveness: this pathway to growth is unfortunately not acceptable in the world of the woke. How can anybody want to live in a world where there is no hope for redemption?

Divide and Conquer

The devil, whose very name, *diabolos*, is rooted in the Greek word meaning "to divide,"[38] does his best work amid chaos. Thus, the latest tactic of

---

[38] Philip Kosloski, "How division is a primary tactic of the devil," *Aleteia*, June 4, 2020, https://aleteia.org/2020/06/04/how-division-is-a-primary-tactic-of-the-devil/.

the "father of lies" is to implant false accusations of injustice everywhere and turn lies about race and sex into popular opinion, thereby fanning the flames of division, disorder, and ultimately, destruction.

Observe the "fruits" born by the woke world. Are *any* of them *not* "rotten"?

Think again of the very term, "woke." It implies that before the woke movement came along, we were the opposite of awake — otherwise known as asleep. The last I checked, sleeping is inherently peaceful. And in places where people have become "woke," peace has vanished.

Woke warriors will tell you our society was not sleeping in relative peace prior to the launch of their campaign, but that there has always been an undercurrent of extreme injustice that they, as heroes, have only recently exposed and are now seeking justice for.

Men have no more time to understand anything.
They buy things all ready-made at the shops.
But there is no shop anywhere where one can
buy friendship, and so men have no friends
anymore. (Antoine de Saint-Exupéry)

Certainly, injustice is inescapable in our fallen world, but if it has really been as prevalent and damaging as they say, why are we collectively much more stressed, anxious, overweight, addicted, and unhappy as the woke agenda makes the world a "better" place than we were when the so-called injustices were running rampant?

Prioritizing Peace and Purpose

Returning to our opening theme of priorities, regrets, and making the most of the time God has gifted us, I'd wager no one has ever come to the end of her life and said on her deathbed, "Man, I wish I'd spent just five more minutes staring at a screen."

Or standing bleary-eyed in line at Walmart to buy cheap Chinese junk I didn't need.

Or sitting in traffic to and from a job I hated.

Or looking at photos on Facebook of food a person I never met ate for dinner.

Or spiking my blood pressure and anxiety levels by consuming more doom and gloom from the omnipresent 24/7 news cycle.

Or arguing incessantly and to no end about gender identities and pronouns.

Or spending my evenings after work away from my family at contentious school board meetings.

Or trying to prove to an angry world that I'm not a racist, or a xenophobe, or a homophobe, or an extremist, or toxic, or...

Gasp!

A Call to Passive Arms

There's a trope common in romantic dramadies and sappy country music songs — two of my favorite things — that warrant their repetition: if you knew you had only a few months left to live, what would you change now? Or, if you were somehow able to live your life over again, what would you do differently? (Spoiler alert: you would *not* stay up later drinking more.)

Most of us would make more time for the important things, prioritizing our prayer life, our relationships, our health, and the simple experiences that nurture our souls. We'd ignore the propaganda blitz the tech giants, multinational mega-corps, and billion-dollar media conglomerates are constantly bringing into our homes and turn our attention to the things that truly matter.

We would stop worrying about artificial "microaggressions," "triggers," and "safe spaces." And instead of playing whack-a-mole with the attacks leveled at our Judeo-Christian, American values, we would turn our focus toward living out those values and ending our days in satisfying peace, making more time *now* to love, serve, and enjoy our neighbors in opposition to the modern spirit of division and conflict that pervades our existence.

We would find, too, that in shutting out wokeness and the mediums that breed it, not only would our own lives be made more peaceful and meaningful, but society as a whole would become this way. The woke agenda relies for its very existence on getting a reaction, and with the NOR-MALs — remember, we're the majority — paying it no heed, wokeness would disappear. Once you realize the left has reached a level of absurdity that doesn't deserve being dignified with a response, you will be free to pursue your higher purpose — to the benefit of everyone and everything.

> "I wish it need not have happened in my time," said Frodo. "So do I," said Gandalf, "and so do all who live to see such times. But that is not for them to decide. All we have to decide is what to do with the time that is given us." (J.R.R. Tolkien)

You don't have to wait for a grim medical diagnosis or near-death experience to pursue a more fulfilling life. But in a world that is so fast-paced, hostile, and loud, how can a single person with a modest income and virtually no platform possibly hope to change a country that is consumed by fake controversies that have all-too real consequences?

You are normal. You love America. You love your family. You love your neighbors. You know they're worth fighting for. You want everyone to be content, to enjoy liberty, and to thrive. You see the violence and depression erupting from the woke culture war, and you ache most of all for the innocent young casualties lost by the lies of radical progressives.

You know that, despite our astounding technological advancements and widespread material wealth, we, as a nation, have higher depression, fewer friends, and greater alienation than our parents or grandparents. Something has been lost. But what is it? And how do we get it back?

Let's recognize that the causes of our dissatisfaction are globalization, centralization, and politicization, all of which set the perfect stage for the woke masterminds to advance their agenda. We buy things from far away, receive edicts from on high, and are force-fed policies contrary to our consciences that work for thee but not for me.

In just one hundred years, America has moved from a rural, agricultural, family-based society to one that is urban, corporate, and hyper-individualistic. We've transitioned from a nation that would not think twice about rationing, growing a victory garden, or eagerly signing up for the draft, to a generation of entitled toddlers who will throw a tantrum the second their Wi-Fi slows down.

A growing sect of our society is lazy and selfish, leaving NORMALs a formidable task. But you now know most people in America think and feel the same way you do (for now). You're willing to stand up and do your part for the greater good. But you're not sure where to start.

You don't have to live in fear and anxiety. We still have the blueprint for the throwback lifestyle of the Good Old Days, and it turns out there are millions of NORMALs already leading happy, healthy, holy lives. This book outlines numerous steps — from the simple to the more committed — that you can take today to insulate yourself, your family, and your friends from the pointless, power-hungry madness destroying our world, to safeguard your minds, bodies, and souls from being targets of the woke agenda, and to find purpose and peace amid the chaos.

Let's get to work.

You are the light of the world. A city set on a hill cannot be hid. Nor do men light a lamp and put it under a bushel, but on a stand, and it gives light to all in the house. Let your light so shine before men, that they may see your good works and give glory to your Father who is in heaven. (Matthew 5:14–16)

2

What's at Stake
Ignore It, and It Won't Go Away

I'm going to Lowe's if anyone needs anything," my brother announced as he headed toward the door.

"Lowe's?!" I protested. "Why? Didn't you see they just sponsored some 'critical race theory challenge' at their company?[39] Why don't you go to Hometown Electric instead?"

"I guess I could. But they'll be twice as expensive."

"Is saving a couple bucks on lightbulbs more important to you than sticking it to a woke corporation that insists white employees 'cede power to people of color' and claims 'people of color can't be racist'?"

"Well, I need to buy a few two-by-fours, too."

"Forcey's Lumber carries those! And Judy's house is on the way. We can honk on the way by and make her day. You know she'll be sitting on her porch..."

"Then I'll have to stop *two* places."

"But we can go to Gio's on the way home and bring some barbecue back for mom and dad and support another local, Christian

---

[39] Tyler O'Neil, "Bank of America, Lowe's sponsored CRT training urging Whites to 'cede power to people of color,'" Fox News, August 19, 2021, https://www.foxbusiness.com/politics/bank-of-america-lowes-sponsored-crt-training.

business-owner. We'll all have supper together like they did in *The Waltons* and save America!"

"Okay, fine. Let's go."

This exchange is based on a true story. All but the bit where I delivered an articulate, inspiring, patriotic speech urging my brother to boycott a woke corporate giant. (I think I actually said something to the effect of, "Yeah but we'll get to visit Bruce's cute dog downtown and get brisket afterward," and my kindhearted brother relented.) The point is, though, we've all found ourselves in this position: mega-corporations came along and put small, family-owned companies on the endangered species list. With few options left, we gave in and gave the Amazons, Targets, and Walmarts of the world our money.

After pocketing our billions, woke corporations are pulling the rug out from under us, strong-arming us with our hard-earned dollars to support social agendas that are completely out of line with our morals and turning the "land of the free" into the land of the canceled and the "home of the brave" into the home of the woke warrior.

> Broadmindedness, when it means indifference
> to right and wrong, eventually ends in a hatred
> of what is right. (Bishop Fulton J. Sheen)

The truth is, we can do a lot better than fund Lowe's and Walmart's race-baiting,[40] Target's LGBTQIA+ Pride line of merchandise,[41] the $4,000 stipend Amazon offers employees to travel for abortions,[42] and

---

[40] Christopher F. Rufo, "Walmart vs. Whiteness," City-Journal, October 14, 2021, https://www.city-journal.org/walmart-critical-race-theory-training-program.

[41] "LGBTQIA+ Team Members & Guests," https://corporate.target.com/sustainability-ESG/diversity-equity-inclusion/team-members-guests/lgbtqia.

[42] Jeffrey Dastin, "Amazon to reimburse U.S. employees who travel for abortions, other treatments," May 2, 2022, https://www.reuters.com/business/

the ever-growing politically charged initiatives hijacking traditional enterprise. We may not be as individually wealthy as these corporations are — not by a long shot — but for the time being, we still have our freedom. And there are more of us. And they need us more than we need them.

Some more encouraging news: a 2018 study on "Experimental evidence for tipping points in social convention" by University of Pennsylvania researchers found it takes roughly 25 percent of the population to overturn established social behavior, with the authors noting, "The only incentive was to coordinate."[43]

It's critical we join forces and strike — in a peaceful, bucolic way — before it's too late. We know the woke minority is well-funded, well-coordinated, and shrill. But it is my hope that this book will inspire enough NORMALs with "the incentive to coordinate" and be a guide for tipping social convention in an organized, powerful fashion before our nation's values are eroded beyond recovery.

It's tempting to turn a blind eye to pervasive woke trends, try to ignore them, and live your life. After all, "love is love" seems innocent enough, right? "Clean energy" is a noble pursuit, isn't it? Other races and classes of people have been mistreated historically, so giving them a little extra boost now won't hurt, will it?

The truth is, though, these woke concepts amount to mere slogans that distract and disguise a much more sinister agenda. It reminds me of a billboard advertising a "FREE KING-SIZED MATTRESS!!!" Millions of people drive by the sign every day and take it at face value. When they show up at the furniture store, however, they are gutted to learn that

retail-consumer/amazon-reimburse-us-employees-who-travel-treatments-including-abortions-2022-05-02/.

43 Damon Centole, Joshua Becker, Devon Brackbill, Andrea Baronchelli, "Experimental evidence for tipping points in social convention," *Science*, June 8, 2018, https://www.science.org/doi/10.1126/science.aas8827.

"terms and conditions apply." The fine print stipulates that the "free" mattress is only for customers who spend $5 million. Oh, and the offer is subject to change. Also, it is only valid on Leap Day, 2023. Which doesn't exist. There is also fine print; "side effects include": alienation, loneliness, anxiety, depression, obesity, shortened life span, and terminal misery. But no one takes the time to read that part. They read the big, woke billboard and believe it.

Think about the precepts of the woke cult, the inroads they've already made in a few short years, and what's at stake if we sit idly by and allow the mob to continue imposing its wicked agenda on our world. As you'll see in the following pages, it's more than cheery rainbow flags and feel-good affirmative action diversity. It's called the "culture of death" for a reason.[44]

Know Thy Enemies

Wokeness, as we've noted, rears its ugly head in numerous forms, the telltale signs of which involve woke masterminds creating a "problem" to which only they offer the "solution." The problem is based on a lie, and the solution involves NORMALs being controlled, compelled, condemned, and punished, our choices restricted, our lives made worse. The people who invented the problem make themselves out to be the heroes, always personally benefiting from the solution. A select group of elite bullies at the top gains special treatment, prestige, and huge sums of money — without sacrificing a thing.

To fight well, you must know what you're facing, how the enemy operates, what motivates the enemy, and why fighting is necessary.

---

[44] Richard M. Doerflinger, "False Freedom and the Culture of Death," *United States Conference of Catholic Bishops*, https://www.usccb.org/committees/pro-life-activities/false-freedom-and-culture-death.

The greatest kindness one can render
to any man consists in leading him from
error to truth. (St. Thomas Aquinas)

"Enemy" you say? Isn't that a bit extreme? Not everyone who is taken in by the woke agenda is evil, of course. But in its most basic form, there are two types of people: the NORMALs, who want to be free to serve God and love their neighbor as themselves, and the woke, who are not satisfied unless they're controlling everyone. Remember that the devil tempted Adam and Eve "to be like gods" (Gen. 3:5). Satan likewise tempted Jesus in the desert, assuring Him of "all the kingdoms of the world in their magnificence" (Matt. 4:8–9) if Jesus made Satan His idol.

As I'll illustrate further on, the elites orchestrating the woke charade know exactly what they're doing. They aren't motivated by their selfless love of others. They want to be like gods, to make men women and women men, to control the population, make themselves the center of the universe, and profit magnificently. You can actually buy "It's all about me" T-shirts and bumper stickers and flaunt the modern-day equivalent of Satan's "*Non serviam*" ("I will not serve"). Many have given into the devil's temptation, and many are receiving the earthly prize Satan promised, though, of course, it isn't enough. Fulton Sheen, in his must-read *Peace of Soul*, noted that famed psychotherapist Alfred Adler "said that neurotics are animated by an unruly ambition to be 'like God.'" To strive to be like God when you're a lowly human must truly be maddening, for, as we witness, the woke are certifiable.

Woke Weapons

The woke will try to outsmart God, to be too clever by half — skirting the laws of nature through weight loss pills, happy pills, cosmetic surgeries — *anything* but practice the introspection and discipline that have proven from time immemorial to satisfy man's longing as much as is possible in this world. What the woke rejects is that God *is* the "one weird trick!"

> The secret of happiness is to live moment by moment and to thank God for what He is sending us every day in His goodness. (St. Gianna Molla)

When presented with alarmism that stokes fear and that compels you to take part in something you'd rather not be part of, it is wise to reflect on who benefits from the division. As previously noted, there's always someone or a group of elite people at the top sacrificing nothing and benefiting richly by stirring the pot, robbing everyone of their tranquility, and taking advantage of the ensuing discord. They pull the fire alarm, so to speak, so they can steal your peace and freedom.

NORMALs cannot allow the woke to use us to their satanic ends. In this next section, we'll briefly break down the major woke weapons, why they're more dangerous than you may think, and most importantly, how the woke-proof lifestyle is an antidote to these social pollutants.

Woke	Woke-Proof
Big Tech	Real life
Race baiters	Nice neighbors
LGBTQIA+ gender benders	Nature lovers
Climate-change czars	Weather realists
DEI, ESG	DIY

Technology: Resource or Recourse?

Big Tech is a big problem. Physically, mentally, *and* spiritually, it is capable of ruin on all levels. *If* we let it. It is through Big Tech, after all, that so much woke influence is born, bred, disseminated, and festers.

We must ask ourselves if we're using our remarkable technology as a resource — discovering or communicating fruitful news and information, being fortified by a community, taking part in a health-giving routine, and so on — or if our devices are a recourse for filling time. We've all seen it and likely done it ourselves: we're told to sit down and wait at a doctor's office, at the airport, in line at the post office, and the first thing we do is pull out our phone. For what? It didn't ring or buzz. We didn't receive a message. We're looking for a distraction, for momentary entertainment. The time we used to fill by striking up a pleasant conservation with our neighbor, saying a prayer, philosophizing internally, or musing on the way interior paint colors are developed is now filled with silent head noise, as we're all absorbed in a virtual world that's filling our time and keeping the brain just-amused-enough so that it doesn't have to think for itself.

Let us harken back once more to a time when people weren't worn thin by the constant pings, dings, and rings of their cell phones. Chats on the telephone took place at convenient and appropriate times — not unexpectedly at any and all hours of the day and night, while driving, grocery shopping, or hiking in the forest. They were generally planned, polite, and purposeful.

News and information were relayed, as we blissfully reminisced already, for an hour in the evening and *only* for an hour in the evening, as well as in publications that were (mostly) thoughtfully written, printed, and mailed out, to be consumed in a measured manner.

Entertainment, too, was something to be sought-after, not thrust upon you first-thing in the morning with a video of a Filipina TikToker "lip-syncing and bopping her head to the rhythm of the viral Millie B song."[45] (This mind-numbingly inane 10-second video has racked-up 683.4 million views on TikTok.)

----

[45] Dave Johnson, "The Most Viewed TikTok Videos Of All Time," *Alphr*, August 24, 2022, https://www.alphr.com/most-viewed-tiktok-videos-of-all-time/.

We need to find God, and he cannot be found in
noise and restlessness. God is the friend of silence.
See how nature—trees, flowers, grass—grows
in silence; see the stars, the moon and the sun,
how they move in silence.... We need silence
to be able to touch souls. (Mother Teresa)

Now of course, texts, emails, "news," and entertainment are every-where. Data reports vary on the amount of time the average American spends in front of a screen, but even the low-end estimates are ap-palling: in 2018, a *New York Post* story reported, "Americans spend nearly half of their waking hours (42 percent) looking at a screen."[46] Statista reported that in 2021, "adults in the U.S. spent an average of 485 minutes (eight hours and five minutes) with digital media each day."[47] For kids aged 11–18, the average time spent online using social media, gaming, shopping, video chatting, and texting is 10 hours and four minutes a *day*.[48]

In 2022, data revealed the average person spent two hours and 27 minutes a day on social media.[49] The COVID pandemic's lockdowns,

[46] Tyler Schmall, "Americans spend half their lives in front of screens," *New York Post*, August 13, 2018, https://nypost.com/2018/08/13/americans-spend-half-their-lives-in-front-of-screens/.

[47] A. Guttmann, "Average time spent per day with digital media in the United States from 2011 to 2024," *Statista*, January 9, 2023, https://www.statista.com/statistics/262340/daily-time-spent-with-digital-media-according-to-us-consumsers/.

[48] Joy Pullmann, "Study: Outside Of School, America's Teens Average 70 Hours Per Week Glued To Screens," *The Federalist*, October 31, 2022, https://thefederalist.com/2022/10/31/study-outside-of-school-americas-teens-average-70-hours-per-week-glued-to-screens/.

[49] "How much time does the average person spend on social media? (2012–2022)," *Oberlo*, https://www.oberlo.com/statistics/how-much-time-does-the-average-person-spend-on-social-media.

researchers found, led to increased cell phone addiction. Scientists in 2021 declared smartphone overuse "a hidden crisis in COVID-19," reporting that "COVID-19 related lockdown policies might lead to the overuse or excessive usage of smartphones." This set of researchers recommended using a "screening tool" to identify "people who might have problematic use of smartphones or other smart devices," to develop and implement psychiatric intervention, and to consider classifying smartphone overuse as an official diagnosis.[50]

Let that sink in.

Now consider that too much screen time, in addition to being a waste of time, increases: inactivity, obesity, isolation, depression, anxiety, eye strain, poor posture, wrinkles, and sleep irregularities. Despite being a supposedly "social" platform that makes communication easier, social media makes us lonelier. It's designed to suck us in and keep us checking up on other people, and research has found apps like Facebook, Snapchat, Instagram, and the like to be more addictive than smoking and alcohol (and, as we'll see later on, just as harmful).[51] Much like its fellow vices, social media adheres to the law of diminishing returns: another study found that limiting social media usage to a maximum of 30 minutes a day significantly reduced users' "anxiety and fear of missing out (FOMO)."[52] An even more alarming study found that "mobile phone addiction during

---

[50] Zubair Ahmed Ratan, et. al., "Smartphone overuse: A hidden crisis in COVID-19," March 1, 2021, *National Library of Medicine*, https://www.ncbi.nlm.nih.gov/pmc/articles/PMC7825859/.

[51] "Social media more addictive than cigarettes, alcohol: Study," *The Economic Times*, February 6, 2012, https://economictimes.indiatimes.com/tech/internet/social-media-more-addictive-than-cigarettes-alcohol-study/articleshow/11779580.cms?from=mdr.

[52] Melissa G. Hunt, Rachel Marx, Courtney Lipson and Jordyn Young, "No More FOMO: Limiting Social Media Decreases Loneliness and Depression," *Guilford Press Periodicals*, December 2018, https://guilfordjournals.com/doi/10.1521/jscp.2018.37.10.751.

the COVID-19 quarantine period could, directly and indirectly, predict suicidality five months later when the pandemic was in remission."[53]

Technology is a wonderful blessing from God, but cell phones are designed to addict us and distract us from God and from the needs of our neighbors. Phones are also the way woke ideology is granted a platform and works its way into the collective psyche.

Our human appetites are boundless, which is why God provided very clear-cut guardrails for how to moderate ourselves. With their "Do what makes you happy" (provided it does not involve self-restraint) creed, wokeness rejects all that archaic self-control. *Ha! How repressed these crazy NORMALs are!* If decadent food, booze, drugs, sex, and public validation make you happy, wouldn't *more* of these things make you *more* happy?

The Secret to Happiness Is No Secret

The thing is, the "secret" to happiness is no secret. God isn't mean. He didn't plop us on this planet and wish us luck figuring it out while He burned rubber in His 6-Series on His way back to Heaven. He's spelled out in endless ways — through not only Holy Scripture and tradition and through the examples of countless holy believers, but through obvious earthly cues as well — how to live in a way that is pleasing to Him. Ever notice how gluttony results in obesity and myriad painful diseases? Or how promiscuity (lust) does the *opposite* of make people happier?[54] ("Research suggests that promiscuity is not associated with increased happiness and, in fact, that the number of sexual partners needed to maximize happiness is exactly one.") The long-term effects of infidelity

---

[53] Gangqin Li, et. al., "Adolescent mobile phone addiction during the COVID-19 pandemic predicts subsequent suicide risk: a two-wave longitudinal study," August 12, 2022, *National Library of Medicine*, https://bmcpublichealth.biomedcentral.com/articles/10.1186/s12889-022-13931-1.

[54] Marina Adshade, "Does sleeping around make people happier?" *Big Think*, August 26, 2010, https://bigthink.com/guest-thinkers/does-sleeping-around-make-people-happier/.

are well-documented[55] — by scientists and daytime soap operas and country music songwriters. The effects of the deadly sins touch everyone, and they're all bad. It's almost as if God told us so.

> Happiness can only be achieved by looking inward and learning to enjoy whatever life has and this requires transforming greed into gratitude. (John Chrysostom)

NORMALs realize that, as C. S. Lewis put it, "God cannot give us a happiness and peace apart from Himself, because it is not there. There is no such thing." We are to follow His commands, do His will, and love our neighbor as ourselves. It isn't always easy to do, but it isn't difficult to understand. God loves us and wants us to love Him and be with Him in His kingdom for eternity, so He isn't trying to confuse us down here on Earth.

So try as they might, the woke will never find happiness or peace in their worldly, materialistic, hedonistic pursuits. They will only become more discontent as they seek to satisfy their insatiable appetites by eating and drinking themselves into ill health, indulging in every sexual urge, and, in a desperate attempt to win approval from a notoriously fickle, virtual audience, spend their time posting views online that they've been convinced are valuable.

"Did it for the 'gram" is a common expression among social-media users that means doing something for the sole purpose of posting it to Instagram (or another social media platform). *Bustle* reported on a 2014 survey that found nearly one-third (29 percent) of Americans had taken part in this phenomenon in an attempt to project to their followers: " 'I'm adventurous' (30 percent), 'I'm successful' (28 percent), and 'I have a

---

[55] Marissa Moore, "Long-Term Psychological Effects of Infidelity," *Psych Central*, October 29, 2021, https://psychcentral.com/health/long-term-psychological-effects-of-infidelity.

lot of friends' (24 percent)."[56] Some people (one survey puts the number at 9 percent of social media users) are so obsessed with appearing fashionable that they will actually go to the trouble of buying an outfit, taking a picture wearing it, and after the social media post has been made, returning the clothes.[57]

Everyone's jealous of everyone, despite hardly anyone sharing an accurate depiction of their lives.[58] The result is an unhappy, unloved, and unloving populace searching for meaning from an unforgiving group of people with impossible standards. People are so busy trying to earn everyone else's approval, they never stop to think, "Does their opinion matter?"

At work, too, our phones are a menace. They make us less productive, as the *Wall Street Journal* reported: "using a smartphone, or even hearing one ring or vibrate, produces a welter of distractions that makes it harder to concentrate on a difficult problem or job. The division of attention impedes reasoning and performance."[59]

> Beware of practicing your piety before men in order to be seen by them; for then you will have no reward from your Father who is in heaven. (Matthew 6:1)

[56] Catie Keck, "We Know You're Faking It On Social Media," *Bustle*, October 9, 2014, https://www.bustle.com/articles/43577-ever-do-something-just-so-you-can-post-about-it-on-social-media-youre-not-alone.

[57] Hanna Kozlowska, "Shoppers are buying clothes just for the Instagram pic, and then returning them," *Quartz*, August 13,2018, https://qz.com/quartzy/1354651/shoppers-are-buying-clothes-just-for-the-instagram-pic-and-then-return-them.

[58] Jessica Stillman, "Shoppers are buying clothes just for the Instagram pic, and then returning them," *Inc.*, https://www.inc.com/jessica-stillman/people-are-revealing-truth-behind-their-happy-looking-social-media-posts-its-heartbreaking.html.

[59] Nicholas Carr, "How Smartphones Hijack Our Minds," *Wall Street Journal*, October 6, 2017, https://www.wsj.com/articles/how-smartphones-hijack-our-minds-1507307811.

Our phones are also making us dumber and less friendly. An eye-watering NBC News report in 2018 revealed our phones negatively affect our ability to remember basic information and to think "deeply, attentively and conceptually." Even when we aren't using them, one study reported that "the mere presence of a smartphone seemed to reduce the quality of conversations."

Here's the real kicker of the NBC report:

Even basic human decency may be sacrificed. Research suggests that smartphones can inhibit people from offering help to strangers on the street, reduce how much we smile at unfamiliar faces in a waiting room and even lessen our trust of strangers, neighbors and people of other religions or nationalities.[60]

The effects of screen time on children are even more startling. According to the CDC, "1 in 5 children, either currently or at some point during their life, have had a seriously debilitating mental illness." The NBC article reported on a "troubling correlation between when smartphones became popular and when rates of mental health problems among teens and young adults began skyrocketing."

It gets worse. MedicineNet.com reported in 2021 that the time children spend on cell phones, "is not just bad for the brain but can affect a child's psychology, thinking patterns, sleep cycles, and behavior, shortening their attention span and potentially encouraging violent or aggressive behavior."[61]

The report further found that "Brain scans have shown that kids who spent excessive time on their screens had a premature thinning of the

[60] Lynne Peeples, "Can't put down the phone? How smartphones are changing our brains — and lives," *NBC News*, December 14, 2018, https://www.nbcnews.com/mach/science/surprising-ways-smartphones-affect-our-brains-our-lives-ncna947566.
[61] Dr. Jasmine Shaikh, MD, "How Do Cell Phones Affect a Child's Brain?," *Medicine Net*, August 4, 2021, https://www.medicinenet.com/how_do_cell_phones_affect_a_childs_brain/article.htm.

cortex. The cortex is the outermost layer of the brain that is involved in processing different types of information from all five senses. Cortical thinning at a young age thus indicates that children are maturing earlier from the use of cell phones."

Brace yourself. If you think these statistics are scary, we're about to add a layer of totally creepy.

I spoke to Rob Shavell, CEO of the data privacy firm DeleteMe, for a podcast about the consequences of a tech-saturated society and how to protect yourself and your children from powerful online algorithms that are eerier than anything George Orwell imagined.[62] Shavell's revelations were startling, to put it mildly.

Big Tech Knows More Than Parents

Over time, the amount of data collected is becoming more enormous and far-reaching than any busy parent can imagine. And it's happening earlier and earlier. This generation of children is growing up with the Internet, and that means that companies, especially social media companies, have a data set over time that is incredible. They can actually use [Artificial Intelligence] algorithms to analyze how your particular child is developing, potentially better than you can as a parent.

That to me is scary, because [companies] run predictive behavior over many, many millions of profiles. A parent could never do that, and [tech companies] can predict effectively things you may not be comfortable with and things you would never be able to predict yourself: what might your child's behavior look like over the next five years. Not just what they will be buying, but how successful will they be, what things will they take up, what kind

---

[62] Teresa Mull, Rob Shavell, "Podcast: Ignoring the dangers of Big Tech will tear America apart," *The Spectator*, September 13, 2022, https://thespectator.com/podcast/podcast-ignoring-the-dangers-of-big-tech-will-destroy-our-country/.

of friends will they have, and how will those events, as they move through time, predict their outcomes as a young adult, and on and on and on. The ability for Big Tech to know more than a parent knows about their own child leads to all kinds of bad scenarios.

Shavell's safeguards are, blessedly, relatively simple:

Reduce your digital data footprint by limiting screen time. Don't allow your child to binge-watch shows and videos and be on social media platforms chatting away all day, every day.

Educate children on what these platforms are doing with their data. I explain to my own daughter how YouTube ads are using what she's just seen to sell her a product. Educating children on what's behind the curtain and what these companies are doing is helpful. Kids pick up more than we parents think they do. Explain to them, "This is a business, and you are an audience member who's a participant in a business that's not always in your best interests."

In an ideal world, Shavell says parents on every account would be able to get a full and transparent report of the data brokers, data collectors, activities, ads, and so forth that are interacting with their child, so they would have a "clear understanding of what data is out there and how it's being used."

Either make the tree good, and its fruit good; or make the tree bad, and its fruit bad; for the tree is known by its fruit. You brood of vipers! how can you speak good, when you are evil? For out of the abundance of the heart the mouth speaks. The good man out of his good treasure brings forth good, and the evil man out of his evil treasure brings forth evil. I tell you, on the day of judgment men will render

> account for every careless word they utter; for by
> your words you will be justified, and by your words
> you will be condemned. (Matthew 12:33–37)

To thwart Big Tech's data extraction and tracking practices, Shavell encourages people to use a different profile with a different email address every time they register an account for social media, YouTube, and so forth. Email accounts are essentially "identifiers to compartmentalize users' activities," so, Shavell says, "don't always be the same person with the same profile. This helps break the tracking that happens across these networks."

Finally, Shavell recommends people consider removing their personal information from data brokers. DeleteMe offers this service, though Shavell notes, "There are also free ways to do it."

These are just the physical and practical effects of screen time. Now let's delve into the psychological and spiritual effects.

Big Tech Is the New Big Tobacco

"If we don't take action soon, I do really think we're going to see a public mental health crisis among the teens and kids who are growing up on social media today," Clare Morell, a policy analyst at the Ethics and Public Policy Center, told me in an interview for an article I wrote for *The Federalist*.[63]

The data is clear, Morell says, that social media apps cause anxiety, depression, self-harm, eating disorders, and suicide. "We're going to see an epidemic — and it's already starting — of online pornography addiction, and what that means for the future of our country is the destabilization of marriages and families. I don't think it's inappropriate to say without

---

[63] Teresa Mull, "Big Tech Is the New Big Tobacco," *The Federalist*, August 31, 2022, https://thefederalist.com/2022/08/31/big-tech-is-the-new-big-tobacco/.

taking any action, within a few years, within one generation, we could be headed toward a civilizational crisis, like in Japan, where the birth rate has fallen below replacement."

Morell co-authored the report, "Protecting Teens from Big Tech: Five Policy Ideas for the States,"[64] that warned:

> One day, we will look back at social media companies like Byte-Dance (TikTok) and Meta (Facebook and Instagram) and compare them to tobacco companies like Philip Morris (Marlboro) and R. J. Reynolds (Camel). For a time, Big Tobacco enjoyed immense profits and popularity. But eventually, Big Tobacco's culpability in causing immense physical harm to Americans — and in trying to obscure the science regarding that harm — became known. They were eventually held accountable for their deceptive advertising to children using "Joe Camel." We are living at a moment when we are just learning of the social and psychological harms of social media, and of Big Tech's efforts to obscure those harms from the public.

"The Loneliest Generation"

"Social" media, despite its name, is a leading cause of loneliness, especially in young people. *Psycom* reported on a study by the *American Journal of Preventative Medicine*,[65] which found:

> Young adults with heavy use of social media platforms — two hours a day — have twice the chance of experiencing social

---

[64] W. Bradford Wilcox, Clare Morell, Adam Candeub, Jean Twenge, "Protecting Teens from Big Tech: Five Policy Ideas for States," *AEI*, August 24, 2022, https://www.aei.org/op-eds/protecting-teens-from-big-tech-five-policy-ideas-for-states/.

[65] Brian A. Primack, et. al, "Social Media Use and Perceived Social Isolation Among Young Adults in the U.S.," *American Journal of Preventative Medicine*, March 6, 2017, https://www.ajpmonline.org/article/S0749-3797(17)30016-8/fulltext#secsect0075.

anxiety, according to a 2017 study. The study's researchers also found that participants who are online most frequently — defined as 50 or more visits a week — have *three times the odds* of perceived social isolation as those who went online less than nine times a week. And it isn't just young adults affected by the social media-loneliness conundrum. It can be adults, stuck in their routines and feeling unable to discover new ways to find and foster friendships offline.[66]

The effects of loneliness are devastating. According to the American Heart Association:

Social isolation and loneliness may increase the risk of having or dying from a heart attack or stroke.[67] A 2018 survey by the Kaiser Family Foundation [found] more than 1 in 5 U.S. adults said they often or always felt lonely or socially isolated. While life changes such as losing a spouse or retiring can result in fewer social connections and interactions for older people, another survey cited in the report said it's young adults ages 18 to 22 who are now considered the loneliest generation, spending more time on social media and less engaged in in-person activities than previous generations.

Another study, reported on by the University of New Hampshire in 2022, found that Big Tech is the new Big Tobacco in more ways than one: "According to the National Institute on Aging the health risks of prolonged isolation are equivalent to smoking 15 cigarettes a day. Social

---

[66] Sherry Amatenstein, "Not So Social Media: How Social Media Increases Loneliness," *Psycom*, November 15, 2019, https://www.psycom.net/how-social-media-increases-loneliness.

[67] American Heart Association, "Social isolation, loneliness can damage heart and brain health, report says," *American Heart Association News*, August 4, 2022, https://www.heart.org/en/news/2022/08/04/social-isolation-loneliness-can-damage-heart-and-brain-health-report-says.

isolation and loneliness have even been estimated to shorten a person's life span by as many as 15 years."[68]

A friend and I went on a long bike ride in a nearby state park last summer. We rode by a beautiful old hunting camp set back off a dirt road. I admired it, and my friend told me it used to be the site of a huge family reunion every year. "They don't do it anymore," she said. "People get busy, I guess," she mused. I shrugged and guessed she was right. We *are* all very busy these days, aren't we?

Or are we? Do we have to be?

> The biggest disease in North America
> is busyness. (Thomas Merton)

Are we truly busy — productively so — or just distracted? Or are we just "too busy" freaking out over the latest mainstream media news story, or envying how comfortable and convenient our neighbors' lives are, or trying desperately to convince them that *our* lives are perfect, to attend a family reunion? What could be more important than getting together with family once a year, in the woods, where there's no cell phone service, but there is sunshine, warmth, tall, perfumed pine trees, a cozy cottage, a campfire, laughter, nature, love, and joy? What's the point of everything, if not an annual family reunion in the forest?

Wokeness Lives and Dies Online

In addition to the physical and mental-health problems screen time causes, our phones, tablets, computers, and televisions are also arbiters

---

[68] Michele M. Kroll, "Prolonged Social Isolation and Loneliness are Equivalent to Smoking 15 Cigarettes A Day," *American Heart Association News*, May 2, 2022, https://extension.unh.edu/blog/2022/05/prolonged-social-isolation-loneliness-are-equivalent-smoking-15-cigarettes-day.

of not only biased "news" manufactured to arouse fear and division, but also woke messaging. Nearly 70 percent of adults and some 80 percent of young people use social media,[69] and the top social media platforms are owned by outspoken liberals. Though they deny partisan censoring practices, Pew Research found in 2020 that their users beg to differ: "Majorities in both major parties believe censorship is likely occurring."[70] And, of course, the more time you spend consuming information from these sources, the more likely you — and your children — are to be exposed to woke propaganda.

In *The Chaos Machine: The Inside Story of How Social Media Rewired Our Minds and Our World*,[71] author Max Fisher details how "moral outrage" posts get the most play. Fisher told NPR on *All Things Considered* how these platforms increase political polarization in our communities: These "incredibly sophisticated automated systems that are designed to figure out exactly what combination of posts, what way to sequence those posts, how to present them to you will most engage certain very specific cognitive triggers and cognitive weak points that are meant to get certain emotions going.[72]"

---

[69] Aaron Smith, "Record shares of Americans now own smartphones, have home broadband," *Pew Research Center*, January 12, 2017, https://www.pewresearch. org/fact-tank/2017/01/12/evolution-of-technology/.

[70] Emily A. Vogels, Andrew Perrin, and Monica Anderson, "Most Americans Think Social Media Sites Censor Political Viewpoints," *Pew Research Center*, August 19, 2020, https://www.pewresearch.org/internet/2020/08/19/ most-americans-think-social-media-sites-censor-political-viewpoints/.

[71] Max Fisher, "The Chaos Machine The Inside Story of How Social Media Rewired Our Minds and Our World," *Little Brown*, September 6, 2022, https://www. littlebrown.com/titles/max-fisher/the-chaos-machine/9780316703314/.

[72] Ari Shapiro, Michael Levitt, Christopher Intagliata, "How the polarizing effect of social media is speeding up," *NPR*, September 9, 2022, https://www.npr. org/2022/09/09/1121295499/facebook-twitter-youtube-instagram-tiktok -social-media.

Fear is the woke mob's main tool, and it's an effective one. Think about the first thing an Old West bad guy does before he robs a stagecoach: he holds up a gun and orders the passengers to get out with their hands up and lie on the ground. Under the control of fear, the victims will do anything to stop the worst thing from happening, even if other bad things (such as their possessions being stolen) happen, too.

It's the same with woke ideology. You're afraid of being called racist, so when the radical woksters hold a verbal death sentence to your head, you'll undergo diversity training, even if you know it's a waste of time and does nothing to end racism. You're afraid the penguins will drop over dead, so instead of driving to see your old college roommate who's three hours away, you keep your evil, earth-killing machine in the garage and miss out on feeding your soul and making memories you'll cherish for a lifetime.

Because it's made up, the woke agenda lives and dies in the media — on television and through online social platforms. "Wokeness" didn't exist before cell phones did, because without a way to broadcast bogus instances of discrimination and fake outrage, the rest of us, living as NORMALs, would have no idea any of the woke offenses were going on (because they aren't). If it weren't for hashtags and the corporate media pushing the radical, woke narrative, nothing *would* be going on.

After all, if you had a noble thought or did a woke thing and didn't post about it on social media, did it really happen? As social media influences the world, we are trained to think and behave identically — like one big high school peer group. As Big Tech homogenizes our lives, Big Tech homogenizes our minds.

It reminds me of an interaction I had with a sales representative from an Irish gun manufacturer. We were at the Shooting Hunting Outdoor Tradeshow in Las Vegas, and we got to talking about gun control laws. Ireland's are extremely restrictive, and I was amazed that any gun makers manage to survive at all on the Emerald Isle, or in the U.K. This man then tip-toed around asking what the U.S. is *really* like, revealing that from news reports, he had expected the streets of America to be rife with carnage — just a daily rerun of *Tombstone*. "It doesn't seem very violent to me?" he said delicately. Could the media be *exaggerating* — lying, even — to vindicate taking our guns away? Indeed, I assured him, FBI crime data reveals that outside of Democrat-run inner cities,[73] the U.S. is a very safe place.

> If you know the enemy and know yourself, you need not fear the result of a hundred battles. If you know yourself but not the enemy, for every victory gained you will also suffer a defeat. If you know neither the enemy nor yourself, you will succumb in every battle. (Sun Tzu, *The Art of War*)

Cancel Them First

Not long ago, my mother mistook my phone for hers and drove off with it — an hour away. I knew she wouldn't be back for some time, but I needed to get in touch with a friend to help me move a piece of furniture. It had been a while since I hadn't had access to my cell phone. I didn't remember my friend's number off the top of my head (had I ever memorized it?). I managed to log into my laptop and find it in one of my emails, but how was I to call him anyway?

I decided to drive around our small town. First I went to where I thought he would be, mowing grass. Then I drove out to a state park nearby where he often goes on Sunday afternoons. He wasn't there, but I found myself enjoying the "hunt." It was a gorgeous day, and each time

---

[73] GianCarlo Canaparo and Abby Kassal, "Who Suffers the Most from Crime Wave?" *The Heritage Foundation*, April 12, 2022, https://www.heritage.org/crime-and-justice/commentary/who-suffers-the-most-crime-wave.

I stopped to look for my friend, I found myself instinctively reaching for my phone in the passenger seat. Driving back to town, I realized even in the absence of my phone, there was a pulling feeling in my mind, as if there was a nagging something I had to do. Check my messages? I guess that was it. Or maybe just "be available." Vague enough, but that was part of it, too. Answer a work email? My work rarely contacts me on weekends, and even if they did, it could wait 'til Monday. But, you know ... just in case.

By the time my third phoneless hour rolled around, and I'd spent a few hours driving all over town, enjoying the sunshine, and looking for my friend, to no avail, I felt free — as if in accidentally taking my phone, my mother had taken a persistently looming but intangible "responsibility" from me. I realized much of that feeling of obligation is self-imposed, imaginary, even, and largely unnecessary. Just because everyone else is trained to expect an immediate response, to know every news event instantly, and be "plugged-in" and "informed," doesn't mean we NOR-MALs have to live this way.

You'd think with all these modern-day conveniences and technologies making so much of our existence streamlined and automatic, we'd be less stressed out, not more so. It's as if we're trying to keep up with the fast-paced technology *we* invented for making our lives easier. Instead, our stress has amounted to an "unforced error" in tennis. We bring into our lives "unforced stress" by taking upon ourselves a second life of sorts (as if one isn't stressful enough!) — one full of scorn, perversion, division, and despair that is never silent, but which can, thank God, be *silenced*.

If you've been out of cell phone range recently, on, say, a camping trip, you've likely felt a sense of relief that your absence from the fast-paced world of texts, emails, phone calls, pop-up ads, and the news cycle was "excused" by the circumstances of nature. Well, it turns out you can excuse yourself from the fast-paced world, too. Just blame it on nature. *Human* nature.

Cal Newport authored the bestseller *Digital Minimalism*,[74] a delightful little book outlining how our society has become overwhelmed by technology addiction. Newport explains how to conduct a "thirty-day digital declutter" to cut out "optional online activities" for a month. People who do this, he shows, experience "massively positive changes by ruthlessly reducing time spent online to focus on a small number of high-value activities," such as taking walks, talking to friends in person, engaging your community, reading books, and staring at the clouds. All — not so coincidentally — woke-proof-approved activities!

Newport also acknowledges the obvious: that used properly and in moderation, technological resources — think Google Maps, online healthcare portals, and so forth — are "triumphant innovations!" Yet to allow optional online activities — such as over-consumption of news and social media — to disrupt our lives not only causes us increased anxiety and loneliness; it also tends to lead to a feeling of inadequacy, as we compare our lives to those "perfect" people online. With our phones glued to our hands, we also tend to spend more money — to the tune of about $1,000 a year in unplanned purchases when we shop distracted by our phones.[75]

You're bored? That's because you keep your senses awake and your soul asleep. (St. Josemaría Escriva)

In addition to trying the digital declutter, I urge NORMALs to ask themselves the purpose of their screen time: is it a resource or a recourse? Is your social media usage bringing you closer to God by strengthening

---

[74] Cal Newport, *Digital Minimalism: Choosing a Focused Life in a Noisy World*, (Penguin Business, 2019).

[75] Kali Coleman, "The One Shopping Habit That's Making You Spend More Money, Study Says," *Yahoo News*, October 22, 2020, https://www.yahoo.com/lifestyle/one-shopping-habit-thats-making-004239947.html.

Christ-centered relationships, supplying you with a community of like-minded believers who inform, inspire, and invigorate your life? Or is it diverting you from the beauty of God's creation, distracting your attention from His goodness, and, as Newport puts it, negatively "manipulating your mood"?

Remain attentive to these questions and use your devices as tools — and sparingly. Remember that online bullies can't "cancel" you if you cancel them first (you know darn well these trolls would never confront you in person!). Don't allow them to agitate you unreasonably and uselessly. Think of them as children throwing a tantrum and let them cry it out. Do not engage.

Be selective in what your eyes and mind absorb. You wouldn't open your mouth and let random strangers put any sort of unknown substance into your body, would you? Then why risk the same thing with your eyes, mind, and soul? You are what you eat. And watch, and hear, and read, and so forth. By consuming whatever Big Tech (including the mainstream media) throws at us, we're essentially filling our minds with junk food, and it has the same negative effects on our souls as cheap, mass-produced, fake fast food has on our bodies.

Woke-proof ways:

+ Designate phoneless areas of your home and commit to phone-less activities: walking in nature, going to the gym (you'll make more friends without your earbuds!), dinnertime, waiting in waiting-rooms, and so on. If your phone causes you to sin, cut it off: leave it at home, in your purse, whatever.
+ Consider significantly reducing your social media usage, or getting rid of social media all together.
+ Limit your consumption of news to an hour a day. Find *one* woke-proof news program to watch, or *one* newspaper to read, or *one* podcast to listen to, and leave it at that.
+ Wear a watch. If you're like me, you use your phone as a time-piece, but checking it can lead to reading emails and texts.

Googling something, clicking on a sponsored ad, getting lost in the world wide web. You can also turn off notifications, but watches are classic and cool and need to be encouraged.

LGBTQIA Is Not ROY G. BIV

The Bible is unequivocal in its condemnation of homosexuality and other forms of "grave depravity" that contradict God's natural law. In *The Rise and Triumph of the Modern Self*, Carl R. Trueman explains how the sexual revolution, "the radical and ongoing transformation of sexual attitudes and behaviors that has occurred in the West since the early 1960s," is distinctive in the way the movement "normalized" sexually explicit behaviors — homosexuality, pornography, and sex outside the bounds of marriage — as mainstream elements of culture.[76]

Read a book, listen to a song, or watch a film from or set pre-1960 and compare the attitudes regarding sex found there to the bawdy, casual take on sex that characterizes modern media. While we're on the subject of pre-woke works, it's worth noting that not only has the sacrosanct nature of sex been defiled, but artistic output has deteriorated along with it. Works produced with a pre–sexual-revolution mindset are often much more enriching — more imaginative in their language and more emotionally enthralling, too, as "the battle of the sexes" and associated concepts supplied endless entertainment, until the very concept was deemed politically incorrect (Pepé Le Pew, anyone?).

These days, even many so-called "conservatives" support homosexuality and same-sex marriage, forgetting — or willfully ignoring — that the point of sex is procreation, and the point of marriage is to rear children, making "same-sex marriage" an oxymoron. To point out this truth in our woke world is to be labeled "homophobic" (though no one I know

---

[76] Carl R. Trueman, *The Rise and Triumph of the Modern Self*, (Wheaton, Illinois: Crossway, 2020).

who professes the truth about marriage is "afraid" of homosexuality), "intolerant," "judgmental," or "bigoted."

> As the family goes, so goes the nation and so goes the whole world in which we live. (St. John Paul II)

"Why can't you just let two people who love each other be happy?" they'll say, painting you as some romantic Scrooge. It's tempting, as always, to do the easy thing, to look the other way, and for a long time the prevailing attitude has been, "so long as you don't bother me about it, I don't care what you do." But it is your duty to care what people do. Christians are not "anti-love." Rather, we understand that loving another person is much more than getting along well with that person or having chemistry. Thomas Merton, in *No Man Is an Island*, explains it perfectly:

> To love one another is to will what is really good for him. Such love much be based on truth. A love that sees no distinction between good and evil, but loves blindly merely for the sake of loving, is hatred, rather than love. To love blindly is to love selfishly, because the goal of such love is not the real advantage of the beloved but only the exercise of love in our own souls. Such love cannot seem to be love unless it pretends to seek the good of the one loved. But since it actually cares nothing for the truth, and never considers that it may go astray, it proves itself to be selfish. It does not seek the true advantage of the beloved... It is not interested in the truth, but only in itself. It proclaims itself content with an apparent good: which is the exercise of love for its own sake, without any consideration of the good or bad effects of loving.[77]

---

[77] Thomas Merton, *No Man Is an Island*, (New York: Dell, 1955), 27.

If you see someone doing something you know is harmful to their mind, body, and soul, you are obliged to speak up. True love is wanting what is truly best for the other person, and sometimes, true love is extremely difficult, which is what makes it so rare and so powerful. In fact, the most loving thing you can do is steer someone away from spiritual harm.

Supporters of LGBTQIA (for those not up to woke speed, that's "Lesbian, Gay, Bisexual, Transgender, Queer, Intersex, and Asexual," though don't ask me to explain what these terms mean) have found in the movement an easily manipulated societal linchpin. No one wants to be seen as being anti-love, and so their live-and-let-live, you-do-you apathy easily took hold.

With a firm foothold, they moved on to undermining traditional marriage. And now we see their true aim: no long can libertarian types dismiss the LGBTQ movement with a "just don't bother me about it" shrug. We are now being *forced* to fund LGBTQ agendas in public schools[78] and to pay for sex-change surgeries.[79]

The woke, as we've noted, are crafty. They always present the LGBTQ movement as something happy and liberating. Bright, cheerful colors. Smiling same-sex couples. Finally! Half the population heretofore living deprived, repressed, loveless, lying lives are free to express themselves, find true happiness, be comfortable in their own skins, and live happily ever after experimenting with as many gender-fluid partners as they can find.

---

[78] Richie Malouf, "CDC allocated $85 million for grants requiring schools to start student-led clubs supporting LGBT youth," *The Center Square*, October 2, 2022, https://www.thecentersquare.com/national/cdc-allocated-85-million-for-grants-requiring-schools-to-start-student-led-clubs-supporting-lgbt/article_3784d282-18e7-11ed-af0b-a7db9311335d.html.

[79] Todd Blodgett, "Taxpayer-funded transgender services jeopardize Medicaid," *The Des Moines Register*, March 14, 2019, https://www.desmoinesregister.com/story/opinion/columnists/2019/03/14/costly-taxpayer-funded-transgender-services-undermine-medicaid/3155724002/.

Except LGBT is not like tasting all the colors of the rainbow. It isn't going to the ice cream counter and sampling every flavor, each one more delicious than the last, to the point that you can't decide which one to order a double scoop of. Heartbreaking research from the American Psychiatric Association shows these lifestyles often involve immense pain and suffering:

> LGBTQ individuals are more than twice as likely as heterosexual men and women to have a mental health disorder in their lifetime. They are 2.5 times more likely to experience depression, anxiety, and substance misuse compared with heterosexual individuals.[80]

According to The Brain Center, "LGBTQ youth are much more likely to contemplate or attempt suicide than their straight counterparts. They're also more likely to report feeling sad or hopeless."[81]

> America, it is said, is suffering from intolerance—it is not. It is suffering from tolerance. Tolerance of right and wrong, truth and error, virtue and evil, Christ and chaos. Our country is not nearly so overrun with the bigoted as it is overrun with the broadminded.
> (Bishop Fulton Sheen, *Old Errors and New Labels*)

Among transgender people, the statistics are even more troubling: A 2020 Yale University study found, "transgender individuals who had received a diagnosis of gender incongruence were:

[80] "Diversity & Health Equity Education: Lesbian, Gay, Bisexual, Transgender and Queer/Questioning," *American Psychiatric Association*, https://www.psychiatry.org/psychiatrists/cultural-competency/education/lgbtq-patients.
[81] "Depression in the LGBTQ Community: Facts & Stats," *Brain Therapy TMS*, June 10, 2021, https://braintherapytms.com/depression-in-the-lgbtq-community-the-facts-you-need-to-know/.

- six times more likely to have a mood or anxiety disorder than the general population.
- three times as likely to be prescribed antidepressants and antianxiety medications.
- more than six times as likely to attempt suicide resulting in hospitalization."[82]

These statistics are devastating. But it's likely many of the mental health battles young people experience are winnable. Gallup found that 3.5 percent of the population identified as lesbian, gay, bisexual, or transgender in 2012;[83] in 2021, that number was 7.1 percent,[84] with young adults representing the highest number of "not straight" responders. Yet it turns out that, left to their own devices, *without* their devices, the vast majority of kids would never think for one second that changing their gender was possible, or even desirable.

"The spike in teens using social media and identifying as transgender is no mere coincidence," reported Heritage Foundation researchers Jared Eckert and Mary McCloskey in 2022. "Behind those screens, sexual and transgender content saturates the digital spaces where most teens hang out."

The report notes how "digital spaces are ever more designed to promote sexual and transgender content," and "some platforms are even designed to hide youth's activity from the watchful eye of their parents."[85]

[82] Colin Poitras, "Transgender individuals at greater risk of mental health problems," *Yale School of Public Health*, August 24, 2020, https://ysph.yale.edu/news-article/transgender-individuals-at-greater-risk-of-mental-health-problems/.

[83] Frank Newport, "In U.S., Estimate of LGBT Population Rises to 4.5%," *Gallup*, May 22, 2018, https://news.gallup.com/poll/234863/estimate-lgbt-population-rises.aspx.

[84] Jeffrey M. Jones, "What Percentage of Americans Are LGBT?" *Gallup*, March 3, 2022, https://news.gallup.com/poll/332522/percentage-americans-lgbt.aspx.

[85] Jared Eckert, Mary McCloskey, "How Big Tech Turns Kids Trans," *The Heritage Foundation*, September 15, 2022, https://www.heritage.org/gender/commentary/how-big-tech-turns-kids-trans.

The researchers cite a 2021 study conducted by a Rhine-Waal University professor faculty member showing "the majority of those who transition were persuaded to do so online through social media, blogs, and YouTube."[86]

The Federalist's Joy Pullmann (interviewed, along with her husband, in chapter three) highlighted a Brown University study released in 2018 indicating, "'Rapid-onset gender dysphoria' among teens and young adults may be a social contagion linked with having friends who identify as LGBT, an identity politics peer culture, and an increase in Internet use."[87]

Vox reported glowingly in 2021 on "How TikTok became a haven for queer and questioning kids," calling the app's transformation filters, which change a user's facial features from those of a stereotypical man to a stereotypical female (I'm shocked *Vox* acknowledges that such a thing as "stereotypical features" exist!) with the blink of the eyes "a beautiful thing to witness."[88]

> If you can redefine human nature, if you can actually get everyone to believe, or if not believe at least say that a man is a woman and a woman is a man, you can redefine anything. (Michael Knowles)

[86] Elie Vandenbussche, "Detransition-Related Needs and Support: A Cross-Sectional Online Survey," *Journal of Homosexuality*, April 30, 2021, https://www.tandfonline.com/doi/full/10.1080/00918369.2021.1919479.

[87] Joy Pullmann, "Explosive Ivy League Study Repressed For Finding Transgender Kids May Be A Social Contagion," *The Federalist*, August 31, 2018, https://thefederalist.com/2018/08/31/explosive-ivy-league-study-repressed-for-finding-transgender-kids-may-be-a-social-contagion/.

[88] Rebecca Jennings, "How TikTok became a haven for queer and questioning kids," *Vox*, August 3, 2021, https://www.vox.com/the-goods/22606245/tiktok-queer-fluid-bisexuality-nonbinary-filter.

There is nothing less "beautiful" than a nation tormented by anxiety, depression, substance abuse, and thoughts of suicide. Yet our society — especially our youth — is so desperate for attention, acceptance, support, and something they perceive to be love that they're willing to engage in behaviors that invite misery. In their struggles and confusion, they will forever alter the beautiful person God made in His own image and likeness through hormone therapies. They will mutilate themselves irreversibly. They will engage in behaviors the Bible makes clear are not in accord with God's plan, "unnatural relations" and "dishonorable passions,"[89] at the expense of their earthly peace and well-being and at the cost of their immortal souls.

Why do the LGBTQ peddlers turn a blind eye to the repercussions of the conduct they encourage? They will tell you the anxiety and depression are the fault of the people who do not "accept" the LGBTQ lifestyle and are due to a lack of gay and trans "rights." Yet being gay has moved way beyond the point of being acceptable and mainstream. Today, it's mark of distinction.

LGBTQ people are now celebrated more than our nation's scientists, engineers, firefighters, and war heroes. They're granted special scholarships and promotions, and they're on every media platform. Netflix has an entire section dedicated to "Gay & Lesbian Movies & TV" with the tag: "Love is love. Drama is drama. Comedy is comedy. This diverse collection of movies and shows celebrate gay, lesbian, bisexual, transgender and queer stories."

The woke are certainly selective in their fight for "equality." What about the anxiety and depression and "rights" of the young Virginia girls who were sexually assaulted by a gender-fluid perpetrator in an all-female

---

[89] "What Are the Bible Passages That Deal with Homosexuality?" *Catholic Answers*, https://www.catholic.com/qa/what-are-the-bible-passages-that-deal-with-homosexuality.

school bathroom?[90] What about the pain and suffering of a California girl emotionally traumatized by seeing male anatomy in the women's locker room?[91] What about the girls who are seriously injured because they're forced to play sports with biological males?[92]

These people don't matter, because they aren't useful in furthering degeneracy and power. Just think how much control you can have over a man if you're able to convince him he's a woman, and how much control you can have over a populace that believes a man can get pregnant. Once you've done that, you've reached the level of ultimate manipulation, by which you can do anything.

The most outspoken LGBTQ activists revel in the perverse, defiantly making a mockery of tradition for the shock value and attention it generates. Singer Sam Smith comes to mind. At the 2023 Grammy Awards show, "they" dressed up as the devil and writhed around in a cage with flames dancing all around him and his fellow demons to sing a song called "Unholy." Billboard lambasted those who labeled the performance satanic for not "celebrating the fact that the [singers] made history for the LGBTQ community that night."[93]

90 Caroline Downey, "'They Failed at Every Juncture': Loudoun County Mishandled Bathroom Sex Assault, Grand Jury Finds?" *National Review*, December 6, 2022, https://www.nationalreview.com/news/they-failed-at-every-juncture-loudoun-county-mishandled-bathroom-sex-assault-grand-jury-finds/.

91 Dana Kennedy, "'17-year-old scolded for crying over transgender woman's penis at YMCA" *New York Post*, January 14, 2023, https://nypost.com/2023/01/14/sighting-of-trans-womans-penis-in-ymca-locker-room-sparks-tears/.

92 Holt Hackney, "'Professor Maintains that Trans Athletes Causing Serious Injuries to Girls," *Sports Law Expert*, December 12, 2022, https://sportslawexpert.com/2022/12/12/professor-maintains-that-trans-athletes-causing-serious-injuries-to-girls/?utm_source=rss&utm_medium=rss&utm_campaign=professor-maintains-that-trans-athletes-causing-serious-injuries-to-girls.

93 Stephen Daw, "Sam Smith & Kim Petras' 'Unholy' Grammys Performance Deemed 'Satanic' & 'Evil' by Conservatives," *Billboard*, February 6, 2023, https://www.billboard.com/music/awards/sam-smith-kim-petras-unholy-2023-grammys-satanic-evil-1235213736/.

> Whoever causes one of these little ones who
> believe in me to sin, it would be better for him to
> have a great millstone fastened round his neck and
> to be drowned in the depth of the sea. Woe to the
> world for temptations to sin! For it is necessary
> that temptations come, but woe to the man by
> whom the temptation comes! (Matthew 18:6–7)

Some of the growing LGBTQ trend among young people may amount to typical teenage rebellion. Yet many of these children are desperately crying for help. They come from broken homes. They are neglected, unsupervised, left to absorb hours and hours of perverse media every day. Eventually they decide to adopt the LGBT lifestyle. A 2014 study published by the National Library of Medicine concluded that, "Maltreatment, including sexual abuse, can have persistent effects on mood and behavior, which may increase likelihood of same-sex sexuality."[94]

To "indulge in unnatural lust,"[95] as the Bible puts it, and to reject and go to great lengths to alter the identity and body a person is born with are signs of a troubled soul. Either the woke refuse to recognize this, or they do see it and don't care. Rather than provide LGBTQ people with a nurturing, safe, supportive community in which to be loved and navigate their interior struggles, the woke mob assures them they'll be more popular, more in vogue, more "true to themselves" if they reject the body and identity they were born with and adopt a lifestyle the hallmark of which is pride — the chief deadly sin.

---

[94] Andrea L. Roberts, M. Maria Glymour, and Karestan C. Koenen, "Does Maltreatment in Childhood Affect Sexual Orientation in Adulthood?" *National Library of Medicine*, September 14, 2012, https://www.ncbi.nlm.nih.gov/pmc/articles/PMC3535560/.

[95] "What Are the Bible Passages That Deal with Homosexuality?" *Catholic Answers*, https://www.catholic.com/qa/what-are-the-bible-passages-that-deal-with-homosexuality.

The woke are never more enthused than when they are advocating for and reveling in a person's "gender-affirming care" — despite the fact that this type of "care" *denies* people's gender and instead affirms people's convictions that they are something other than what they truly are. This has historically been known as insanity, and in modern times, as "dysmorphia." The woke cheer on and celebrate depravity in all its forms — the more debauched the better! — never pausing to consider the torment of the souls they lead astray. If it's weird, kinky, experimental, controversial, and non-traditional, it's to be encouraged, no matter what.

The woke profess to care *about* one another, but they never bother to care *for* those who need it most, which is telling in their simplistic "love is love" mantra. Anyone who's ever been to a wedding knows love is much more dynamic than that. It entails a whole list of attitudes and behaviors (which is why it's so hard sometimes!). Love is patient, love is kind. "Love is not pompous, it is not inflated ... it does not seek its own interests." Something tells me this type of love would not have a parade for itself.

Nothing is sweeter than love; nothing stronger,
nothing higher, nothing more generous, nothing more
pleasant, nothing fuller of better in heaven or on earth;
for love proceeds from God and cannot rest but in
God above all things created. (Thomas à Kempis)

This is not to say, obviously, that people who ascribe to an LGBTQ lifestyle are incapable of love, but the love described in the Holy Bible contrasts sharply with the "love" flaunted by many LGBTQ activists. True love wants what is best for the other person, i.e., to help lead that person to Heaven, not simply what makes them "feel good" in the passing moment.

We are called to minister to all people in Christ's name. That means accepting people with LGBTQ tendencies "with respect, compassion, and sensitivity" and prayerfully guiding them toward the proper understanding of human sexuality.[96]

Climate Changers vs. Weather Realists

"Climate change" is yet another avenue by which the woke choreographs a culture of fear and control. Once you're afraid, you'll do what they say. You'll give up your gas stove, your woodstove (yes, those are on the chopping block, too![97]), your gas-powered car, your plastic straws, your cheeseburgers. You'll end your weekly trips to see Grandma, because she lives too far away. She'll die of loneliness, but at least we cut down on our carbon footprint! You'll forgo eating hot food. You'll freeze in the winter. And you'll be forced to rely on the benevolent government even more than you already do for life's necessities.

So-called "climate change" is my favorite woke cause because of how shamelessly phony its proponents are. For starters, the very phrase "climate change" is an evolution (puns always intended!) of the term "global warming," adopted, obviously, when the Chicken Littles realized their scare tactic was flawed. Parts of the world are, in fact, cooling.

To admit that the streets of Fairbanks, Alaska aren't on the verge of turning into a balmy beach anytime soon, the global warming alarmists had to change their narrative, and quick! So "climate change" was born, and, like all second-born kids, is conveniently blamed for everything so

---

[96] "Ministry to Persons with a Homosexual Inclination," *United States Conference of Catholic Bishops*, November 14, 2006, https://www.usccb.org/resources/ministry-to-persons-of-homosexual-iInclination_0.pdf.

[97] Rosie Frost, "These clean air campaigners are calling for wood-burning stoves to be banned," *Euro News*, October 18, 2021, https://www.euronews.com/green/2021/10/18/are-wood-burning-stoves-really-as-green-as-they-seem.

that the progressive left can justify anything. It didn't take long for them to advocate for abortion as a way to "help" the climate.[98]

I hereby command you: Be strong and courageous; do not be frightened or dismayed, for the Lord your God is with you wherever you go. (Joshua 1:9)

Let's say the earth's "changing climate" *were* about to melt every single ice cap, dehydrate every last emperor penguin, boil every ocean, and spontaneously combust every one of Al Gore's eyesore solar panels.[99] You'd never know, judging from the behavior of the climate change czars squawking the loudest, that this was the case.

Think about it. If you really, *truly* believed, in your heart of hearts, that climate change is "the single most existential threat to humanity we have ever faced, including nuclear weapons,"[100] (per Joe Biden), and that your modern lifestyle was causing it, wouldn't you do … *something*? Wouldn't you take drastic measures to change your lifestyle in a major way, and do everything in your power to get everyone you know to do likewise?

As we know, however, the most ardent climate change czars are the wealthiest, most powerful people, with the most to gain from

[98] Robert N. Proctor and Londa Schiebinger, "How Preventing Unwanted Pregnancies Can Help on Climate," *Yale Environment*, July 21, 2022, https://e360.yale.edu/features/unwanted-pregnancy-contraception-abortion-climate-change.

[99] Drew Johnson, "Al Gore's Inconvenient Reality," *National Center for Public Policy*, August 1, 2017, https://nationalcenter.org/ncppr/2017/08/01/al-gores-inconvenient-reality-the-former-vice-presidents-home-energy-use-surges-up-to-34-times-the-national-average-despite-costly-green-renovations-by-drew-johnso/.

[100] Steven Nelson, "Biden calls global warming bigger threat to humanity than nuclear war during NYC speech," *New York Post*, January 31, 2023, https://nypost.com/2023/01/31/biden-says-global-warming-is-bigger-threat-to-humanity-than-nuclear-war/.

perpetrating the "climate anxiety" that now affects some two-thirds of Americans — and 84 percent of children — and which is so helpful in controlling them.[101] At least in celebrity circles, there appears to be a direct correlation between how much a person harps about the environment and the size of his carbon footprint.

In fact, Mr. Gore himself is the perfect example. The John Locke Foundation analyzed the environmental impact of the eco-warrior's home in 2017, with many "shocking" (*hardly*) findings, including, "Gore guzzles more electricity in one year than the average American family uses in 21 years."[102] Leonardo DiCaprio, meanwhile, a U.N. "climate change ambassador" who proclaimed climate change to be "the most urgent threat facing our entire species," is fond of using his private jet and a superyacht, the latter of which reportedly "demands fuel worth $339,712 to fill its tank."[103]

If the greatest fear-mongers themselves are not losing any sleep over "climate change" or changing their ways at all, why should the rest of us?

The Big Scam

"Over the past 50 years, we've gone from 'global cooling,' to 'global warming,' to 'climate change,' to 'extreme weather,' to 'weird weather,' " Steve Milloy told me.

Steve is a biostatistician, securities lawyer, and writer (among many other accomplishments), who served on the Environmental Protection

[101] Stephanie Collier, MD, MPH, "If climate change keeps you up at night, here's how to cope," *Harvard Health Publishing*, June 13, 2022, https://www.health.harvard.edu/blog/is-climate-change-keeping-you-up-at-night-you-may-have-climate-anxiety-202206132761.

[102] Mitch Kokai, "Al Gore's carbon footprint detailed," *John Locke Foundation*, August 7, 2017, https://www.johnlocke.org/al-gores-carbon-footprint-detailed/.

[103] Doha Madani, "Leonardo DiCaprio gets called out for boarding superyacht: 'eco-hypocrite,'" *Geo News*, January 10, 2022, https://www.geo.tv/latest/392622-leonardo-dicaprio-gets-called-out-for-boarding-superyacht-eco-hypocrite.

Administration transition team under the Trump administration. Steve has worked in the environmental sector in varying capacities for 30 years. He knows the industry inside and out, which is why he calls climate change "the biggest scam humanity has ever created."

Steve says that, if the climate change alarmists got their way, millions of people would die almost instantly. People who live in cities, especially, who have no idea where their food comes from or what's involved in producing it, would be destroyed immediately, as would people relying on prescription drugs, dialysis, and so on. Everything in life as we know it would be altered drastically, and much of it would disappear entirely.

Here are insights Steve shared with me about how the climate change alarmists operate:

> This notion that we can go back to the pre-Industrial Age and still maintain our standard of living today, with all the people we have — no way.
>
> There's nothing that happens in today's world that does not depend 100 percent on fossil fuels. And if there were not fossil fuels, we would be back to pre-Industrial conditions, which would be a disaster for humanity.

"We will never be free of fossil fuels"

> For people who think wind, solar, "emission-free" technologies are the way to go, none of that stuff can be made without fossil fuels. It can't happen. It's not going to happen, and I don't think it's intended to happen. I don't really think the people who are pushing this agenda are really that stupid. They know everything depends on fossil fuels and all this effort we've put into [alternate energies] is not working. Absent some truly revolutionary technology, which is not foreseeable, we will never be free of fossil fuels. Fossil fuel technology is the greatest thing ever to happen to mankind. We went from 1 billion people in the pre-Industrial Age to 8 billion people now. That's impossible without fossil fuels.

Their plan is to reduce the population

The [climate change crowd's] whole plan is to reduce the population. Paul Ehrlich — who wrote *The Population Bomb* in 1968 — his vision was that the Earth had a carrying capacity of 2 billion people, and here we are at 8 billion. The greens don't like that that many people are on the planet, and they would like to reduce the population, and that is why they deny energy to poor people, they're threatening our food supply. They would like to rid the planet of the poor among us. The 1993 book, *Malaria Capers*, summarizes Third World people as "better dead than alive and riotously reproducing."[104] This is not a new policy.

Green policies "are not meant to work"

These policies are not meant to work; they're actually meant to reduce the number of people on the planet. For some reason, these people want to tell everyone else what to do, and perhaps they feel that they can accomplish that with 2 billion people instead of 8 billion people. I don't really understand the mentality myself. I don't really try to figure it out anymore, I just look at what their policies are intended to do, and their policies are not intended to help people thrive; they're intended to reduce people's standard of living. And when you do that to poor people, you are threatening their well-being and their lives.

Al Gore was behind one of the fist bills proposed on "climate change." Back then it was a lot of money, not so much now, but it was $5 billion, and one-third of that bill was going to go to "family planning." Which is abortion and birth control. And it was "international," which means for black and brown people. So it was also racist.

---

[104] Dr. J. Gordon Edwards, "Malaria: The Killer That Could Have Been Conquered," *21st Century Science & Technology*, Summer 1993, https://calepa.ca.gov/wp-content/uploads/sites/6/2016/10/CEPC-2013yr-Feb28-Comments-AppA_Ex17.pdf.

"Most people can't believe these people are that evil"
These thoughts are unfathomable to most people. Most people can't believe these people are that evil. But look at history. People can be this evil. When they banned, for example, [the insecticide] DDT in the United States, they knew that would be propagated around the world, and of course tens of millions of poor black and brown people have died because of that.[105] They know the effects of these polices, yet they don't care. They're hoping that, because they've camouflaged themselves behind this "earth-friendly" façade, that no one will question them.

The climate has always changed, slowly, sort of imperceptibly. The climate was as warm a thousand years ago as it is today, and in between, the thirteenth through the sixteenth centuries were relatively cool; it was a period we call the "Little Ice Age." Things change all the time.

"Climate deniers were the first people canceled"
The greens willfully misrepresent everything, and because they have the biggest megaphone, they think they can get away with it.

Climate is the way they make their whole agenda come true, because they can control everything through climate. That is why "climate deniers" were the first people canceled. People like me were canceled a long time ago — we were canceled in the 2000s.

"Good-hearted people have been hijacked"
Climate change activists are always talking about "well, before people were here." Well, if it weren't for people, then who would care? The earth would literally just be the third rock from the sun.

---

[105] Annabel Ferriman, "Attempts to ban DDT have increased deaths," *National Library of Medicine*, May 26, 2001, https://www.ncbi.nlm.nih.gov/pmc/articles/PMC1173321/.

There are some people for whom this is religion, but for the people in charge, it's a political agenda. They only want 2 billion people so they can control them. But there is a whole army of people who are tree-huggers. Or animal lovers — I mean in a religious sense. These are good-hearted people who have been hijacked.

"Everyone is propagandized"
Even most conservatives don't really understand it and have fallen for the non-stop propaganda. The people who promote what passes for environmentalism today have captured essentially every institution in America. It takes an extraordinary knowledge base not to fall for it. I've worked on this stuff for thirty years, and I realize none of it is true.

It's shocking we've gotten this far. But this is what has been happening with our school system. Everyone is propagandized. You have these teachers who are just left-wing bots, spitting out left-wing propaganda, testing kids on it, and that is what they learn. It happens in public schools, private schools, charter schools. If you were taught since kindergarten that every bit of bad weather was caused by fossil fuels, that's what you're going to believe, and that's what people do believe.

"It's not science, it's alarmism"
The greens don't care about anyone alive today — all the poor people in Africa and India and people being oppressed in China. They don't care about the environment in China today or anything like that. It's always "in one hundred years." A lot of these climate predictions are for the year 2100. "The year 2100 is going to be five degrees warmer." None of this is science. Science is making a prediction, testing it, and seeing if it's true, not making some prediction that is untestable. It's not science, it's just alarmism.

Discrimination Is Everywhere! (And So Is Violence)

For the woke, "discrimination" is as certain as death and taxes. Someone is *always* discriminating against some class of people for something. Black Lives Matter, antifa, and other radical woke, progressive groups claim discrimination any time a white law enforcement officer acts in defense against a so-called "person of color," or POC. A transgender inmate recently cried "discrimination!" because (s)he(?) was denied a vaginoplasty in prison.[106] Asking the morbidly obese singer Lizzo to cover up her cellulite-ridden bottom in public is considered "fatphobic" — and racist, too, of course, because Lizzo happens to be black.[107]

You know the drill. It's easy to be momentarily annoyed, roll your eyes, and go about your day. But while you're busy contributing to society, working hard to put food on the table, paying your bills, supporting your family, and honoring your country, the woke are working, too. Not in any useful way, but to stoke the fires of wokeness. And fires, shootings, robberies — all means of senseless violence — are what woke ideology brings about.

The woke but godless, the arrogant but ignorant,
the violent but physically unimpressive, the degreed
but poorly educated, the broke but acquisitive, the
ambitious but stalled—these are history's ingredients
of riot and revolution.[108] (Victor Davis Hanson)

---

[106] Jon Brown, "Minnesota transgender inmate sues after being refused surgery in prison," *Fox News*, June 12, 2022, https://www.foxnews.com/us/minnesota-transgender-inmate-sues-refused-bottom-surgery.

[107] Doha Madani, "Lizzo tearfully calls out 'fatphobic' and 'racist' hate following 'Rumors' release," *NBC News*, August 16, 2021, https://www.nbcnews.com/pop-culture/pop-culture-news/lizzo-tearfully-calls-out-fatphobic-racist-hate-following-rumors-release-n1276920.

[108] Victor Davis Hanson, "The Fragility of the Woke," *National Review*, July 9, 2020, https://www.nationalreview.com/2020/07/woke-protesters-historys-ingredients-riot-revolution/.

Think about it: to discriminate in the way progressives define the term (not to be confused, for instance, with a "discriminating taste") means to maltreat because they belong to or "identify" as belonging to a particular physical, racial, gender, or sexual-preference group. This kind of discrimination is wrong. But to constantly "point" fictional acts of discrimination have only one purpose in mind: to cause division, provoke anger, encourage retaliation, and justify violence.

And that, of course, is just what's happened. As the Heritage Foundation's Mike Gonzalez points out, social-justice warriors, in the name of "diversity, equity, inclusion [DEI], and (now) *justice*," think nothing of inciting violent riots.[109] So, "the sustained, often violent street actions . . . [became] a recurring feature of American urban life in 2020" and were "almost entirely driven by left-wing protestors."[110]

Physical violence is not the only way the race-baiters elicit division. A 2016 *New York Post* story reported how administrators at the Bank Street School for Children on New York's Upper West Side aimed to "fight discrimination" by "teaching white students as young as six that they're born racist and should feel guilty benefiting from 'white privilege,' while heaping praise and cupcakes on their black peers."[111]

A 2023 Fox News story reported how Lane Cogdill, a Maryland middle school teacher and Black Lives Matter supporter who simultaneously

---

[109] Sheila Callaham, "Does 'Black Lives Matter' Hinder Or Help Universal Equity? Three Diversity Executives Speak Out," *Forbes*, August 23, 2020, https://www.forbes.com/sites/sheilacallaham/2020/08/23/does-black-lives-matter-hinder-or-help-universal-equity-three-diversity-executives-speak-out/?sh=5128507a1967.

[110] Mike Gonzalez, "For Five Months, BLM Protestors Trashed America's Cities. After the Election, Things May Only Get Worse," *The Heritage Foundation*, November 6, 2020, https://www.heritage.org/progressivism/commentary/five-months-blm-protestors-trashed-americas-cities-after-the-election.

[111] Paul Sperry, "Elite K-8 school teaches white students they're born racist," *The New York Post*, Jul 1, 2016, https://nypost.com/2016/07/01/elite-k-8-school-teaches-white-students-theyre-born-racist/.

uses "ze/zir," "they/them" and "he/him" pronouns and "admitted to intentionally concealing students' gender changes," uses race to justify BLM's rioting and looting. "As far as I'm concerned, as a white person, and as a history teacher, if your ancestors built this country, you have the right to burn the motherf----r to the ground,"[112] Cogdill said.

Social "justice" is concerned not with justice nor with making everyone equal, but rather is set on punishing a group of people for a crime they didn't commit. It isn't about acknowledging racial and cultural differences and celebrating what we, as humans, have in common; it's about labeling white people as "wrong" because they are not POC. Through Critical Race Theory, or CRT, an entire generation of young people is being trained to judge their neighbors by the color of their skin. "At its core," explains Tennessee Senator Marsha Blackburn, "CRT segregates people into two main categories: oppressors or victims.[113]"

> I'm sorry for something I didn't do
> I lynched somebody, I don't know who
> You blame me for slavery
> A hundred years before I was born ("Guilty
> of Being White," Minor Threat)

If children happen to be white, they are brainwashed to feel shame and guilt about it. If they are a POC, they are told they are entitled to preferential treatment and are encouraged to disparage non-POCs. How

[112] Hannah Grossman, "Middle school teacher claims it's 'White supremacy' to oppose thievery: 'Burn this motherf----- to the ground'," *Fox News*, February 19, 2023, https://www.foxnews.com/media/teacher-claims-white-supremacy-oppose-thievery-burn-motherfcker-ground.
[113] Marsha Blackburn, "Why Is Critical Race Theory Dangerous For Our Kids?," July 12, 2021, https://www.blackburn.senate.gov/2021/7/why-is-critical-race-theory-dangerous-for-our-kids.

are such lessons helpful in building a nation full of culturally and ethnically diverse citizens who value one another and will work together to build a great future? Such a reality is not the woke mob's goal. They think selfishly, in terms of "how can I benefit in the here and now?" A generation of children who are ashamed to be American[114] and who are convinced they owe an unforgivable debt is the perfect prerequisite for all kinds of self-centered and sinister ends.

Final thought: remember the woke movement is characterized by a few puppet masters benefitting personally from the fear and division they bring about, and then recall that BLM spent $12 million on luxury properties.[115]

DEI and ESG

You'll notice how the woke like to give their initiatives easy-breezy abbreviations that flow off the tongue effortlessly and work their way into everyday language. DEI and its cousin ESG (environmental, social, and governance) initiatives are rampant at huge woke corporations, but they're also working their way into small companies that think if they adopt such initiatives, they, too, will land on the Fortune 500 list.

My regional bank has served my family's financial needs for more than a hundred years. I just noticed that sandwiched on the bank's website between the Home Loan Center and Online Services tabs is a DEI link, which takes one to a page that explains the bank's commitment to ESG. Why? What does having a checking account or applying for a mortgage

---

[114] Anika Exum, "Why Williamson County parents are suing school district, state education commissioner," *Nashville Tennessean*, July 11, 2022, https://www.tennessean.com/story/news/local/williamson/2022/07/12/williamson-county-parents-wit-wisdom-teaches-critical-race-theory/10029032002/.

[115] Isabel Vincent, "BLM spent at least $12M on luxury properties in LA, Toronto: tax filing," *The New York Post*, May 17, 2022, https://nypost.com/2022/05/17/black-lives-matter-spent-at-least-12-million-on-mansions/.

have to do with the color of my skin, my cultural heritage, or anything other than the very non-ethnic numbers in my bank account?

The problem with DEI is the same problem all woke concepts have: they don't do what they purport to do. Forcing diversity does not make anyone feel more included. If you truly want an inclusive environment, why harp on people's differences? Ashlynn Warta of the James G. Martin Center for Academic Renewal made the astute observation about how DEI-related funding is not only a waste of college and university resources,[116] but is also *counter*-productive:

> Rather than encouraging diverse, equitable, and inclusive environments, they actually encourage students to conform to predetermined ideologies. More specifically, DEI efforts are narrowing the scope of what is "acceptable" on college and university campuses.

Brian Dapelo is a business strategist and consult who wrote on LinkedIn "7 Ways Your DEI Initiatives Are Harming Your Company and How to Resolve It."[117] Brian granted me permission to cite his important observations in this book, and though the entire article is well worth reading in its entirety, I include a condensed version of it here:

1. *DEI is discriminatory.* It is hard to disagree that firing or declining to hire someone on the basis of religion, gender, or orientation is discrimination and is illegal. Yet, when a POC is treated preferentially in the workplace based on those same characteristics, it is called "diversity and inclusion"? Logic suggests that preferencing candidates based on these qualifications mean that others are intentionally discriminated against based on the same criteria.

---

[116] Ashlynn Warta, "Diversity-Office Funding Wastes UNC-System Resources," *The James G. Martin Center for Academic Renewal*, August 8, 2022, https://www.jamesgmartin.center/2022/08/diversity-office-funding-wastes-unc-system-resources/.

[117] Brian Dapelo, "7 Ways Your DEI Initiatives Are Harming Your Company and How To Resolve It," *LinkedIn*, April 27, 2022, https://www.linkedin.com/pulse/7-ways-dei-harming-your-company-how-resolve-brian-dapelo/.

2. *DEI places undue stress on physical attributes.* Whether intentional or not, DEI programs tend to favor those who look different as opposed to those who are diverse in other areas, like thought, faith, culture, socioeconomic upbringing, experience, and so forth. This is likely because the emphasis on the physical makes DEI programs give more immediately tangible results by making a company *look* more diverse, when in reality the people still think, act, and believe the same to fit in with the company culture.

3. *DEI diminishes the size of the talent pool.* By putting unnecessary limitations on the talent pool because of racial or gender quotas established under DEI programs, the number of qualified candidates that may otherwise be a better fit for the company is significantly reduced. By basing hiring decisions more on the candidate's skills, experience, personality, and motivation instead, there is always a wider pool of applicants to choose from.

4. *DEI decreases performance.* When hiring preference is placed on one's looks rather than skills, experience, and other qualifications, failure is often the result. Two things can typically happen when a significantly underqualified candidate is hired: either the candidate stays with the employer and decreases productivity over time, or else they quit/get fired and their work is passed on to others, decreasing the overall performance of others until the role is again filled with a more qualified candidate, costing tens of thousands of dollars in the process.

5. *DEI is divisive.* When anyone is shown preference throughout their career based on their physical attributes rather than on merit, envy and disdain are sure to occur, causing in-fighting, unnecessary distractions, and ultimately division in an organization. This can significantly decrease morale amongst other employees and even lead to racist/sexist/exclusive behavior that would otherwise not have previously existed.

6. *DEI diminishes accomplishment.* Many DEI programs have caused some people to question whether the beneficiaries of these initiatives are there because of their qualifications, or because they are a "diversity

hire." That is a travesty. It is humiliating to those who genuinely achieved those positions on merit and nothing else.

7. *DEI is distracting.* DEI has become so widely promoted in corporate spheres following the belief that "diversity is strength," that many executives have become obsessed with this notion and gone overboard in promoting it to the point that it has become more of a distraction from much more important corporate objectives aimed at benefiting all stakeholders.

A friend who works for a large international company described how this played out in his business. An employee, who was an immigrant from India, was promoted to managing one of the company's largest offices, just as she was returning from maternity leave. The message the company hoped to send to its customers and competitors: we care about minorities *and* working mothers.

The woke-hire ended up using her power for evil. She used her position to harass her colleagues and bully those who worked for her. She behaved in her own racist ways, suppressing other Indian women who out-skilled her. She manipulated the compensation system to take an unfair share for herself. And above all, she was totally incompetent. She made poor decisions for the business that were quietly corrected behind the scenes by those with common sense and skill. The management quickly realized the mistake it had made, but it was impossible to reverse. Demoting this young minority mother would be seen in the business community as misogynistic and racist. And so, she remained in a position of power, where she behaved in the very manner the company preached against.

If DEI is the interior designer picking out the multi-race colors of the bank offices, then ESG is the contractor telling DEI what cans of paint make the cut, where it can be applied, and if there's enough money to afford the White Privilege hue. ESG, explained in a very basic way, is how woke investors decide whether to fund something. They invest in companies that further the woke agenda — referred to as "stakeholder capitalism" — and see to it that non-woke institutions crash and burn.

Put simply, ESG is the vehicle by which the rich and powerful become even more powerful. With lofty goals as their smokescreen, woke executives dictate which businesses will thrive (i.e., those that embrace the woke agendas we've just gone over) and which will wither and die (i.e., companies that espouse traditional values or that simply refuse to toe the DEI line). ESG is the weapon by which the woke set all their ideological goals in motion. ESG investing "brings the cultural and political dominance of the climate change and social justice narratives into one, mighty fist that is beating its way through one boardroom after another," wrote Kathy Barnett for *Newsweek*.[118]

Rather than investing in industries NORMALs want and need to thrive, such as the oil and gas industry, powerful, woke corporate executives pick and choose the companies that sell their woke souls to curry favor — and lots of money — with investors. This is how NORMALs are left with a diminishing list of options when it comes to non-woke corporations we can conscientiously patronize.

[118] Kathy Barnette, "ESG Is a Woke Scam Infecting Our Corporations and Changing Our Nation," *Newsweek*, November 28, 2022, https://www.newsweek.com/esg-woke-scam-infecting-our-corporations-changing-our-nation-opinion-1761408.

3

What to Expect
Sacrifice, Vigilance, Reward

A friend of mine is a "foodie." He's also conservative and does his best to resist supporting woke industries. So I was surprised to learn he was still frequenting a neighborhood restaurant that celebrates "Pride Month" year-round with rainbow flags permanently on display. "He can't help himself," a mutual friend told me. "He can't resist the sauce on the hanger steak. The food is just too good."

Know this: woke-proofing your life will require some sacrifice. You will be called to deny yourself and stay strong. You'll rearrange some of your priorities, make a concerted effort, take a few extra steps, go out of your way, and become more self-reliant. You must also be brave and speak out.

Most of all, you must remain vigilant. A recent study on the "illusory truth effect" found that "repeated information is often perceived as more truthful than new information."[119]

We also know that we grow numb to things the more often we see them. "Habituation" is the process the American Psychological

---

[119] Aumyo Hassan and Sarah J. Barber, "The effects of repetition frequency on the illusory truth effect," *Cognitive Research: Principles and Implications*, May 13, 2021, https://cognitiveresearchjournal.springeropen.com/articles/10.1186/s41235-021-00301-5#Abs1.

Association defines as "the diminished effectiveness of a stimulus in eliciting a response, following repeated exposure to the stimulus."[120]

In other words, the more we're inundated with woke ideologies, the more likely we are to absorb them subconsciously and allow them to supplant themselves in our minds and in those of our children, our family, our friends, and everyone we encounter. We become desensitized. It's like walking into a room and noticing an offensive odor. Two minutes later, the odor is a part of you; you don't even notice it anymore.

In woke-proofing your life, though, you will reap the reward of your passing discomfort a thousandfold in the friendships you make, the hope you regain, the happiness and healthiness you personally experience, the satisfaction you feel in being able to take care of yourself, and in the beautiful future you help build.

Seek Ye First

The woke-proof lifestyle is anchored in the Judeo-Christian values nearly every American held prior to the Attack of the Woke (doesn't that sound like a horrible science-fiction horror film?), and to which the majority of us still ascribe. It is imperative, then, that in the face of adversity, persecution, and "cancelation," we NORMALs do as King David did, saying, "The Lord is my rock, and my fortress, and my deliverer, my God, my rock, in whom I take refuge, my shield, and the horn of my salvation, my stronghold." (Ps. 18:2–3)

We can do all things through God who empowers us. (Phil. 4:13) We must strive to live in a way that makes God's presence known and felt — a life that brings Him ever closer to our minds, hearts, and souls and to those of our neighbor. We must also avoid those things that shut God out and keeps Him at a distance (here's lookin' at you, screen time).

---

[120] American Psychological Association, "Habituation," *APA Dictionary of Psychology*, May 13, 2021, https://dictionary.apa.org/habituation.

> An excellent method of preserving interior silence is to keep exterior silence.... Even in the world, each one of us can make his own solitude, a boundary beyond which nothing can force its way unperceived. It is not noise in itself that is the difficulty, but noise that is pointless; it is not every conversation, but useless conversations; not all kinds of occupation, but aimless occupations.... There are two ways of separating ourselves from almighty God, quite different from one another but both disastrous, although for different reasons: mortal sin and voluntary distractions—mortal sin, which objectively breaks off our union with God, and voluntary distractions, which subjectively interrupt or hinder our union from being as close as it ought to be. We should speak only when it is preferable not to keep silence. The Gospel does not say merely that we shall have to give an account of every evil word, but of every idle thought. (St. Alphonsus Liguori)

The benefits of a society steeped in religion are numerous. *Live Science* reported in 2015 that "a slew of research has tied being religious with better well-being and overall mental health. A number of studies have found that devout people have fewer symptoms of depression and anxiety, as well as a better ability to cope with stress. Certain religious practices may even change the brain in a way that boosts mental health, studies suggest."[121]

It makes sense. When you believe that God is "gracious and merciful, slow to anger and abounding in love and fidelity," (Exod. 34:6) that He has counted all the hairs on your head, (Matt. 10:30), and that He has "plans for welfare and not for evil, to give you a future and a hope" (Jer. 29:11)

---

[121] Rachael Rettner, "God Help Us? How Religion is Good (and Bad) for Mental Health," *Live Science,* September 23, 2015, https://www.livescience.com/52197-religion-mental-health-brain.html.

you tend to be less worried about the future. When you "look not to what is seen but to what is unseen" and realize that "the things that are seen are transient, but the things that are unseen are eternal," (2 Cor. 4:18) it makes life and its trials a whole lot lighter.

Our natural human inclination is to try to control everything, but once you understand that the one who designed the cosmos, knows everything about everything, has existed for eternity, is in charge of the climate, our relationships, and every other unpredictable element of life that gives us anxiety, you can't help but "let go and let God." It's the most freeing, peaceful, and invigorating feeling in the world.

Author Ericka Andersen has studied this phenomenon. Writing for *USA Today* in 2021, Andersen reported:

> Broad-based evidence demonstrates that attendance at worship services is indispensable to a happy, generous and flourishing society.
>
> Pew Research found that actively religious adults are more likely to be happy, volunteer time to good causes and be more civically involved than non-religious or non-practicing religious folks.[122]

"Happier, Healthier, and More Optimistic"

Speaking to the earthly advantages of religion, Andersen noted to me how trusting in God for all things and relying on His grace and mercy reducing people's anxiety and frees them to be more thoughtful of others:

> Those who are in a committed faith are generally more grounded in their purpose and do not feel they must "control" every aspect

---

[122] Ericka Andersen, "Why going to church during Holy Week (and beyond) is good for your mental health," *USA Today,* March 28, 2021, https://www.usatoday.com/story/opinion/2021/03/28/how-attending-church-during-holy-week-can-boost-your-mental-health-column/4764317001/.

of life. Because of this they are often better parents and spouses, friends, and neighbors. People of faith give significantly more to charity and volunteer work — both in and outside their respective faiths — and are more likely to be civically involved and trusting of their neighbors.

Because they aren't living just for themselves, others are important. Thus, this attitude contributes to the greater good of their families and communities. They are also more emotionally protected, with loved ones there to help, encourage or support when life gets hard. This community aspect of faith is the most powerful part, in terms of how society is affected overall. Those who have a strong faith community are happier, healthier, and more optimistic.

The research in my book, *Reason to Return: Why Women Need the Church & the Church Needs Women,* shows that, regardless of life circumstances, those who are committed to consistent faith community fare better in almost every way. In fact, one study I documented found that the only people who reported improved mental health in the aftermath of COVID were those who attended church weekly (online or in person) throughout 2020 and 2021.

Once again, God provides us with constant reminders that not trusting in and relying on Him is bad for us. The American Psychological Association reports, "Chronic stress is linked to six leading causes of death including heart disease, cancer, lung ailments, accidents, cirrhosis of the liver and suicide."[123] Such research makes one wonder if we're experiencing so much a "mental health crisis" as a "lack of God and community crisis." Being anxious and sad are normal elements of the

---

[123] SLMA Inc., "The Science of STRESS," *South Louisiana Medical Associates,* https://www.slma.cc/the-science-of-stress/.

human condition; it's when we don't cope with them properly that they become a disease.

> Cast all your anxieties on him, for he cares about you. Be sober, be watchful. Your adversary the devil prowls around like a roaring lion, seeking some one to devour. Resist him, firm in your faith, knowing that the same experience of suffering is required of your brotherhood throughout the world. And after you have suffered a little while, the God of all grace, who has called you to his eternal glory in Christ, will himself restore, establish, and strengthen you. (1 Peter 5:7–10)

Another related, kind of odd but interesting (don't ask me how I found this) study published by a University of Michigan Health Behavior and Health Education researcher in 2009 found that

> more frequent attendance at worship services may encourage people to become more humble.... Both formal and informal aspects of religion may encourage people to become more humble.... Perhaps most important, the data indicate that older people who are more humble tend to rate their health more favorably than older adults who are less humble.[124]

For those still on the fence about the whole religion thing, consider this report by StudyFinds.com on research released by the University of Exeter in 2022: "People who go to church are more likely to have a very satisfying sex life, a new study reveals. Researchers in the United Kingdom found that strongly religious individuals are typically more

---

[124] Neal Krause, "Religious Involvement, Humility, and Self-Rated Health," *National Library of Medicine*, August 10, 2010, https://www.ncbi.nlm.nih.gov/pmc/articles/PMC2918920/.

content with their bedroom activities than those who are not religious or engage in casual sex."[125]   *

Alright, we get it: believing in God and going to church are good for us. But ... believing in God, getting someone else to, and strengthening our relationship with the Lord are not as easy as getting the Omega 3 fatty acids and antioxidants we also know are good for us. How does a person who feels a void that the things of the world are not satisfying go about believing, if he or she has never believed before? How does someone reignite his love if he's been a stranger to God for some time? How do we, who have faith already and practice it, grow ever closer to our Lord and share our faith with others?

I've encountered many people in my life who say they don't believe in God, though further discussion reveals they *believe* in God, but they aren't on familiar terms with Him because of some hang-up, often having to do with not feeling God's presence, blaming Him for something, being ashamed to face Him, or a combination of all these things. These people aren't sure how to approach God, thinking of Him more as a stern principal, eagerly dolling out punishment, than as an understanding Father who only wants what is best for His child.

Fr. Terry Brennan is a tirelessly cheerful soul well-attuned to the complexities of the human condition (he was a lawyer before answering his call to become a priest!). His early priesthood was spent as a missionary to the native people of New Mexico, and he now utilizes his boundless energy educating and evangelizing people from all walks of life.

When I asked Fr. Brennan how he recommends a person go about seeking and finding God, he advised:

> If you feel a desire or even an interest in something transcendent, beyond yourself ... even something divine, then be grateful. It is

---

[125] Chris Melore, "God bless: Strongly religious people have a more satisfying love life," *Study Finds*, August 30, 2022, https://studyfinds.org/religious-people -love-life/.

an invitation to something spiritual. If your response is a desire to pursue whatever is good and beautiful and of the Truth, then you can have a quiet assurance that you are on the correct way. Then, your own unique human characteristics are stirred to action, and invite you to respond. This response can be either an inner dialogue or an exterior action; both with the intent of finding a meaning or a purpose to one's self. It all starts with that initial invitation — God's grace, God's invitation to unity.

Ericka said:

> If someone is seeking God or a faith to hold to, I encourage curiosity and prayer. The Bible says, "Seek and ye shall find." You've been invited to the table. Knock on the door and you'll be let in.

There is technically no "wrong" way to come to God. He is everywhere always, and so seeking and finding Him is always a possibility anywhere. That said, some techniques are more linear than others. Dramatic "come to Jesus" stories, such as MyPillow founder Mike Lindell's crack-addict-turned-outspoken-Christian conversion, make for good headlines, but encountering God in a peaceful, sweet, and tender way can be just as life-changing. Bear in mind that, as King David told the people of Israel, "the Lord searches all hearts, and understands every plan and thought. If you seek him, he will be found by you; but if you forsake him, he will cast you off for ever" (1 Chron. 28:9).

I often think about dying and what it will be like the moment after I take my last breath. (When I brought this up during a work happy hour function once, my boss at the time remarked, "I don't know if I'm not drunk enough for this question or *too* drunk for this question.") I struggle with a sense that I talk *at* God but not really *to* Him. As if He's an abstract machine that can control things and with which I deliberate over my course of action, but who is not so much the loving, familiar father He should be, with whom I communicate openly, affectionately, and constantly.

> For prayer is nothing else than being on terms
> of friendship with God. (St. Teresa of Ávila)

"What will it be like when I encounter Him in person?" was my thinking one day, as if God couldn't hear me. Then it dawned on me, brilliant theologian that I am: we are always in God's presence — already! We're encountering Him right now, all the time, forever, whether we recognize it or not. There's no escaping Him. What a silly thing to think — that there will come a time when we will at last be in the presence of the one who made us and who governs everything.

St. John of the Cross provides us this comforting assurance: "In the first place it should be known that if a person is seeking God, his Beloved is seeking him much more." How do we seek God? Here are four helpful tips:

1. *Try.* This is the first thing a person must do to establish or enhance his relationship with God. What do you have to lose? Ask God to help you grow closer to Him. To truly love someone, you must know Him. Get to know God by reading His words in the Holy Bible. Ask a godly friend, relative, coworker, or acquaintance how she fortifies her faith. Ask her to pray with and for you. Accompany her to church. Ask God to make His presence seen and felt in everything you do — in the most mundane chores, in the song of the streams, and in the face of the grocery store cashier.

Ask God, too, to help you submit to your suffering as Christ did His cross — with love and for the benefit of the whole world — and thank Him for all that He wills to send you. I find, too, that because God *is* love, the more loving things you do and the more loving your attitude, the closer to God you inherently become. Little acts of love done in silence and without complaint serve as intimate secrets between you and God. Only He and you know you've done them and why, as you make room for Him to live in your heart and direct your life.

---

*A word, a kindly smile, will often suffice
to gladden a wounded and sorrowful
heart. (St. Thérèse of Lisieux)*

---

2. *Purify your heart.* St. Augustine of Hippo instructs us to "purify the inmost recesses" of our hearts that our Lord might abide there. Our souls should be a refuge for God, a place He delights in dwelling. Once He is there, living in a safeguarded home, He can guide us more fully with His strengthening gifts of grace.

3. *Turn your thoughts into prayers.* The time is always now. You are never alone. God is always there, listening, guarding, waiting for your communication and love. We need only lift our eyes and minds and hearts to Him, to tell Him of our worries, hopes, and joys, to ask Him for help in doing His will and thank Him for His abiding goodness. Rather than merely thinking *about* things, turn your inner dialogue into a ceaseless conversation *with God*, asking Him to guide your thoughts and worries toward wisdom and understanding.

4. *Find God in nature.* Nature helps ease many earthly troubles, and it's helped many find God. Go for a walk (*sans* phone!) and reflect on the varied tones of the leaves and flowers and butterflies and moss and tree lichen. Listen to the music a flowing stream makes and consider what sort of a kind creator would think to make a bird's chirping into a *song*. Look at the design of a snowflake. Why are they intricate and beautiful, when they could be uninteresting blobs? Contemplate the flavors and textures of food and the unending enjoyment we derive from eating, though it be a repetitive enterprise. Reflect on the graceful way the clouds float across the sky, and how the sun makes things gold and sparkly. Ask God to reveal Himself to you everywhere.

---

*Prayer is the place of refuge for every worry,
a foundation for cheerfulness, a source of*

constant happiness, a protection against
sadness. (St. John Chrysostom)

"Proclaim on the Housetops"

As a person of faith, it is your duty to "speak in the light" and "proclaim
on the housetops" (Matt. 10:27). Our Lord instructs us to acknowledge
Him before others, and He will, in turn, acknowledge us before our
heavenly Father (Matt. 10:32). Do not be ashamed of your faith. To
shy away from publicly acknowledging God is to put people's opinions
of you above your relationship with Christ. This does not mean you're
obliged to put a "Jesus Freak" bumper sticker on your car and listen
to nothing but Christian rock. Live a Christ-centered life. Pray before
meals in restaurants. Instruct and minister when the occasion presents
itself. A preachy attitude and tone tend to be off-putting, and unlikely to
be very effective. Think of non-believers and fallen-away Christians as
wild creatures wary of the strange and unknown. Try a gentle approach,
preaching the gospel first and foremost through example.

When I confided in a priest friend of mine to feeling distracted and
distant from God lately, he advised that I begin each day with half an
hour of silence, in which I recite this refrain: "O Jesus, I surrender myself
to You, take care of everything!" I've found that this exercise, combined
with some fresh air first thing and a giant mug of coffee, is enough to
set any day on the straight and narrow. Though I still feel the need to
repeat, "take care of everything!" often throughout the day (and to refill
the coffee cup, too).

Everyone should also give *Trustful Surrender to Divine Providence*
a read at least once a year.[126] It's a short little book that packs a punch,

----

[126] St. Claude de la Colombière, Fr. Jean Baptiste Saint-Jure, *Trustful Surrender to
Divine Providence: The Secret of Peace and Happiness*, (TAN Books, 1980).

reminding us that God knows what He's doing. C. S. Lewis's *The Screwtape Letters* is another resource that is somehow fun to read and also startling in its illustration of how Satan and his devils craftily, constantly, and subtly carry our destruction in our world.

Fr. Brennan has compiled a basic reading list for those eager to learn and grow in sanctity:

Bible and biblical studies

All religious studies begin with and must include the Bible. Choosing a good study Bible (vis a vis a "devotional" Bible) is crucial. But then again, how can anyone base his true devotion on anything other than the truth? So shouldn't every Bible we use be the most authentic Bible, the most accurate rendition, of all the Bibles that are available?

The Douay Rheims Bible, which is grounded upon the earliest sources — many of which no longer exist — the English translation of the Vulgate compiled by St. Jerome, constitutes the best study and devotional Bible. But also keep in mind: as important as it is to rely on a Bible that originates in ancient texts and was compiled by a reliable scribe, it is also important to rely on a Bible that was reliably translated. With so many English translations, how does one choose the best? Again, the Douay Rheims has been relied upon for being a faithful translation from the original Latin.

Having said this, those who study the Bible also seek study materials. The resources available are unbelievably numerous. Here are reliable sources:

- Biblical commentary: *The Great Commentary of Cornelius à Lapide* (Available online: https://www.ecatholic2000.com/lapide/untitled-170.shtml). Written by a Catholic priest. One of the best sources. A real gem.
- Psalm commentary: *A Commentary on the Book of Psalms*, St. Robert Bellarmine. Clear and fresh insights on many levels. The best source.

- Writings of the prophets: *The Prophets*, Abraham Heschel. Written by a prominent rabbi, a unique source to understand the prophets themselves and their inspiration.

Catechism

There are so many — how to choose? Here is a good beginning, but not a list of sole sources.

- *Catechism of the Catholic Church*: Even though this was written for use by bishops and priests and can feel overwhelming, it still is a vital and good source of basic Catholic teaching.
- *Roman Catechism*: This goes by many names; it is the catechism of the Council of Trent, and therefore a rich, accurate, and inspired work.
- Vatican II: Read the four Dogmatic Constitutions and see how the Church still needs to apply these teachings in a correct way, especially *Sacrosanctum Concilium*. Notice the anthropology in *Gaudium et Spes*. Question the characterizations of Judaism and Islam as religions professing the same one God as Christians.
- *Apologetics and Catholic Doctrine*: Archbishop Michael Sheehan. Detailed description of the Faith.

Philosophy

Here, it is as important to avoid certain philosophers as it is to read others. Also, keep in mind that many Catholic writers were both philosophers and theologians. See below.

- *Consolation of Philosophy*, Boethius: One of the earliest Catholic philosophers; he wrote from prison just before his martyrdom. Clear and passionate.
- *Pensées*, Blaise Pascal: In an era of compelling, confusing, and erroneous philosophies, here is a true Catholic holding up the standard.

- *Liberty, the God that Failed*, Christopher Ferrara: By far the best explanation of how seventeenth-century British philosophy influenced our American Constitution and government.

Theology

Theology did not become a systematic study until the advent of universities; earlier writers wrote in various and even extensive ways, but this bibliography begins in the thirteenth century.

- *Summa of the Summa*, Peter Kreeft: Aquinas is the pre-eminent theologian, but his prolific writings can be difficult for the layman to approach. It is hard to find a good summary of his writings. This one is good.
- The works of St. Bonaventure: *Mystical Opuscula, Breviloquium; Opuscula: Second Series; Collations on the Six Days; Defense of the Mendicants*. He is the other great theologian of the Church, easier to read as a primary source than Aquinas.
- *Theology for Beginners*, Frank Sheed: Contemporary and covers a broad subject matter. Noted Catholic author.
- *Veritatis Splendor*, Pope John Paul II: Although all his encyclicals should be read, if there is one that stands out, this is it. Needed in the upside-down world of relativism we are in now.
- *Upon this Rock*, Stephen K. Ray: Papacy has been a central issue for centuries and remains so today.

Early Church

- *Against Heresies*, St. Irenaeus: To read what a saint in the second century believed about the Catholic faith and to compare it to our beliefs today and to see the exact congruity. Richly gratifying.
- *Apology*, St. Justin Martyr: A philosopher convert's explanation of the faith and especially the Mass. Richly gratifying again.

◆ *Didache*: One of the earliest Church writings. Describes the Sacraments and other Church-established traditions.

◆ *Early Church Fathers, The Apostolic Fathers*, ed. Jack Sparks. Read the original sources of any and all of them — from this source or any other.

◆ *Rule of St. Benedict*: to understand the underpinnings of religious life. Then read his biography written by Pope St. Gregory the Great.

◆ *The Philokalia*, four volumes: Writings of the early Church and Eastern religious. Deeply spiritual.

Church History

◆ *History of the Church*, Eusebius: Earliest extant history.

◆ *History of the Catholic Church*, Fr. John Laux.

Saints

◆ *Lives of the Saints*, Alban Butler: Four volumes. There is no better, more accurate compendium of the lives of the saints or inspiration for all Catholics.

◆ *Confessions*, St. Augustine: Great personal insight and inspiration.

◆ *Life of St. Francis of Assisi*, St. Bonaventure: He wrote from a time contemporary with St. Francis.

◆ *Life of Catherine of Sienna*, Raymond of Capua: He was her spiritual advisor and a Master General of the Dominicans. Accurate and moving.

◆ *Autobiography* and *Spiritual Exercises*, St. Ignatius of Loyola: Classics.

◆ *All Will Be Well*, Julian of Norwich: Timeless wisdom from six hundred years ago.

◆ *Apologia Pro Vita Sua*, St. John Henry Newman: First-hand conversion story.

◆ *Story of a Soul*, St. Thérèse of Lisieux: Much-loved for its simplicity and self-revelation.

Education: Take Back the Narrative

Behold, I send you out as sheep in the
midst of wolves; so be wise as serpents and
innocent as doves. (Matthew 10:16)

Woke ideologues are calculated and know that infiltrating government schools and corrupting young minds is their best bet for success. Therefore, the woke-proof education of our children is a critical component of a woke-proof future. To think and act rightly, it is imperative that NORMALs possess an understanding of the world that is informed by the greatest minds who ever lived. This may involve a non-woke re-education of yourself, your family, and friends — of anyone who will listen, really.

But where to begin? There are plenty of resources available for providing children with a traditional education, but what if you're like most Americans who have learned little of value in our government schools and progressive institutions of higher learning?

A traditional education involves developing the mind in such a way that our thoughts bring about virtue, and we are fortunate that many institutions and programs exist to facilitate this type of learning.[127] My alma mater, the University of Dallas, is one such place. UD's stated mission is being "dedicated to the pursuit of wisdom, of truth, and of virtue as the proper and primary ends of education":

> The University seeks to educate its students so they may develop the intellectual and moral virtues, prepare themselves for life and work in a problematic and changing world, and become leaders

---

[127] Madeline Coggins, "As woke curriculum increases, classical education booms: Hillsdale College sees 53% increase in applications," *Fox News*, February 4, 2023, https://www.foxnews.com/media/woke-curriculum-increases-classical-education-booms-hillsdale-college-sees-53-increase-applications.

able to act responsibly for their own good and for the good of their family, community, country, and church.

The University understands human nature to be spiritual and physical, rational, and free. It is guided by principles of learning that acknowledge transcendent standards of truth and excellence that are themselves the object of search in an education.

UD offers a course of study that "preserves what is of enduring value from the past ... and leads students into freedom so that they can help build a civilization of truth and justice." Every undergraduate student completes the study of the "Core Curriculum" that enables them to "see the parts of their education as complementary." Regardless of their major, all students are required to study history, theology, literature, economics, politics, mathematics, physical and biological sciences, language, and the arts.

This kind of education sets NORMALs up for success in our morally topsy-turvy world like none other. Not just material, worldly success — though UD and other classical liberal arts institutions count among their graduates many people who have made their mark on society in remarkable ways — but in equipping people with a true understanding of humanity and with the tools necessary to think critically, self-govern, and act as moral leaders.

An eloquent man must speak so as to teach, to delight, and to persuade... To teach is a necessity, to delight is a beauty, to persuade is a triumph. (Cicero)

Of course, most people aren't able to go back and attain a classical liberal arts education at a college or university. And you don't have to. The pursuit of a classical liberal arts education is one of those things for which the Internet is a blessing.

Hillsdale College offers many free online courses through its "America's Public Education" program, which gives students "an education that pursues knowledge of the highest things, provides insight into the nature of God and man, forms character, and defends constitutional government."

Scholars Online is another good place for self-educators to start. Great Courses offers classes taught by experts and professors on a range of categories that can be worked through at your own pace. My brother listened to just about every course the company offers on the Middle Ages, and after a road trip with him that involved countless "you know, in the Middle Ages…" factoids, I can personally attest to the breadth of what a person can learn through the Great Courses.

The Classical Liberal Arts Academy offers insanely affordable curriculum plans online. William C. Michael is the headmaster of the academy, which provides "classical studies and tutoring for Catholic students of all ages."[128] He has also written and spoken extensively on such topics as where adults should begin in studying the classics, why "you don't need living teachers to study the seven liberal arts," and the "difference between school studies and the pursuit of real wisdom."

I asked Mr. Michael to provide some insight into how to take control of one's education as an adult. He told me:

"It Simply Takes a Sincere and Sustained Interest"
The education of adults differs little, in method, from the education of children, but adults have several advantages:
- They are no longer subject to compulsory K-12 education requirements.
- They can move much more quickly through lessons than children can.
- They have more life experience than children and can understand more of the ideas of wise men.

---

[128] Classical Liberal Arts Academy, https://classicalliberalarts.com/.

With that in mind, adults start from the beginning of the classical liberal arts as children do, and progress much more rapidly through them. Adults can also begin in advanced philosophy and theology studies because their language and comprehension skills are stronger than those of children.

A good model for adults is St. Ignatius of Loyola who, as an adult convert interested in the priesthood, had to start in grammar school and work his way up — and did so.

The key, really, is that adults need to study the master texts, at their own pace, one lesson at a time. If their interest is sincere, they will find that doing so requires no special help or outside teaching. It simply takes a sincere and sustained interest.

Our modern idea of "learning," involving formal study programs and degrees and diplomas, is "arbitrary and artificial," says Michael, because the people who pursue such a course of "education" do so with the goal of checking a box to receive an award that they can take with them to pursue something else — something different from what they studied.

"It's the opposite of the way ancient wise men study and think about study," Michael says. Ancient wise men do not study to make money or get a comfortable job. Whereas the philosophers of Aristotle's day, for example, "studied not to know what good is, but to actually be good men," modern "scholars" simply seek to know what the answers are for a test to get the credit. "Their goal is not to have a living, active, permanent knowledge, but just to get done what is required. The pursuit of real wisdom is quite the opposite."

Blessed is the man that walketh not in the counsel
of the ungodly, nor standeth in the way of sinners,
nor sitteth in the seat of the scornful. But his delight
is in the law of the Lord; and in his law doth he
meditate day and night. And he shall be like a tree

planted by the rivers of water, that bringeth forth his
fruit in his season; his leaf also shall not wither; and
whatsoever he doeth shall prosper. (Psalm 1:1–3)

Michael presents Psalm 1 for guidance on how we are to educate ourselves: we are to "ponder [the Lord's] law, day and night," remain like a tree "planted" beside flowing waters, yielding its fruit in due season. [129] A godly man's method of study involves being rooted in the source of wisdom — Sacred Scripture and Divine Revelation — meditating on the law of the Lord, and delighting in it. Michael expounds:

"The wise man is not caught up in the constantly changing world"

The wise man [described in Psalm 1] has a very simple course of study — it's a program studied through daily meditation. He's not racing through checklists, he's not completing certificate courses, he's not collecting degrees and diplomas. He's got one book that he's studying, and he studies it day and night. What it means to be this blessed man is not to be the so-called "smart person" talking about a thousand different topics with all kinds of trivia knowledge, but the wise man is compared to a tree planted beside flowing waters.

What marks this blessed man is his lasting, permanent character. It's a character that perseveres and bears fruit when it's supposed to, in the end. His leaves never fade, because he's planted in the presence of that which nourishes him.

"All that he does shall prosper." Notice it doesn't say that this is an active, busy man running all over the place, and every random thing he does prospers. This is a man who's planted. This is a stable,

---

[129] William C. Michael, "The Difference between School Studies and the Pursuit of Real Wisdom," *Classical Liberal Arts Academy,* https://www.youtube.com/watch?v=KG47A5ujjlQ.

permanent, planted man. Everything that kind of stable, persevering man, who ponders the law of the Lord does, will prosper.

We're told the wicked are not like this. The wicked are like the "winnowed chaff, which shall be driven away by the wind." That chaff being blown away by the wind is what the Holy Spirit compares ungodly men to. They have no root, they have no permanence, they don't persevere, they blow away. They're like nothing. The wise man is rooted in God Himself and Sacred Scripture. That is the source of his stability. Because his mind is there, he's always focused on Divine Revelation, and he has a divine permanence about him that is rooted in God Himself, who never changes, who is eternal.

The wise man is not caught up in the constantly changing world. He's not following the advice of the scientists and new fads and theories and new programs and new projects. He's not involved in that stuff. That's the world of the chaff, which vanishes. He's focused on those things that never change.

Change, by contrast, is what woke ideology thrives upon. Woke terminology is always being tweaked — is it "black," "African American," "Person of Color," "Black, Indigenous, People of Color"? Is it "homeless person," "unhoused individual," "person experiencing the effects of houselessness"? — causing an existential frenzy for those who care enough to keep up. That's the point. But truth never changes, and so to be affixed to truth and guided by it is to be at peace.

Something else that changes often in our frenetic world is the list of "acceptable" works of literature.[130] If progressives announce that a book should be "banned," buy the book! — or several copies. Read it, and share it with friends. In fact, a "Banned Book Club" among fellow

---

[130] "Banned & Challenged Classics," https://www.ala.org/advocacy/bbooks/frequentlychallengedbooks/classics.

NORMALs sounds a whole lot more fun and edifying than a "Check Your Privilege" party. Start with George Orwell's *1984* and *Animal Farm* and Aldous Huxley's *Brave New World*. Then you can move onto some more pleasurable, "challenged" material, such as *The Call of the Wild, The Sun Also Rises, The Cat in the Hat,* and oh ... let's see ... *Woke-Proof Your Life.*

Another easy (ha!) way to attain a classical liberal arts education as an adult simply involves (ha, ha!) becoming a parent. Absent your own spawn, you can also involve yourself in a child's education as a tutor, babysitter, volunteer, mentor, and so forth. If you have kids in your life, there are many ways to infuse their education with classical principles and learn along with them. As you'll learn further on from parents who have taken their children's education into their own hands, there are many solid resources available, including (yes, I'm biased) the University of Dallas's K-12 Curriculum. UD also offers a Classical Support Team that works with Catholic, public charter, and various private schools to "provide guidance and practical assistance to faculty and administrators at all levels of understanding the liberal arts tradition."

I've spoken to parents and educators who have successfully guided their children to a virtuous adulthood, and to others who are in the process of providing their children with a traditional education. I present excerpts from my conversations with them here:

Homeschooling

Interest in homeschooling has exploded in recent years, especially since the chaos of the COVID-19 lockdowns, masking requirements, and online "learning" (the learning loss attributed to COVID is appalling)[131] opened parents' eyes to some alarming realities of their children's

---

[131] Jessica Dickler, "Virtual school resulted in 'significant' academic learning loss, study finds," *CNBC*, https://www.cnbc.com/2021/03/30/learning-loss-from-virtual-school-due-to-covid-is-significant-.html.

government-school educations. The Public School Exit blog reports on census data that reveals "the percent of school-age children being educated at home is estimated to now be well over … 11.1 percent."[132]

There has never been a better time to give homeschooling a go — especially considering that Harvard researchers report, "Home-schooled kids are 'healthier, happier and more virtuous than public-school graduates.' "[133] There are more fellow homeschoolers to interact with and learn from than ever, and more resources available to customize your child's education to suit his needs and interests. Laws governing and requirements associated with homeschooling vary from state to state; the Homeschool Legal Defense Fund is a great place to get started.[134]

Jenni White, from Oklahoma, homeschooled five of her children; she taught three of the five all the way from the beginning through to their graduation. She also homeschooled a friend's child at the same time she was homeschooling her own.

"We started with one kid"

We started with one kid. The oldest boy is very studious and was being made fun of by students and teachers at his school. I was a public-school teacher. We never started out thinking we would homeschool.

When our son came home crying like that and begging to be homeschooled, I thought, "Well, I'm going to have to figure out what this homeschooling thing is about."

---

[132] Alex Newman, "New Data Shows Homeschooling Explosion," *Public School Exit,* March 30, 2021, https://www.publicschoolexit.com/news/new-data-shows -homeschooling-explosion.

[133] Brendan Case and Ying Chen, "What Home-Schoolers Are Doing Right," *The Wall Street Journal,* November 10, 2021, https://www.wsj.com/articles/home-school ers-schooling-are-doing-right-education-parents-bartholet-harvard-parenting -11636577345.

[134] Home School Legal Defense Association, https://hslda.org/.

Jenni says it was "all God's doing" that she got pointed in the right direction. After three years of homeschooling, she and her son took part in a homeschooling co-op (in which parents and children come together to teach and learn together) that taught the Classical Conversations program. After three years in the co-op, she tutored all her children at home.

Jenni says her children represented the range of learning styles. She had one natural scholar, one who was more "peer-driven," one "who wouldn't do anything," and one "who needed to be pushed." She homeschooled all of them to become thriving adults.

"It's such a relaxed environment"

It really is just nothing but word of mouth and getting together with other parents. I hear people say, "Homeschooling is just too hard; I can't do that." To which I say, "Well you never tried, so how do you know? There's no reason to say that if you never tried." People quickly figure out they can get up in the morning and not go insane getting their kids' lunches ready and getting their breakfasts ready and getting them out the door to school. They realize it's such a relaxed environment when you're doing it yourself — the stressors are so minute.

If parents could just get to that point where they allow themselves to realize that seven hours a day, going from this class to that class — if they get beyond the regimen that's prescribed for education and say, "Education is whatever works for my kids and whatever it looks like is what it looks like," they'd be so much more satisfied. It just has to function for my kid, and that's all it is.

"Do what works for your child"

But instead, we feel like we have to drag the prescription bottle out that says public-school curriculum, public-school timeline, public-school whatever — and translate that into our own home. If it's not going to work for your kid, why would you drag it into your own home? Do what works for your child.

The thing that is probably most empowering to me as a parent, if you can make yourself get there, is that even if you are completely unable to get your child to do anything beyond learning to read and write, and you find yourself in my position, where you're wandering in the desert of education thinking *I'm never going to get this kid to do anything, he's going to be a complete moron, what am I going to do?* — it washes itself out in the laundry. It honestly does.

My kid had anxiety issues and he would not have been a good fit for public school. And I had no choice but to let him do what he wanted to do. The kid is super intuitive about stuff now. He's a good reader and a good writer and he's taught himself Japanese and he's interested in things.

"You're going to be fine"

We, as parents, have got to stop feeling like all of their education rests on us and if we don't do X, fill in the blank, or if our kids don't look like X, or they can't take standardized tests, then we're a failure, or we've miseducated them, and they're going to be outcasts in the world. And I'm sure there are some cases of that, but I really truly believe in the grand scheme of things, in loving homes, you're going to be fine. Your kid's going to be fine. Despite what you think.

Jenni was running an education watchdog nonprofit organization when she was homeschooling her children. She said the family never took big vacations or bought brand-new, fancy cars, but they did not have to make big lifestyle changes to school their children at home. "You had a budget and you stuck to it," Jenni says.

"There were always oopses"

We are super organized people. Organizing the day helped things run more smoothly. I would sit down at the beginning of the school year and plan out lesson plans like I did when I was a teacher — what subject I was covering, what materials to use, how to get books covered, what chapters to go over in a reasonable period of time.

But there were some days we just decided we're going to go to a museum all day. Or somebody's sick. Or let's take a field trip day. There were always oopses — planned oopses. To have a plan was helpful. We did not follow it exactly, but it helped to get work done. Most kids need a schedule and some structure. It's always better to start the structure and have the structure available and deviate from the structure than to say the structure isn't going to work and never even attempt it. Lack of structure — especially in middle school and early high school — is probably the worst thing you can do.

Jenni says homeschooling her children not only enabled her to safeguard their minds from woke propaganda, but it brought them emotionally closer as a family, too.

My kids were with me twenty-four hours a day, seven days a week from the time they were born. So when things would come up, whether it was on the Internet or with friends or what we were reading, I always had the opportunity to come back with a comment or remark or whatever about anything they read or heard, and I was there to answer any questions they had. I tried to teach by the Socratic method, asking them, "What do you think about that then? What would you have done differently?"

We are conservative Christians, so my kids got the conservative Christian take on any question they had. Conversely, my thirty-nine-year-old daughter [who went to public school] did not. She was not under my view, and we did not have much time to talk. She and I have had a very difficult time over the years really sustaining a relationship, because she's adopted quite a liberal perspective on things. I think it's evening out a little bit as she's aging, but when she was young we didn't have much to talk about because she just simply didn't see anything through a lens that I could see through. There was a lot of over-talk and mis-talk and lack of communication and lack of enjoyment of one another's time. We just didn't have enough in common to talk very much. And it got worse when the kids came out of school, because it hit me like a giant ton of bricks — *"oh my gosh, I have so much in common with these kids, I've been with them constantly, and I know pretty much everything about them."*

"That's why God gave them to you"

I just could not encourage people more to homeschool. They may think, "My kids and I talk when they come home, and we have discussions." Well if they're gone seven hours a day, how much do you really converse with them, how much do you really know them? And how much have you imparted your wisdom to them?

And you better be imparting your wisdom, because that's why God gave them to you — for you to be able to teach them what you've learned. Otherwise what's the point? It's been such an absolute blessing to be able to homeschool them.

Janice, also from Oklahoma (the homeschooling laws are really good there!), is a single, homeschooling mother of eight children, aged seven to twenty-seven. She also works!

I think homeschooling was always kind of in the back of my mind. When my oldest boy was four, he was already reading Hardy Boys books. He could read easily. What could kindergarten offer him? Obviously, I taught him to read just fine, so we just kept going.

Over the years, my purpose for choosing this path has fine-tuned. When my first was little, I just really enjoyed being with my kids, so I thought, "Why not naturally just spend more time with them?" As they've gotten older and times have changed, why I homeschool now may be different from why I homeschooled then.

Shocked by standardized tests

When my older two kids were eight and five, and I had been homeschooling for a couple years at that point, I worried if they were learning what they were supposed to be learning and doing what they were supposed to be doing. So I gave them a standardized test in my home. I was pretty dejected after giving that test, but the scores came back, and they both scored over the ninetieth percentile in everything. It really shocked me, because public-school kids are taught to these tests. My children weren't taught to these tests, however, we read a lot. I thought, "What is going on in the public school that the average score is 50 percent, and my kids, who had never heard of some of this stuff, are scoring in the ninetieth percentile?" That really cemented to me that they were where they needed to be and learning what they needed to be learning. And we never did another standardized test again!

"Stop shopping. You don't need it"

I attended a large homeschooling convention that's held every May in Oklahoma to see what was out there. There is always something newer, bigger, better, shinier. You can buy and buy and buy and buy, so at some point I had to come to the realization that what I had was working and if God wanted me to look into something else, he would have to bring it into my life instead of me going to search for it. I've been a lot happier since then. Stop shopping. There will always be something bigger and better, but you don't need it.

Planning ahead

I teach on Tuesdays and Thursdays, so I'm only gone two days a week. A couple years ago, my dad started taking my children to

Bible study on Monday nights, and then they would spend the night with him. He would take them on Tuesdays to parks, the zoo, stuff like that. Up until COVID.

I usually plan two weeks in advance. I find that if I try to plan more than that, something comes up where we have to push lessons back, and then I have to do a lot of erasing and marking in my schedule book. I find that two weeks is a nice period of time to plan ahead.

My kids are pretty independent. I'm just there to check their work when they're done or when they have questions. They have their schedule in their book. It's just non-negotiable not to do their schoolwork. They have chores they have to do, too. Oftentimes, half the year, we don't work on a Friday. Half the year we do. It really depends on the weather and if we want to go do stuff.

"There is a way to do it"

When I first became a single mom, I had so many people tell me, "Oh you're going to have to put your kids in school." And I said, "Oh, well, God called me to homeschool." I believe that very, very firmly. And when I became a single mom, I didn't feel a release on that call at all. If God has called me to homeschool, there is a way to do it.

The first few years — I was finishing grad school at that time, too — it took us a while to get into a good groove of things and figure out what worked for us. But after about three years in, things were going smoothly. It was a call. There was no *not* doing it.

"School revolves around life"

Homeschooling in a family is very different from other types of schools. With homeschooling, school revolves around life, versus in a public school, life has to revolve around school. Give yourself some time to detox from the public-school system and do not try to replicate the public-school system. Children will notice little things and say, "This isn't the way my teacher did it." They need some time to adjust.

Take your time

For parents just going into it and whose kids have never been in the public-school system, I would say better late than early. Let your children mature. Do not try to push your three- and four-year-olds to read if they're not ready. I've had children who have read at four and I have had children who have read at 12. There's a wide range, and so long as there's progress, things are working. Don't try to push them too early.

"Buy what you need"

You don't need to buy the whole curriculum. Buy what you need and honestly, I probably don't spend $500 on all of my children's curricula a year. Use your library. Don't feel like you've got to do every single thing the public-school system does. If your child is interested in something, great; if he's not, just give him a brief overview so he can recognize words and know what these things mean, but you don't have to go super in-depth with everything.

"Homeschooling has helped our family bond"

I've always enjoyed my kids and being with them. I love all the years I was a stay-at-home mom, and I would not trade them for the world. Homeschooling has helped our family bond and grow our family relationships. We've gotten to see how life works through difficult circumstances — death and things that come up. It's allowed us to really live life together. Over the last three years of the pandemic, with the masking and quarantining and testing and virtual learning, I've never been more pleased that I chose to homeschool. We just kept on going. It never gave us any pause at all.

Where I live, just recently, there was an instance in the public school of a transgender student assaulting another student in the bathroom. My children don't have to deal with any of that stuff. They're in an environment where they're not picked on, they're not bullied. They're loved and cared for, and when squabbles arise among siblings, we're able to deal with it in a healthy, constructive manner, whereas most moms don't even know what's going on in their kids' public schools.

"A more realistic way to spend life"
My children are all hard-working, well-mannered, and polite. Three of them work at a restaurant, and their supervisor says they're the hardest-working employees he has. Those things are taught at home. I teach them how to talk to people, how to handle difficult conversations.

Through homeschooling, my kids really figure out what's important in life. It allows their differences and interests to flourish. They can try new things, and I encourage them. It's a more realistic way to spend life.

Brenden Boudreau and his wife Elizabeth live in Michigan and homeschool their growing brood. Brenden shares their experience:

"Learning and growing into it"
A decade ago, we more or less would have considered sending our children to public school, but we now are of the conviction that homeschooling our children, at least in the early years to start, is the best decision. Our children are still young, ages five, three, and one, so we are just dipping our toes into the homeschooling waters. It is challenging and we feel like we are drinking from a firehose, but we are learning and growing in it.

Our faith is foundational to our family. We desire to raise our children in the nurturing and admonition of the Lord, trusting that He will care for them, as they are ultimately His. But they will not come to faith through accident. We regularly attend the public worship services, usually two on each Sunday. This was a concept completely foreign to us growing up, but we have found great blessing to our family through it, as it is twice as much time spent in worship, hearing the Word preached and practiced for our children to understand the importance of church, but it also provides an opportunity for my wife and me to take turns taking care of the children, so that each of us is able to hear at least most of one sermon each Sunday. We also have our children involved in Sunday school and will eventually also have them learn catechism questions and answers.

Family worship at home

We try to do family worship regularly at home as well in the morning before my workday begins. This currently involves reading a story from *365 Great Bible Stories* by Carine Mackenzie and discussing it, prayer, and singing a psalm together. We recently decided that we are only going to do one psalm per month so that our kids can learn it and sing along. The blessing of singing psalms is that we are ultimately singing the Scriptures, which then is in our minds regularly.

We try to emphasize the importance of prayer to our children and try to do so by example. It's wonderful when the kids want to pray before meals, or will ask for prayer when they are sick. Reliance upon God is something we'd love to instill in our children, as well as a clear understanding of the gospel.

"The world is sometimes subtle in its assaults on children"

We don't have cable television and we don't spend much time watching shows. While they do zone-out on shows on occasion, their ability to play independently and their desire to play outside is something we encourage and are grateful to see. The shows they watch, we watch carefully as well, and likewise with the books we check out from the library, as the world is sometimes subtle with its assaults on our children.

Our oldest son George just joined Trail Life USA this year, which is a Christian scouting organization. I was heavily involved in scouting growing up, but Boy Scouts is a shell of what it was when I was in it. In Trail Life, George will be able to learn practical life skills and what it means to be a godly man. I attend the meetings with him, which gives us the opportunity to spend time together and to talk.

"Children need structure"

Discipline and correction are also key parts of parenting. Ultimately, the world is trying to teach people that they can live however they want and do whatever they want, regardless of the consequences, and we see what that has wrought on the current generation. Children need structure. It is important that they know right from wrong, that truth is not relative. But it's also important that they know from us, their parents, that we love them unconditionally. Helping children feel secure in their families is also crucial to their development.

"We cannot parent in our own strengths"

Our families are mostly supportive of our decision-making with the way we are raising our children, though they might not completely understand or agree. At times, it would seem easier just to go the way of the world instead of being particular, but our consciences wouldn't allow for it, even with how difficult it is sometimes to be in the world, but not of it. What we've learned is that godly parenting does not come naturally. It requires holy habits. By that I mean as parents, we cannot be lax in our faith, but must also be growing in grace through prayer, regularly reading the Bible, and relying on God to help us defeat our own sins.

We cannot parent on our own strength, but must be reliant upon Christ in all things.

We are not perfect parents by any measure. We have our weaknesses, good and bad days. But we are trying our best to raise our children in a way that is pleasing to the Lord and praying that He will use our sometimes-feeble efforts to bring our children to faith and to protect them from the evils of this world.

Private School

School choice (also known as education choice) programs have, like homeschooling, taken off in recent years, and Fox News reported that 2023 was set to be the best year yet for this "fast-growing" movement.[135] As more parents experience the freedom of choosing where and how their children are educated, and as they learn about the opportunities other families have, they demand more options.

Simply put, education choice programs take all or a portion of the funding allocated for a child to attend a government ("public") school and give it to the child's family to put toward an educational environment of the family's choosing. The money follows the student, so to speak, and can be used on private school tuition, a private tutor, homeschooling textbooks, commuting money to drive to a charter school, and so forth. Edchoice.org is a wonderful resource for all things education choice.

Joy and Nathaniel Pullmann are parents to six children. Joy works from home as the executive editor of *The Federalist*. She is also the author of *Classic Books for Young Children* and *101 Strategies for Eating Well Amid Inflation*,[136] among other works. Nathaniel is headmaster of Redeemer Classical School, which he and Joy founded.

---

[135] Valeria Gurr, "School choice revolution: Governors driving this fast-growing movement," *Fox News*, February 23, 2023, https://www.foxnews.com/opinion/school-choice-revolution-governors-driving-fast-growing-movement.

[136] https://payhip.com/JoyPullmann.

Nathaniel has an aptitude for engineering and majored in physics and mathematics at Hillsdale College. But then, he and Joy started their family:

> I was sucked in by politics, by which I mean the history of political and moral philosophy. I really loved that when I was introduced to it. I got off the engineering path, though I still love math and physics and get to teach it.

"We couldn't find a school that was the right fit"
When our oldest son was about three, we started thinking about what we were going to do for his education. We couldn't find a school that was the right fit.

Joy was homeschooled. We thought we might do that. We started with a homeschool co-op, and that was fine, but we just thought, for two reasons, we wanted to start a school: for one, we wanted to have some of the advantages that a school has academically, but more importantly, we wanted to build a community around our kids of other kids who are reading the same things, becoming friends with them, spending a lot of time together. Building an alternate society doesn't work if it's just you and your family.

To build that for our kids, so they didn't have to build it all when they grew up, we needed to build a community around them. You can do that with homeschooling — we just found it more difficult. So we decided to build something a little more structured, a little more automatic for them to have that community around them, so we decided we needed to start a school, and three years later, we opened the doors.

Where to start
It completely depends upon the type of people you have around you. A lot of churchgoers [we know] are homeschoolers, and not many of them were early adopters of this crazy idea I had.

We have a lot now, but they were slow to catch on. It was a lot of bootstrapping and doing it ourselves. I'm not great at delegating.

It's great if you have a board, overseeing things like where's the school going to be, making sure it's up to code, how are you going to file taxes, who's going to be in charge of that, approval from the government, what's the curriculum going to be like, how are we going to hire teachers, where are we going to get them from, and so forth. Before you even open the doors, you have to have that nailed down. You have to know these things eight months before you open the doors, so you have answers for people who are looking for a school and who are going to ask you those questions.

"It's going to be really hard, because everything good is"

It's like starting any other organization or business. There is a lot of pre-work that goes into it, figuring out a lot of little details, to make sure the thing is solid when the first customer walks in the door, so to speak. They aren't customers — you can't treat them that way, or else you won't build a community.

I did an apprenticeship with the headmaster of Hillsdale Academy. It's helpful having someone I can email — "Hey, do you have a faculty handbook I can look at?" instead of just making one up myself.

Starting a school is going to be really hard, because everything good is. If you want to do something good in your life, it's going to take a lot of work. If you have children already, you know this. If you're trying to raise them well, it's nobody's definition of easy. This is a similar thing. This is going to be hard, it's going to take a lot of work, it's going to consume your whole life, but so is everything else that has a great prize at the end.

"Lots of people want to help you"

There are way more resources out there right now than there were twenty years ago. Lots of people want to help you. You can find them. And one big piece of encouragement I give to people all the time is: this doesn't have to look like a public school. You don't need a giant building and twenty-five teachers and all the curricula that they have and the labs and whatever else. What you're trying to do is help form the soul of the children who are there. There are lots of ways you can do that that are simpler, classic, and not so complicated, but much more beautiful than what is normally done in schools.

"We're talking about the soul and well-being of your child"

You can do it. The first thing to do is just step out and try. Because it needs to be done. It might be hard, but again, so is raising your children. It's not like you're just *not* going to do that because it's difficult, right? We're talking about the soul and well-being of your child. What else are you going to do? Just like, hope it works out when you send them to the public school? Let a stranger educate your child who doesn't love and care about him or her, actually has completely contrary ends to you, believes things that you find completely repugnant, and then try to teach them to your children and indoctrinate them? You can't do that. It's not even an option.

You need to figure out the best thing you can do for your child, and if that means starting a school, there are dozens of organizations and hundreds of people out there who would love to help you figure out all the day-to-day details of doing it. But that doesn't make the school work. I can give you the handbook, that doesn't make the school work. What makes the school work is that you love the children who are there, and you pour out your life for them, just like you do for anyone you love.

The Pullmanns are living proof that the cookie-cutter, 9-to-5, conventional way to live is not the only one. Nathaniel went without pay for several days as he started the school, and the family found "creative ways to live."

The particular way we went about this isn't something we planned from the beginning. By the time we started the school, this was the life we had, and how we personally figured it out. It wasn't easy, and maybe [foregoing pay] isn't a choice you have to take on. I would recommend trying to find somebody to pay the headmaster's salary for the first couple years. Or a church willing to make it a mission of the church.

"The ease of life has tricked us"

I think we need to stop assuming the way America says we should live — the normal, standard, American way of life — is good and should be our default. That life should be relatively easy — send your kids on the school bus at whatever dark o'clock in the morning, and they come back at 4. Part of the reason we do that is because it's normal and American, part of the reason we do that is because it's easy. We don't have to do the work to get our kids to school, we don't have to do the work to make the lunch for our kids, we don't have to do the work of educating our kids, we don't have to do the work of anything. They just walk out the door in the morning and walk back in nine hours later. And so, that ease of life has sort of tricked us that those are the ways we should live, where that's never been satisfying to people.

It's never been a satisfying life to anybody to take the easiest path all the time and just do the normal thing. You can start a school that looks totally different from other schools, you can live a life that's totally different from the way other people live.

"We have to sacrifice"

We also have to sacrifice. We can't always do the thing we like the most or the thing we most desire. You have to figure out what you need to give up to get what is actually good in life, and maybe what you're going to find out is you didn't really need the thing you gave up.

Go on your phone right now and look at the thing that says "screen time." That's how many hours of time you have in a day to build a school.

"Sometimes it does have to be you"
There are ways to do this that aren't exactly the way we did it. Sometimes it does have to be you. I didn't start a school because I wanted to start a school; I started a school because I had to. Know why you're starting a school, why you're running a school, and build everything from that.

"You have to be the beacon"
Maintain a real vision of what you want the school to be, and don't let the desire for more students or rapid growth or quick success pull you away from that. Families will push back on little things in the corners. I had a family ask that we tone down the number of prayer services we have. Stand firm on your principles. You will become a beacon to the kind of people you want in your community. If you are going to build a community, you have to be the beacon. You have to draw them to you, and the way you do that is by being as faithful to your principles as you can, not by trying to get a bunch of people in the door. You're going to have to tell people, "This school isn't the best fit for you and your family," and accept slow growth.

Be true to your principles, to the faith, to an understanding of what children are, and to the formation of their souls, and you will draw all the people to you that God needs you to have. When things get hard, and you have doubts, pray. And then work harder.

Joy explains that she and Nathaniel were exposed to classical schools and determined that was "the best thing we could give to our kids."

"All the most beautiful things"
She says that when she listens to her children's voices singing the psalms, reading the liturgy, reciting Bible verses, "it's all the most beautiful things

that have ever been said in human history transforming their lives and their hearts from day one, and that's what I wanted."

Investing in a community

Joy acknowledges that her family forfeited millions of dollars in terms of what her husband would likely be earning in the engineering field, but they've chosen to "invest in a community" instead.

> I can't emphasize or even describe what a benefit to our lives it has been — it's just priceless. God has already granted to us inde-scribable returns. It's a happiness no amount of money can buy. And we are not impoverished by any means. We both get tired from working. I have to schedule times to talk to my husband. My children fight. Life is never going to be utopia, but I've found if you orient your life around your kids and increase the ratio of goodness and faith that are available, you can have a piece of heaven in moments that punctuate your life every day.
>
> I can't control where people end up in life. I can't ensure my children's salvation, but I think it's every parent's and church's duty to provide the best for their children and take care of their souls, regardless of the outcome, because that's in God's hand.

Consider life-shadowing a family or school

> I would really encourage people to go life-shadow a classical Chris-tian home and visit a classical Christian school. I think that is the best way to catch a glimpse of how wonderful and full of meaning a life like that is. You can see the baby vomit on his mother, but you can also see that that baby gives his mother a reason to get up in the morning. You can see the kids complaining that they have homework, or they have to practice their piano, but you can also see these kids are learning a second language at age eight. That they are talking about poetry, they are singing hymns in the hallway and it sounds like the voice of angels, and there's almost nowhere else that that is common.

"People have to prepare to challenge themselves"
Creating that existence is lot of work. People have to prepare to
challenge themselves. There's not going to be any free ride or free
lunch. But a couple of years in, you can have a couple children
singing with the angels and you joining in in the morning every
single day, and it completely reorients your life. And when you
have those moments when you have grief and suffering, and we
all have them, and sometimes they may last for a long time, you
have something to get you through.

Go in the direction of what obviously seems good, and if it
doesn't seem good to you, try trusting God a little bit. Just a little
bit. Start with that. What's one action of faith you can take? What's
one life-affirming thing you can do? Do that!

Dave Seminara, an author and prolific writer (and former diplomat!),
"fought the public school on everything." What pushed him over the edge
was the recommended reading books for children on display at a school
he and his wife visited while deciding where to enroll their children in
Florida. Of the four books on display, two of them were LGBTQ-related.

"There is no way we're sending our son here"
They didn't have them somewhere in the stacks so kids would
have to go searching for them — they were right there on the
table. I said, "there is no way we're sending our son here." I sent
the school an email and was sent a generic statement about "trying to represent diverse demographics of students."

Dave and his wife send their sons to Catholic school.

"Completely worth it"
It's a big financial sacrifice, and I think it's completely worth it.

Dave acknowledges his young boys are "addicted to TikTok just like
everybody else," though he tries to limit their exposure to social media
to no more than thirty minutes a day.

Expose them to valuable ideas

Parents are busy. Monitoring what your children are consuming all the time is a really difficult thing to do. I can't control everything they see, but you can expose them to what you want them to listen to. I put the Morning Wire podcast on in the car in the morning, so I expose them to ideas I think are valuable.

Charter Schools

A charter school is technically a public school, in that it is tuition-free, yet they are independently run. The U.S. Department of Education considers them "schools of choice," though they are a hybrid public/private school. *Education Week* notes, "Charters frequently take alternative curricular approaches or emphasize particular fields of study, such as the arts or technology, or set out to serve special populations of students such as special education or at-risk students."[137]

Terrence O. Moore started Ridgeview Classical Schools, a top-ranked K-12 charter school in Fort Collins, Colorado that has been the model for many other charter schools. Moore is also the Executive Director of Classical Academics for Responsive Education Solutions.

"The teachers didn't inspire"

I went to public high school and was very politically engaged as a young student. But I was bored at school. The newer teachers were nice; they weren't bad people by any means, but they had been trained in the wrong methods of education. They didn't inspire and they weren't worthy of the curriculum.

Moore came across schoolbooks that had belonged to his grandfather, who had been a doctor in Austin, Texas.

---

[137] Arianna Prothero, "What Are Charter Schools?," *Education Week*, August 9, 2018, https://www.edweek.org/policy-politics/what-are-charter-schools/2018/08.

"I felt cheated"

The books they were reading in middle school and high school were amazing. They were reading Milton, they were reading full novels, Benjamin Franklin's autobiography. I felt cheated.

When it came to choosing a college, because I was an avid reader, I went to the most countercultural Great Books college that was around, and the juxtaposition between a University of Chicago education and what I had at school was just a very different thing. I thought, "We should be doing this in public schools, not just in private schools where affluent parents can afford it."

"It's what the founders would have wanted"

As Thomas Jefferson says, if we're making citizens, we can't just keep to the upper crust — we need to teach the rest of the public as best we can to make responsible citizens. It's what the founders would have wanted.

There is nothing wrong with sending your child to a private school if you want to. There is a rich heritage behind that. But not every person can afford it, and what are we, as Americans, who are paying for education one way or another, saying about our future citizens and the fate of the republic if we don't have the right sort of education institutionalized?

Parents deserve choice. Parents have different perspectives and want different things for their children. A child may need a bilingual education if he's living on the border of Texas, for instance.

"A lot of happy families"

If you start with the right kind of mission and stay true to the mission, if you build a lot of credibility with parents, and do what you're claiming you wanted to do, then you end up having a lot of happy families.

Board conflicts and lack of understanding can compromise the mission. Instability can arise within charter school boards; there will be friction with parents and boards if teachers don't believe in the school's real mission. I would not say it's a rose without thorns, but charter schools do offer a possibility you would not have if you stayed complacent within your public schools, hoping your kids got in the talented and gifted programs.

"It gives you hope"

To see joy in kindergarteners' eyes as they're learning phonics and true handwriting and lovable nursery rhymes and also learning how to sit still and pay attention when they're supposed to, and if you go all the way up to the high school, and you see students carrying on really deep and meaningful conversations about aspects of our nation's founding, about the civil rights movement, about great works of literature, and you see these are soon-to-be responsible adults who are being taught to have knowledge and heart at the same time, it gives you hope.

"It's how we get back to what this country is"

That's what you see in these schools if you're doing it right, and really doing justice by tradition and what education ought to be. It's how we get back to what this country is and how we have human flourishing. I see [elsewhere] boredom, dependency on technology, children being completely unable to do anything without an app attached to it, and a complete lack of happiness.

"Start with your community"

Look at different examples and schools. Ultimately, what you have to do is start with your community. Sometimes, you can find former teachers. Know your state laws to know how feasible starting a charter school is. Visit other school's websites. Perusing their Facebook pages can also be helpful. Visit schools and sit in on some classes. Talk to parents and students to know what the school's social life is like, how much are they learning, and so on. See if they're truly learning and if they're truly happy.

"We're sending them to school to learn to be responsible human beings"
We should see the fruits of the tax money we are paying. Families should have choice for their own children to have a good education and an education that's in line with their own thoughts, principles, and values. We're not just sending our kids to school so they can have a job when they graduate. That's the easy part. We're sending them there to learn what it means to be a good, responsible human being and to help create beauty in the world and enjoy it and add to it. That is only going to be in a place that really speaks to their minds and hearts and imagination, and schools are very important in that, and parents can't do it alone.

There are different ideas of what education should look like, which is why we have charter schools that all parents can afford.

Government or Public School

Though the tide is changing, public schools are where most American children — some 72 percent — are educated.[138] Certainly, some public schools offer a high-quality education and state-of-the-art amenities. Many also employ dedicated, talented teachers. Yet there's been a mass exodus of public-school teachers in recent years.[139] The quality of America's public-education system is abysmal, and getting worse. Our government school's tendency to focus on indoctrinating children with a woke ideology will harm not only our children's minds,

---

[138] Alejandra O'Connell-Domenech, "Nearly 2 million fewer students have enrolled in public school," *The Hill,* August 16, 2022, https://thehill.com/changing-america/enrichment/education/3604392-nearly-2-million-fewer-students-have-enrolled-in-public-school/.

[139] Harry Zahn and Winston Wilde, "Why teachers in America are leaving the profession in droves," *PBS,* August 20, 2022, https://www.pbs.org/newshour/show/why-teachers-in-america-are-leaving-the-profession-in-droves.

hearts, souls, and well-being, but it's also harming our economy and American society.[140]

Still, some families may feel they don't have any choice but to send their child to the nearest public school. All is not lost. Katy Faust is the author of *Them Before Us: Why We Need a Global Children's Rights Movement* and a forthcoming book about "raising conservative kids in a woke city." She sends her children to public school in Seattle, and assures parents it's possible to "raise sane kids"[141] and "fight assimilation into cultural leftism"[142] when public school is your only option.

Katy offers parents this encouraging pep talk, though parents also ought to read her contributions to *The Federalist* (see footnotes) for more detailed pointers:

Your children are not doomed

Is social media gunning to take out your kids? Yes indeed. Are schools hellbent on destroying the values you are instilling in your kids? 1,000 percent. Do you suspect that even the churches in your world are compromising or being silenced by the woke mob? You're not wrong.

Are your children doomed? No, they're not.

Whether you are homeschooling your kids in the reddest of red states or, like me, sending them to public school in Seattle, your children do not have to be victims of our woke culture. If you

---

[140] Kimberly Amadeo, "U.S. Education Rankings Are Falling Behind the Rest of the World," *The Balance,* March 17, 2023, https://www.thebalancemoney.com/the-u-s-is-losing-its-competitive-advantage-3306225.

[141] Katy Faust and Stacy Manning, "How To Raise Sane Kids When Leaving Public Schools Is Not An Easy Option," *The Federalist,* April 6, 2022, https://thefederalist.com/2022/04/06/how-to-raise-sane-kids-when-leaving-public-schools-is-not-an-easy-option/.

[142] Katy Faust, "4 Ways To Help Your Kids Fight Assimilation Into Cultural Leftism," *The Federalist,* December 13, 2019, https://thefederalist.com/2019/12/13/4-ways-to-help-your-kids-fight-assimilation-into-cultural-leftism/.

are intentional, strategic, and take your role as primary educator seriously, your children can become *transformers* of culture, rather than be *transformed by* the culture. Indeed, that's the only formula for both saving your children, and saving this nation.

College

There are enough news stories about the horrors happening on woke college campuses to cause any NORMAL family to wonder if higher education is worth it. Reports in recent years have shown that the value of a college degree has steadily decreased.[143]

There is dignity to be found in any work that does not contradict God's commands. In a wonderful piece published by *The Atlantic* in 2014, Scott Samuelson explained "Why I teach Plato to plumbers."[144] Samuelson noted that the goal of education is not "simply economic advancement and technological power," and that the study of the liberal arts is valuable because "we should strive to be a society of free people, not simply one of well-compensated managers and employees." He added that in his experience teaching philosophy at a community college, he encountered "among future plumbers as many devotees of Plato as among the future wizards of Silicon Valley."

Love everyone with a deep love based on charity ... but form friendships only with those who can share virtuous things with you. The higher the virtues you share and exchange with others, the more perfect your friendship will be. (St. Francis de Sales)

[143] Peter Clark, "Why College Degrees Are Losing Their Value," *FEE*, December 19, 2021, https://fee.org/articles/why-college-degrees-are-losing-their-value/.
[144] Scott Samuelson, "Why I Teach Plato to Plumbers," *The Atlantic*, April 29, 2014, https://www.theatlantic.com/education/archive/2014/04/plato-to-plumbers/361373/.

Nevertheless, rest assured: there are still plenty of colleges and universities cultivating virtuous patriots through rigorous, traditional, truth-focused scholarship. Numerous online lists of "non-woke conservative colleges" exist, and I can personally vouch for the University of Dallas (my alma mater) and Hillsdale College (alma mater of my twin brother and of the Pullmans) for their solidly conservative curricula and campus environments.

I am grateful I followed in my siblings' footsteps and attended the University of Dallas. I knew that after graduation I wanted to do something in the literary realm, and if I had my way, I would have limited myself to four years of straight English and literature classes. Yet UD required that I expand my horizons, and I can appreciate now being "forced" to encounter a much broader, enriching course of study. I can also attest to how many classmates were assured of their major as freshmen, only to change their minds and avert a "wasted" degree after two years of exposure to a variety of disciplines.

If you're in the market for a college that requires students to complete coursework in *all* the liberal arts — composition, literature, foreign languages, U.S. government/history, economics, mathematics, and natural science — the American Council of Trustees and Alumni awarded "A" ratings to seven schools in 2023:[145] Christopher Newport University, Magdalen College of the Liberal Arts, Patrick Henry College, Thomas Aquinas College, Thomas More College of Liberal Arts, University of Dallas, and University of Saint Katherine.

The Cardinal Newman Society also recognizes colleges "for their commitment to a faithful Catholic education" and "strong Catholic identity." These colleges are named in the Newman Guide, which they publish for free online.[146]

---

[145] "What Will They Learn? A guide to what college rankings won't tell you," American Council of Trustees and Alumni, https://www.whatwilltheylearn.com/schools/compare?grade=A.

[146] https://cardinalnewmansociety.org/college/.

A Fox News article reported in March of 2023 that "The Heritage Foundation president [Kevin Roberts] recommended several colleges for young adults who don't want a 'woke' education. The top five are Grove City College, Hillsdale College, St. John's University, University of Dallas and Wyoming Catholic College.... Roberts said he would encourage Americans to 'give up on those institutions that have given up on America ... and let's build those [colleges] and expand that list. And if we do that, then we will grow out of this de-spiritedness, and in 10–20 years, wake up and realize we've taken back this great republic."[147]

It's possible, certainly, that after being educated in the classical tradition, a high school graduate could experience four years of woke academia and emerge unscathed. He may even develop firmer convictions and an enhanced talent for debate. But he may also feel lonely and isolated during his college experience, and will certainly be subject to a lot of time wasted on nonsense — not to mention the woke agendas your tuition money will fund.

What's more — and again, I can attest to this — being surrounded by like-minded students makes the learning experience not only more pleasant, but easier. When you know that your classmates are striving toward the same goal, it makes the give and take of ideas exciting and rewarding. You're on a journey together as comrades, studying the same great texts, aiding and inspiring one another in the acquisition of wisdom and virtue. A bond formed on such a quest is deep, profound, and often leads to lifelong friendships — and, as many a liberal arts college alumni (including the Pullmans) will tell you, many marriages as well!

When it's time to consider a college, consult the lists, talk to friends, other parents, recent graduates, acquaintances from church. Visit college campuses and absorb the atmosphere. Look for signs of woke seminars

---

[147] Ashley Carnahan, "Merchant Marine midshipmen warn of 'wokeness' in the academy: 'We're no longer focused on excellence,' " Fox News, March 5, 2023, https://www.foxnews.com/media/merchant-marine-midshipmen-warn-woke-ness-academy-no-longer-focused-excellence.

and clubs and sit in on some classes. Observe the interactions of students. Peruse coursebooks and read course descriptions. Talk to students about what life is like at their school.

I also recommend using Thomas Sowell's *Choosing a College: A Guide for Parents and Students* as a jumping-off point for what to look for in a college. The book was published in 1989 but contains timeless guidance of what to consider and what questions to ask when choosing a college.

Money Matters

Money talks, and companies NORMALs have loved for years are pulling the rug out from under us, using our money to talk the woke talk and walk the woke walk.

Dave Seminara, whom we met on page 129, wrote a piece in 2020 for the *Wall Street Journal* lamenting "When Your Favorite Companies Go Woke."[148] The commentary received nearly two thousand comments and prompted Dave to compile a list on his personal website of the growing number of companies that are openly dedicated to furthering woke causes.

Dave graciously permitted me to reprint his boycott list here. It's a big list, intimidating, and growing. Dave is constantly having to update it, and it's worth revisiting his website often.[149] In fact, save his blog as a bookmark; his other humorous and insightful writings will help you feel less alone. As so often happens between like-minded NORMALs, Dave and I connected through a shared outlook and have developed a friendship. Highlights of a conversation we had regarding what to do when your favorite companies go woke, how to boycott strategically so

---

[148] Dave Seminara, "When Your Favorite Companies Go Woke," *The Wall Street Journal*, August 5, 2020, https://www.wsj.com/articles/when-your-favorite -companies-go-woke-11596664277.

[149] Dave Seminara, "Complete List of Woke Companies," *Dave Seminara*, 2023, https://daveseminara.com/complete-list-of-woke-companies-condemning-so bing-called-racist-voting-laws/.

it doesn't ruin your life, what to do when your kids don't care about woke companies, and more are published after this eye-watering list.

> If I stopped buying products from woke companies, I'd be eating nothing but Goya food and wearing loincloths made from Mike Lindell's pillows. (Dave Seminara)

It's worth reiterating that the woke-proof lifestyle is about prioritizing a family and community-centric mindset and approach to create a simpler, more meaningful existence. As Dave acknowledges, you can drive yourself crazy trying to avoid every woke influence. Doing what you can not to fund such institutions is important, but by shifting your focus to higher ideals and concentrating your energy on prioritizing high-quality relationships, a cultural boycott will come about naturally. A *New York Times* article examining the effectiveness of boycotts by Americus Reed concluded that action followed by sustained effort to keep the boycott going is the most effective way people can "vote with their wallets." "If the boycott reflects a movement — rather than a moment — it can change the world around it,"[150] wrote Reed. Remember how M&Ms' special-edition, female-only, and size-inclusive (genius marketing!) candies lasted, what, a week? Consumers quickly said, "Enough is enough!"[151] You know it's bad when people ditch a beloved chocolate candy brand because of its politics.

---

[150] Americus Reed, "Social Media Boycotts Succeed When They Reflect a Movement," *The New York Times*, February 7, 2017, https://www.nytimes.com/roomfordebate/2017/02/07/when-do-consumer-boycotts-work.

[151] Stephen M. Lepore, "M&M's launches woke female-only special edition bag of candy featuring 'lesbian' green and brown chocolates, as well as new plus size purple sweet who represents body positivity," *The Daily Mail*, January 7, 2023, https://www.dailymail.co.uk/news/article-11610317/M-Ms-launches-woke-female-special-edition-bag-candy-featuring-lesbian-green-brown.html.

Please see appendix 1 for lists of companies that publicly opposed Georgia's election integrity law and Florida's Parental Rights in Education Act (the "Don't Say Gay" bill) and that support radical LGBTQIA+ and BLM campaigns, abortion, climate change, or other woke causes, including vacating Twitter when Elon Musk took over.

Time to yank out all your electric cords, smash your screens, hitch up the mule, get the old plow back in action and oil up Great-Grandma's spinning wheel, because the woke tentacles touch everything.

Just kidding. Fear tactics are weapons of the woke, not of the NOR-MALs who are "guided along right paths" for the sake of the Lord's name (Ps. 23:3). It is true that many of the biggest, most well-funded companies are the worst woke offenders. Notice how many on this list are venture capital, investment, and consulting firms. It seems as if money *is* the root of all evil.

Several of these are umbrella corporations that own a lot of the products that have become integral to American life. Johnson & Johnson, for instance, makes Tylenol, Neutrogena, Aveeno, and Listerine. Mondelez International makes Oreos, belVita biscuits, Cadbury Dairy Milk products, Toblerone chocolate, Sour Patch Kids, Trident gum, Honey Maid graham crackers, Ritz Crackers, and Philadelphia cream cheese. Paramount is somehow involved in CBS, Showtime Networks, Paramount Pictures, Nickelodeon, MTV, Comedy Central, BET, Paramount+, Pluto TV, Simon & Schuster, and other media, reports *Forbes*.[152] If you're a cereal fan, good luck eating breakfast without patronizing Kellogg's and its "Together with Pride" pronoun cereal.[153]

Two other big repeat offenders you'll notice are technology and online service companies. We've chronicled the destructive tendencies

---

[152] https://www.forbes.com/companies/paramount/?sh=6095d17c7f2c.
[153] "Kellogg's releases 'Together With Pride' cereal celebrating preferred gender pronouns," *Fox Business,* May 27, 2021, https://www.foxbusiness.com/lifestyle/kellogg-company-releases-pride-cereal-to-celebrate-freedom-to-choose-preferred-pronouns.

140

of screen time, and these companies readily promote and take advantage of our fast-forward world to advance the woke agenda.

It's tempting either to give up completely on boycotting corporations with such long arms and sticky fingers, or to obsessively play boycott whack-a-mole with every subsidiary you uncover. Let me tell you, though — as someone who grew up forbidden from eating General Mills brand products and from watching Sesame Street and the Disney Channel — you'll survive. Boycotting is not that bad. You get used to doing without certain things, and eventually, you don't even miss them. You kind of put on blinders, not even considering certain products as an option, as people who suffer from shellfish allergies do to the "from the sea" section of the menu and I do to attractive married men.

Plus, refusing things out of principle lends an air of mystery and superiority to you — or so I imagined as a high-school senior, explaining to my friends that I'd never had a Pop Tart. (I did actually try one when I got to college — sorry, Mom — and it was cardboard garbage.)

What does it profit a man, to gain the whole world and forfeit his life? (Mark 8:36)

We live in an age of abundance, so despite a handful of investors seemingly owning *everything*, there are still plenty of companies with conservative values and companies that keep out of culture wars altogether. Please turn to appendix 2 for a list compiled by Dave and added to with a list the Concerned Women for America Legislative Action Committee granted me permission to use.

"A-Hunting We Will Go!"

Also keep in mind there are many ways to boycott. You don't have to boycott *everything*, and you don't even have to boycott anything *all* the time. Choose one woke company to boycott at a time, then add another when you're able. Don't buy anything online for a week; then try two weeks, then try a month. When you're limited in what you can (or want) to buy, it can actually be a rewarding challenge — like a hunting expedition. It also trains the mind and soul to focus less on material things and more on the best things in life and those that transcend the physical world.

Start by doing what is necessary; then do what is possible; and suddenly you are doing the impossible. (St. Francis of Assisi)

Here are three simple tenants to focus on when you feel trapped in a maze of woke corporate walls:

1. *Rely less on technology.* Every click, swipe, and tap means more money for a company that's probably woke. Plus, going on a so-called "cash diet" can help protect your identity and save you money, as parting with real money, not "future," plastic money, has been found to be "psychologically more painful."[154]

2. *Simplify.* When a few woke companies own so much, spending and consuming less in general hurts their bottom line. It's easier to talk yourself out of a third pair of sandals and a lipstick for your *other* purse when you know your unnecessary purchases are funding something wicked. Distract yourself from whatever it is your closet/house/patio "needs" by saying a prayer, walking away, and, perhaps, heading to the antique store! (see chapter four)

3. *Become more creative and resourceful.* With your time, money, and possessions. Learn to fix/repurpose something you

---

[154] "Cash vs. Credit Card: Which Should I Use?," *Ramsey Solutions*, March 16, 2023, https://www.ramseysolutions.com/debt/cash-vs-credit-card.

already own rather than buying a new one; rent or ask to borrow something you don't need really to own from a friend, a neighbor, or a relative; grow some of your own food, cook more at home, get crafty and hands-on. Spending money on stuff is our modern default, but it doesn't have to be that way.

We'll go over these principles in greater depth in the coming chapters, but let's pause to hear the woke-proof journey of Dave Seminara, our woke list mastermind:

"There are ways to micro-boycott"
I have been able to reduce my spending at various woke companies, but I have not been able to stop completely. I don't spend as much at Amazon, for instance, but I cannot eliminate Amazon. We're all busy. There are ways to micro-boycott, too. Go to Walmart only for batteries, for instance, and let the big companies know they offend us.

"Supporting really small businesses is the way to go"
Supporting really small businesses is the way to go, though. This used to be something that really was more of a "crunchy" thing to talk about. It's interesting now how liberals purchase from woke corporations. In my college years, corporations were conceived as Republican. Now everything has changed. Conservatives are going to farmer's markets and striving to be local. There's a lot of crossover now between the tenets of what we think of as liberals in Portland, for instance, and the new conservative mindset. They're just doing it for different reasons.

Do your best with your kids
I have two teenagers, and they want iPhones. They like Nike sneakers. Every time they want to get Nike sneakers, I say, do you really want to support Colin Kaepernick? It becomes harder to boycott

corporations when you have kids — they don't care. They want to
fit in, and they like this brand and that brand for whatever reason.
Do your best with the spending. It's up to parents to be as vigilant
as they can, and drive your kids crazy.

Make some changes, make some sacrifices, be strategic
If you're willing to make other changes in your life and make
some sacrifices and take some effort and be strategic, you can
significantly reduce your support of woke companies. Sometimes
you have to do without.

I was in Tampa Bay with my wife, for example, and she wanted
some ice cream. We pulled up to a shop, and it was Jeni's ice cream.
That's Nancy Pelosi's favorite brand. I didn't want to go in here,
but I did want ice cream, and thought what the hell. The first thing
I saw was a BLM sticker. I literally could not do it. I did not go
in. I did not get ice cream. The same thing happened at a coffee
shop. I saw a BLM flag, and I walked right out.

Dave agrees that though extreme boycotting is difficult and unpracti-
cal for most people, there are upsides, like discovering new neighborhoods, for instance, or bonding with your kids while doing something
inside the home, such as making homemade ice cream.

> The closer one approaches to God, the
> simpler he becomes. (St. Teresa of Ávila)

"I ended up falling in love with a little tennis shop the size of a closet"
I was really angered by Dick's Sporting Goods, one of first companies to pay women to have abortions. I teach tennis and didn't
want to buy tennis balls from Dick's. I ended up finding and falling
in love with a little tennis shop about the size of a closet. I don't
know if the owner is a Democrat or a Republican, but it's run by

a small businessperson, and I'd rather be supporting him than Dick's Sporting Goods.

"I like to put woke companies on notice"
I like to put woke companies on notice. I don't just let it slide. I follow up. I want to let them know — you're not getting this past me. I was at Barnes & Noble and saw this whole display of liberal children's books and asked to speak to the store manager. I said, "What's up with this?" I know they're not going to do anything about it. But I want them to know we don't like it, and we're paying attention. Because if we don't say anything then they think what they're doing is fine, and it's not fine. And all of us need to do that. I want that bookstore to get a hundred complaints. We're just chipping away at a large problem here, but it's worth doing.

Complain like hell, let your voice be heard, and don't feel like the boycott has to be complete. Because you can still spend money on Amazon, but if you spend fifty bucks a month on Amazon, compared to three hundred bucks, that hurts.

Dave also recommends the PublicSq. app, which advertises itself as "America's Marketplace: the largest community of freedom-loving, patriotic consumers and businesses the nation has ever seen." Through this app, Dave found Conservative Grounds near his home, so he needn't support Black Lives Matter when he craves a coffeeshop cappuccino anymore.

Mammoth Nation is another option. I haven't personally used the service yet, but it markets itself as "a membership-based online shopping platform that features American-owned and operated businesses, while also openly supporting America First candidates and causes."[155]

To combat ESG, American Conservative Values ETF is an investment advisor that "seeks to boycott as many companies hostile to conservative values as possible, while remaining confident that it can provide

---

[155] https://mammothnation.com/.

large-cap performance and risk." I cannot personally vouch (yet!) for this company's work, but they're worth investigating; plus, the "worst of the worst" list of companies they refuse to invest in is helpful for anyone looking to avoid funding the woke mob.[156]

Finding a Woke-Proof Doctor

Dr. Andrew Mullalley practices at Credo Family Medicine in Indiana. He told me that when he was preparing to graduate from medical school in 2013, he could see woke influences starting to take hold in healthcare:

> One of the classes was on "racial differences in healthcare." I was misinformed and thought it was going to be about giving everyone the best care, because different genetics have different side effects to medicine, but it was all about, "is there any way you're microaggressing against someone else?"
>
> The medical community was a quick adapter to woke things, mainly because it's so academic.

"Woke agendas are more of a distraction from finding cures"
> Much of this woke stuff is driven by academics, who, at least in my experience, are doctors who don't even care for patients. They're really pseudo-politicians or bureaucrats, and this is the ordained course of action, and they're going to enforce it on everyone else. Whereas if you're out caring for patients, and trying to help people, you realize people don't actually want any of this stuff, and the perceived benefits you're looking for, or if you're trying to avert some harms, those boogeymen don't exist in the real world. You just don't see them. [Woke agendas] are more of a distraction from finding cures.
>
> The woke stuff exists mostly in training; 99 percent of doctors totally ignore it and pretend it doesn't exist because it doesn't

---

[156] https://acvetfs.com/boycotts/.

impact their life. So much of [med school] is subjective and based on your supervisors not hating you that there's a huge coercive element when your faculty advisors advocate for something that you kind of have to ask, "how high?" when they say "jump," or else you won't pass.

There are a lot of people who are coerced into silence, and it gives this false impression that there are more people interested in this than there really are.

How to survive woke schooling as a non-woke student

You have to be clever to keep your conscience intact. You have to be the first one there and the last one to leave. If you're an average doctor and you don't dance to the woke stuff, they'll crucify you. If you're there earlier and stay later, and you cover for people on call and everybody owes you a favor, they can't really get too mad at you, even if you're not woke.

I would be the first person to help somebody out of they needed help. If you're friendly and helpful to people, even if they don't care for you or if they disagree with you, it's really hard for them to hate you. So love them into submission, so to speak.

God has not called me to be successful; He has called me to be faithful. (Mother Teresa)

"It's just a total sideshow"

In medical school and residency, we have to go through woke training. In practice, most patients don't know what you're talking about if you ask, "What are your preferred pronouns?" They'll say, "What are you talking about? My back hurts. I'm worried I have cancer." It's just a total sideshow, but it's driven by trying to cater to a very vocal minority.

"The federal government can be very coercive with regard to woke healthcare"
In medicine, most everything is financed through Medicare and DHS [the Department of Health and Human Services], so the federal government, depending who is in power, can be very coercive with regard to woke healthcare.

An example is HHS Rule 1557. It was an Obama-era rule — Congress never voted on it — that said if you prescribe hormones for any reason, you have to prescribe them for gender transitioning. So doctors who may prescribe them for infertility at times would also have to prescribe them for men who want to transition to women. We'd have to prescribe testosterone for women, too. Trump got rid of that rule, and Biden brought it back.

There is a large amount of federal influence tied to Medicare. These things can be challenged through the courts, but somebody's got to take five years off for a court case.

If you get kicked out of Medicare, all the other insurances kick you out as well. So there are a lot of coercive items the federal government does to get doctors to be more woke.

Finding a woke-proof doctor is "critical"
Finding a woke-proof doctor is critical. Maybe even more so than other areas, because it's an area that does not get talked about very much. I think there's such a weight of woke pressure, if we don't push back pretty hard, there's a lot of inertia behind that movement. Standing up for your values, for commonsense, and objective biology is critically important, because as these folks get in, and really a lot of them are already in positions of authority, then they're going to have direct say over daily life.

One thing I think is good that's come out of this wokeness so far, over the past two or three years, is that you see a level of engagement at the school boards. How long have we totally abdicated curriculum choices to totally random people who, if you knew them, you probably wouldn't even let them babysit your kids, let alone teach them? And we're paying them to teach our children.

Physicians, I'd say, are very much in a similar boat. When a patient presents to a doctor, the doctor has a fiduciary duty. The patient has to trust him, because the doctor is giving advice on issues the patient doesn't have enough information to make excellent decisions about without getting help.

If the doctor asks the parent to leave the room: hard stop
One of the things we do is called standard of care. After a child is nine or ten years old, at their wellness exams we're supposed to ask the parents to leave the room so the doctor can talk to the child privately. The goal is that the child will maybe share stuff with the doctor that he or she would not share with their parents.

That seems like a terrible idea to me. The secular organizations that determine the standards of care say, "this is what you're supposed to do," and what they're thinking is the child is experimenting sexually, and hurry up and get them on birth control. Or the child's actually gay, and you can encourage them in their gayness. If the doctor asks the parents to leave the room, I'd say that's a hard stop. I would not recommend that doctor. That's a bad idea.

That would be a very salient example. We know a lot of the surveys now, a lot of Gen Z, 40 percent or so identify as something other than heterosexual, which is super scary. Standard doctors who don't care about this stuff are going to do what they're taught, which is to encourage and affirm the kids in whatever weird idea processes they currently have.

You have to trust your healthcare providers. A good doctor should act as a consultant, not a dictator. I give advice, you make decisions. Everyone has ideas of what is good/normal, preferences and biases. If you don't know them or they are not your own, they may be antithetical.

Finding a woke-proof doctor, measures to take, and questions to ask
Look into telemedicine if you can't find anyone locally. I think in-person is much better, but if the alternative is going to someone who's going to poison the mind of your child or not treat you as a person, yeah, give me telehealth.

You may need to be outspoken to make sure they know your belief system.

Try these alternative resources:
https://www.cathmed.org/
https://onemoresoul.com/
https://mycatholicdoctor.com/
https://doctordoctor.org/
And, of course, there's word of mouth.
Definitely screen doctors for abortion and euthanasia at least.

Have two people at every visit; two against one and two people to advocate.

Some questions to consider asking:

+ Do parents leave the room in teenage wellness checks?
+ What questions or advice do they have for kids going through puberty?
+ We recommend abstinence for our kids, will you support us in this?
+ What information would you keep confidential from us if our child shares it?
+ How familiar are you with NFP? Which methods?
+ What do you do for miscarriage care?
+ Do you refer for abortions?

I make myself rich by making my wants
few. (Henry David Thoreau)

Making Your Voice Heard

Speaking of making your voice heard, there isn't much point to boycotting a company if they don't know why you're doing it. Say something to the manager. Write a boycott email or letter. Make a phone call. It shouldn't be mean-spirited or threatening. Strive for a clear, firm, and polite message. Here's a sample template:

> *My family and I enjoy [product/service], but your support of [woke initiative] is at odds with our [traditional/Judeo-Christian/patriotic] values. We respect that you are free to express support for any cause you support, but we wish you would stick to [occupation]. We would like to continue patronizing your company, but will have to [stop/ significantly reduce] supporting a business that does not represent our values. Thank you for your time.*

Or, if you have the time and think it worthwhile, you could go into teaching mode. Here's a letter I recently wrote to my bank that readers are urged to replicate and tweak as need be:

> *Dear [Bank Board of Directors]*
>
> *My family has entrusted [your bank] with the management of our finances for four generations. I am alarmed by a recent change I've noticed within your institution that I am convinced will degrade the services upon which we've relied for decades.*
>
> *I'm referring to the "Diversity, Equity, and Inclusion" and "Environmental, Social, and Governance" initiatives you are promoting.*
>
> *I have always found [your institution] to be an organically diverse, equitable, and inclusive place, and so the new DEI agenda appears to be seeking to solve a problem that doesn't exist. More than simply constituting a waste of time, the bank's adoption of trendy DEI initiatives will not improve banking services or enhance "social justice." It will increase discrimination, as candidates for employment and current employees are judged by their physical attributes, rather than their*

merits. This situation will cause discord among your employees and will harm customers via decreased output. Less-qualified employees will be hired and promoted on the basis of their sex, skin color, race, "sexual identity," and so forth, rather than on their ability to understand and manage financial systems.

Regarding "ESG" investing, it is your job to oversee the growth of my money and not to dictate what sort of moral causes my money backs. ESG investing is notorious for financially supporting many causes to which traditional Christians, such as myself, are opposed — including abortion.

I am unable to reconcile the convenience of doing business with [your institution] with my morality. If the DEI and ESG initiatives are not done away with, I will be forced to take my business elsewhere.

Thank you for taking my concerns into consideration.

Remember, the woke-proof lifestyle is all about banding together with like-minded NORMALs. Share your letters and emails and phone calls with friends and relatives, and ask them to speak up, too. And don't forget to thank the good guys for taking a stand. Keep them motivated!

Thank you for having the courage to [hang an American flag/display a cross/stand up for traditional values/etc.] at your business. I am excited to support a company that represents my beliefs, and I will encourage everyone I know to do the same. Your bravery is appreciated. Keep it up!

The Nutshell

Woke poison is everywhere, but if enough people speak up, vote with their wallets, and create a woke-proof movement, the tide will turn. There are many ways to boycott a business, and minor sacrifices and perceived inconveniences will often result in beautiful, surprising serendipity.

WOKE-PROOF WAYS

- Instead of spending $300-per-person-per-day on a trip to Disney, try something simpler and more local. Take a road trip three hours from your home, stay at a little inn, and explore a state park.

- Try a cash diet. Start with "cash-only Fridays"; then build up your plastic/online immunity.

- Visit your local library to borrow books and movies instead of buying them from Amazon.

- Start your own Free Little Library and stock it with *Woke-Proof Your Life*.

- Find a nearby farm, orchard, or family-owned market that you can work into your shopping routine.

- Start a woke-proof CD, record, or DVD collection (thrift stores are great for this) instead of streaming everything. Start a "cancelation collection" of books, movies, etc., before they were stripped of their authenticity by "sensitivity readers." This doesn't apply exclusively to old stuff; even modern media — *Friends, Parks and Recreation, The Office* — is rife with content that has become unacceptable in just a few short years

- Make your engagement with media more intentional. Focus on enjoying music, television, and film that expresses traditional, uplifting sentiments.

- Listen to the radio — it's free, and you get to hear about local businesses and happenings, and sometimes, if you're lucky, outrageous accents.

- Learn to ask locals for recommendations, directions, and advice rather than relying on the internet for everything.

- For goodness' sake, get rid of your Amazon Alexa/Echo devices! Especially if you have kids.

- Read chapter 8 on self-sufficiency to learn the value of doing and making some stuff yourself.

Do not love the world or the things in the world. If
any one loves the world, love for the Father is not
in him. For all that is in the world, the lust of the
flesh and the lust of the eyes and the pride of life, is
not of the Father but is of the world. And the world
passes away, and the lust of it; but he who does
the will of God abides for ever. (1 John 2:15–17)

My advice to anyone working for a woke company is … run! It's not worth selling your soul, and "my God will supply every need of yours according to his riches in glory in Christ Jesus" (Phil. 4:19).

Transitioning from working for a woke company could take a little time, creativity, and, as you'll learn from model Jason Morgan's riveting story on page 161, guts. Jason attests that in speaking the truth, he's gained more through a network of new, wonderful people in his life than he ever would have by remaining silent. It's hard enough to stomach using a computer manufactured by Woke, Inc., let alone give your time and talent toward aiding a company that's hellbent on destroying society.

Ripping the Band-Aid off and starting anew isn't easy. Ultimately, though, you'll be much more satisfied. You'll work alongside people you like, doing something that doesn't lead to annoyance or guilt (not to mention all that time wasted on diversity seminars and sensitivity trainings). Some things to keep in mind as you stand with your toes on the edge of the woke high board, ready to dive into the sparkling sea of non-woke possibilities:

Making Life More Expensive Than It Needs to Be

Money isn't everything, and you probably think you need more money than you really do. For one thing, look at Dave's boycott list! You've halved your spending already, simply based on everything you're going to cut out, right? Plus, if you're significantly cutting down on your screen time, you won't know about all those things the targeted advertisers convince you that you "can't live without." I'm being a little absurd for fun, but it is true that most of us make life more expensive than it needs to be.

Secondly and thirdly: this book will inspire you, I hope, to save money by simplifying your life, becoming more self-sufficient, and rather than filling your life with streaming services and Made in China *stuff*, you'll enrich it with *experiences* and *relationships*. Trust me — when you're down at the firehall during a gun raffle fundraiser listening to Greg recount a youthful escapade, you won't miss that HBO Max subscription.

Also, you have likely already considered moving to a place that's more rural and inexpensive and that allows you more time to do the things you are paying someone to do for you now.

I'll add just one more word of inspiration for those thinking of jumping the woke ship for a more streamlined, throwback lifestyle: Maintaining a household is a lot of work, especially if you're blessed to have children. Even without kids, the cooking, cleaning, laundry, budgeting, gardening, and so on never ends. Until relatively recently, sole-breadwinning families were much more common (as were two-parent families). Scott Winship, a senior fellow at the American Enterprise Institute and director of the Center on Opportunity and Social Mobility, released a study in December 2022 on whether "trends in men's pay weakened the traditional family."[157] Winship reported:

> I find that however one views the transformation of the American family, the causes have little to do with changes in men's breadwinning ability, since men are as able as ever to meet economic marriage ability thresholds. To the contrary, family change reflects the rising affluence of the United States, which has manifested in greater economic opportunities for women, an expanding safety

[157] Scott Winship, "Bringing Home the Bacon: Have trends in men's pay weakened the traditional family?" *American Enterprise Institute,* December 2022, https://www.aei.org/wp-content/uploads/2022/12/Bringing-Home-the-Bacon-Have-Trends-in-Mens-Pay-Weakened-the-Traditional-Family.pdf?x91208.

net for single parents, and a variety of economic and cultural shifts that have affected family life.

Where I live, sole-breadwinning families are not the norm, but they aren't unusual, either. A mom or a dad stays home, works from home, or works part-time. Families save money on childcare, housecleaning services, exorbitant pre-made meals, landscapers, fuel for commuting, wear and tear on vehicles, and so forth. Society says a person doesn't have meaning if he or she doesn't leave the home for a "career," but how often does this amount to a misplaced, manufactured "vocation"? Devoting one's life to one's household and family is nothing to be ashamed of.

If you want to bring happiness to the whole world, go home and love your family. (St. Teresa of Calcutta)

Connecting the people who will "rebuild American civilization"
Depending on your career and industry, you may be able to avoid the influence of woke corporate America by switching to a smaller company or making a career change. And you may be able to live a happier life with less income and more freedom.

Though modest living has its advantages, being woke-proof doesn't mean you have to be broke. Nate Fischer is the founder and CEO of New Founding, a network that's "organizing and connecting the people who will rebuild American civilization."

I spoke to Nate about how New Founding can help NORMALs who are looking for an alternative to woke corporations when it comes to building an economic and cultural network of like-minded people:

The central theme is that we are building a network and a community that is aligned around a vision and designed to advance that vision, which is in the interest of Americans on the right.

It seems to me that a lot of Americans feel they don't have any institutions looking out for them. Especially in the commercial world — they feel betrayed by brands and companies they thought were either on their side or neutral, or it wasn't a political domain, and now they realize how alienated they are.

We're building this network that is going to be on their side. At the consumer level, you can think of it as a Costco, in a sense. Not exactly in how it's organized, but you have this company that goes and negotiates on your behalf and collectively looks out for you.

You can think of it as: come here to better align your life, especially in the commercial and technological space, with your values, as people recognize that many of the companies they've done business with for many years are very hostile to their values.

Silicon Valley networks are untenable
According to Nate, the networks created by Silicon Valley companies are "broad in scope in the people they're trying to serve, but very narrow in their focus" of technology and industry.

These networks are untenable. First of all, there are irreconcilable differences that are dividing those networks, and second of all, that's just not a very natural, human way of organizing. People don't build deep relationships around a particular technology or narrow segment of life. Natural networks are actually much deeper, and they're built around shared vision and values.

The alternative is recognizing that there's a much deeper opportunity for something that organizes people around very important shared traits, especially those that are underserved.

"A network of trust"
New Founding is a network of trust, Nate says, that enables people to find jobs and employees (sometimes for people who aren't public about

their politics), business partners who are aligned with the same vision, and recommendations for everything from lawyers to babysitters.

Our talent program matches people around jobs, drawing on the network. Contrast that with Silicon Valley, where it's a standalone thing, and you have to build a network around jobs. Your job is a small portion of your life, so we draw on networks that already exist, kind of like a church or a country club.

New Founding also publishes a newsletter that guides people in a conservative lifestyle. "Don't buy from businesses that hate you" is a core principle of New Founding, which also helps companies grow their digital sovereignty and avoid cancelation.

A lot of times companies have a problem because many media models are very dependent on hostile platforms, like Facebook, and that's a precarious place to be, given our values. New Founding can help.

If you're working for a woke company, don't get in too deep

Every time you get to make a decision, be investing in relationships and networks that are going to be durable. That generally means — you may have thought most companies were friendly or neutral; they're not. Investing any portion of your career into a company that's hostile is something that can further trap you there. If you're learning valuable skills that are transferable, then that can make sense. If you're earning money that can get you to financial independence, that can make sense. But the question is, are you moving toward greater independence, or are you actually moving toward greater *dependence*?

There are a lot of times where you might invest a lot of effort in a job, and the primary payoff is the potential for promotion several years down the road. And it can be a good return if you plan to stay at the company, but if you don't align with the values, then it's kind of a wasted investment, and you'd be better off putting that investment toward, say, a side-hustle that gives you money that makes you more financially independent, or into something completely different if you're planning to leave.

Beware of wasted efforts

Think of where you're putting your real energy and always be trying to move toward that greater alignment, and when you're forced to do business and you're an employee of a company that doesn't align with your values, just think of it in a more instrumental sense. If you're getting some money from them, that's great. You could opportunistically be looking for the right opportunity to pop up. But it could be similar to putting a lot of effort into getting into a private school that turns out to be hostile to your values, and that school ends up being a wasted effort.

"Real change is not going to come through conventional politics"

The more independent you are, the less leverage [the woke] have. Build your business with positive pipelines of people who agree with you. Hire on our platform, within your church. It's not a question of publicly turning down people who disagree with you, but proactively seeking out people you want to work with. When you pro-actively organize your life, it helps eliminate a lot of potential problems.

I absolutely think [cultural change] can be accomplished, and the reason I am where I am is because I think change can come through this phase. I think a lot of people were disappointed with the outcome of the [2020] election. I don't think the election changed much, because my view has always been that real change is not going to come through conventional politics. That's defensive at best. We face so many structural impediments. Real change is going to come from disruptive alternatives in really leveraging our technology.

The technology space is the space that offers way more rapid organization and change. I think many of the organizations we think are incredibly powerful, like Google, are far more vulnerable than many people assume. It's widely recognized that Google search results are increasingly spam, they're increasingly less useful. I think that flows from their poor grasp of the nature of humanity itself. The types of networks they build are unnatural networks, and that weakens them. We [at New Founding] understand humanity in a way that they don't; they have important blind spots, and that offers a path to build much more compelling products.

"We believe in people"

The sort of network we're building here is not just a refuge for people whose values align, but it will actually end up being a much more dynamic place generally and a more compelling type of network to be a part of. If that's the case, it will keep growing, to the point of disrupting a lot of the incumbent players who seem dominant now but who are actually unsatisfactory in what they offer. You'll be part of building something that actually has the potential to change the direction of the country meaningfully.

We fundamentally believe in people, and they don't believe in people. Why does Google try to replace people with machine learning algorithms so much? Silicon Valley fundamentally has a pessimistic view of humanity all the way up to themselves, even — they think they'll be replaced by AI. I don't. I think we are unique, special, created in the image of God, and there's something different there that isn't going to be replaced by technology, and I'm willing to bet on that. And I think those who bet on that will prove right in very important ways.

I have learned, in whatever state I am, to be content. I know how to be abased, and I know how to abound; in any and all circumstances I have

learned the secret of facing plenty and hunger,
abundance and want. (Philippians 4:11–12)

Handling Cancelation

Jason Morgan is a supermodel. He has starred in campaigns for Armani, among other high-profile brands. His image is his livelihood. But when he revealed his opinion to be different from the fashionable views of his industry, he was ostracized by followers, then ultimately canceled on Instagram, showing how absolutely the woke will disregard reality to realize their agenda. Jason Morgan is objectively a stunning specimen; canceling him is not only a crime against free speech, but against humanity.

Jason told me that he never meant to be *that* kind of poster boy:

It's not something I even really wanted to step into — it just happened. I feel like it was almost forced upon me in a way. I wasn't really outspoken before, but when Trump got elected, I saw the way, not just the fashion industry, but everybody was reacting. I wasn't a huge Trump guy in the beginning when he won, but then I thought, even if you don't like it, let's see what he can do.

I was back in New York a few days after that, and I couldn't even get to my apartment because people were protesting his election. It didn't make a lot of sense to me. I was annoyed with that, and I was annoyed by some of the reactions from people in the fashion industry. I started paying more attention to what the media was saying about Trump, and I realized they were lying so much. It just made me like the guy more because I knew what he was up against. I guess I became a Trump supporter, but I didn't talk about it.

Through a connection he made in New York, Jason was invited to at Mar-a-Lago, where he met President Trump and Tucker Carlson.

It was a really special night. I had my dad with me and my brother, and I thought, *I can't even share this [on social media], and this is one of those big things you would share with people.* I'm thinking, *I can't even share this because I know how the fashion industry would react.* And I thought, the hell with this. I'm just doing it. So I posted a picture with Trump in the background, and all it said was, "What an honor." And I posted a picture of Tucker Carlson, saying what a gentleman he was. And I lost like twenty thousand followers.

"They know I'm not a racist or a homophobe or any of those things"

Everyone in the fashion industry unfollowed me. There was quite a bit of backlash on my Instagram. And it made me angry. It made me really angry. Especially with the people who know me in the fashion industry. They know I'm not a racist, or a homophobe, or any of those things. I thought they knew who I was as a person. I knew there were so many people who felt the way I did, but they were just too afraid to speak out. And I thought maybe the world would look a lot different if people were honest and said what they really felt. I couldn't be a hypocrite anymore and not do it myself. Because whatever small following I had, I just felt like I can't get mad at celebrities and people with big followings who are being silent when I'm doing it myself. I just felt like it was my duty to speak out. Because I know how important culture is, especially to younger people. They look up to celebrities and influencers.

The backlash made me — it made me double-down almost. I hate lies. I hate liars and I don't like when people are lied to. It was just one thing after another. I met Trump on March 7, 2020. The next day, people were freaking out about COVID. The world shut down a week later.

"Group think, that's all it was"

I was against it all. I felt the duty to speak out about that. More people got mad at me. BLM happened. I knew that was nonsense.

I looked at the data. I know cops. I know cops aren't racist. I couldn't stand seeing them portrayed that way. I knew every model was posting a black square [in solidarity with BLM] on social media.

Group think, that's all it was. And I saw how powerful it was. Black squares, get vaccinated. I took it as a duty to speak out about all of it. I pretty much had the opposite view on all this stuff. I'd lose more followers, offend people in the industry, although a lot of people in the industry secretly [messaged] me to say, "Thank you so much for speaking out."

I'd say, "You can do this too, don't thank me. You're just letting us get fed to the wolves. I appreciate you thanking me, but why can't you speak out? It's cowardice."

"You can't cancel everybody"

I really feel like we're losing this country because people are so afraid to speak their minds. And if everyone just spoke their mind — you can't cancel everybody.

It's definitely hurt my career, but at the same time, I've gained a lot from it. I've lost money, but I know who my real friends are now. I just feel like I can look at myself in the mirror now and know I've done everything I can as far as sticking to my beliefs, and there's a certain amount of pride with that, and it's led me down a whole different path in life with spirituality — it's pretty crazy where it's taken me.

I see how evil it all is. This doesn't end well, and I have a head start as far as what a lot of people are going to be feeling, but they don't realize it yet.

No one is going to really speak out until they feel pain in their life, and by then it's going to be too late. The country will be gone by then. It's going to take a lot to win this culture war because all these institutions are so heavily infested with this nonsense.

I see a lot of similarities with the Bolsheviks and what's happening now. Wokeness is like a religion to these people. You're seeing it right now with free speech stuff. They don't want free speech. We are the evil ones, and they're willing to do whatever it takes to destroy us. It's a war, it really is.

I got my Instagram deleted — permanently deleted — over something silly like a Bill Gates Halloween costume meme that everyone was posting. I was earning some revenue with Instagram, getting free stuff. I know there are people who didn't book me because of the way I spoke out, but I'd get also messages from photographers and clients and had some bookings through that platform. It'll hurt me, but at the same time, it was a double-edged sword.

"You're getting work and money, but at what cost?"
At the end of the day, you have to be true to yourself. If you're not being honest — you're getting work and money, but at what cost? You really are selling your soul, and it doesn't feel good.

I've been poor and I've had money, and once you get over that certain amount of money and your bills are paid, it doesn't matter.

My grandfather's brother died in WW II. I've always admired people who served, and I've always been interested in heroic people. My uncle was a fireman. That kind of life was always kind of calling me, and maybe I feel like this is our war. The small sacrifice I made by speaking out is the least I could do. And I met so many really, really amazing people, and I would have never done that had I not spoken out.

And that's the thing. When you start speaking the truth and telling people how you really feel, yeah, you might lose some friends. I've even had some family members cut me off, and it's caused quite a rift with a lot of families, and that's no fun, but you really do gain a lot. Those are the people you want to be around.

You can be yourself, they're funnier, they're more entertaining, they've got your back. It's pretty cool.

"What kind of world are you leaving your kids?"
I would tell people not to be afraid. I don't have kids, and I know it's a totally different thing when you have children to support, but what kind of world are you leaving your kids, if you just allow wokeness to win? We've been letting this happen for longer than I realized, until I really started evaluating this stuff. It's been going on for decades.

If you open the door even a little bit, you're letting in really demonic forces. I was looking for answers with all this: why is there so much evil taking over our country? And when you start seeking wisdom, it's going to lead you to Christ. I really believe that. That's what happened to me. I'm looking for what's real, what's truth. He is the only truth. The Crucifixion and how Christ died for us. Some of the bravest people I've seen through all this, they're all Christians, and that's not by accident. They're willing to stick to truth and principles more than any other people I've seen, and that's because of Christ.

The only thing that's stopped me from having rageful anger toward the people who destroyed my career, and the only thing that can save us, is if we find Christ. I went to Catholic high school, because it had a good hockey program and was a good school, but I didn't really go to church before that. I didn't get it. I thought it was all fairy tales. It wasn't until I saw real evil with all this woke stuff going on that I realized, okay, there is evil, and there is Satan, then there is a God. I started praying and things started changing. It gives me a lot of peace, because I know in the end God has the last word.

Love and practice simplicity and humility and don't
worry about the opinion of the world, because if

the world had nothing to say against us, we would
not be real servants of God. (St. Padre Pio)

"I'm a totally different person now"

Once you establish a relationship with Christ, it changes everything. It really does. You can handle anything. You don't care so
much about worldly stuff, approval, any of that. I am appalled by
the way I used to act and the things I used to believe. I'm a totally
different person now. And it's about repentance, and it's beautiful.

I still struggle every day, and I'm still tested every day. We're
in a spiritual war. It's not left and right, these people are under
a satanic spell. We never had debates over what a woman was
before. This is apocalyptic.

I used to be so combative, but I've realized the only way you
can win is by living a moral life and leading by example. Just show
them — this is the way I live, and hopefully it rubs off, and it will.

If You Want Something Done Right ...

Sometimes you do have to start your own school, your own company,
turn a hobby into a lucrative career or a cottage industry into a substan-
tial business.

I interviewed three people who make a living with their small businesses. The incessant dedication required that would deter so many
wasn't something any of them mentioned — it was only acknowledged
in passing when I brought it up. All of them spoke of the intense satisfaction that comes in building something they truly own and can control.

Paul runs a butcher shop in my town. It's been in his family since
1928. Two of his regular employees have been with him for going on
thirty years, and photos of all of them and their families are displayed
in the shop. The employees are welcoming to everyone, and many of
their customers are regulars. "You have a reputation to uphold when

your name's on the sign and the business has been going for over ninety years," Paul says.

Paul makes it a rule to keep politics out of his business.

> My dad used to say, "When you're in business, you don't talk politics, because you always have half the people mad at you."
>
> It's a losing proposition. It's just like talking politics at a party. You're going to tick somebody off, because not everybody is like-minded.
>
> We treat every person just the same as everyone else. Your money is just as green as anyone else's. It doesn't matter what your viewpoint is. You deserve respect because you are a person. You can be sincere about your point of view, and you can be sincerely wrong.

"It's kind of like a big family taking care of each other"
Paul reflects on how he gets to know his customers for years. His work has much more meaning as he interacts on a personal level with the people whose life stories he becomes intimately acquainted with, people he cares about. (He remembers my mother coming into the store while pushing me in a stroller!) Paul caters local fundraisers and events and is a friendly fixture in the community.

> The federal government is spending money on countries that don't even like us. Don't you think it's better to shop locally — where that money is employing local people and the wages stay in the community? It's kind of like a big family taking care of each other.

Paul's customers have a more enriching shopping experience than they would at a big box store where a different robotic cashier — or an actual robot cashier — rushes them through the checkout each time. The tightknit nature of Paul's business also affects the quality of his products. He gets his meat from local family farms, with whom he's established a trusted relationship over time. The meat doesn't have to travel as far, and in addition to being fresher, Paul says there's better quality control.

> If you ever notice the meat recalls they have, it's always hundreds of thousands of pounds of meat, and where's that meat coming from? It's coming from these great big plants out in the Midwest or wherever. You never hear of recalls from small, local plants, so that tells you something right there. If you came in and asked me, "where did this roast come from?" within a day I could tell you the exact farm where it came from. You go into any supermarket and ask where your roast came from, they can't tell you.

Paul remembers when the Walmart in the next town opened up. The small downtowns were booming back then, with small-business owners who knew you by name and would go out of their way to provide you the best service; now, these Main Streets are largely rundown and abandoned.

Paul took a trip to Italy once and marvels at his memory of the way that people in a little village he visited helped one another prosper:

> There was a flower shop, a butcher, a place to buy produce, a cheese shop. People would go down every day or so and spend their money right there. The butcher would make some money and spend it on the produce; the produce person would spend some money at the bakery. The whole community was thriving, because they're not sending their money out to foreign places. These people were specializing, growing one thing, and selling it right away. There was nothing frozen — they were straight to the source.

Lloyd owns a used car dealership, repair shop, and metal roofing company in our community. He has a sign out front of his business that says, "We want your freedom back." He moved from the more populated southern part of Pennsylvania to the north-central region twenty years ago for "hunting and just to get away from the rat race," he tells me.

"I won't go along with it"
I think we probably have more freedom, being up here in the wild. We have so many freedoms that they're trying to take away from us. Really, we haven't had to deal with it all yet, because we're out in the country, and people who deal with it are mostly in the city. And I know we're going to get it sometime. I'm a Christian. So much of what they're trying to do is non-biblical. I won't go along with it. I will not tolerate it whatsoever. And there's a lot of people who won't. There's a higher power that takes care of us.

Dave has run his family's restaurant for forty years. When I ask him about the independence he enjoys, despite the never-ending grind, he tells me, "We make our own rules. And everybody knows it."

Reflecting on the woke world, Dave adds:

One of the biggest gripes I have is, [the woke] section everything off. If you're American, that's the end of the story. I don't care if you're female, black, orange, Catholic, Jew, Protestant — it don't make any difference to me. We all should be playing on the same level. I don't think we should be segregating, with this group saying — we deserve this, we deserve that. I don't care if you're a Native American Indian or an Indian from India — you're an American, and that's as far as it goes! I don't care if you're a firefighter or a dishwasher here, it don't make any difference. Everyone should be on the same level.

Tim, who owns and operates a family truck-driving business, chimes in from a table away:

"Everyone you cut, we all bleed the same"
Everyone you cut, we all bleed the same. A black person is no more African American than I am English American. We were all born in America.

Dave and Tim trade stories of what they've seen in their travels. Dave was a cross-country truck driver before he turned to running his restaurant full-time, and seeing what he saw in the cities has made him appreciate the quiet country life:

> Most of these outside problems don't affect us here. It's creeping in, but it's nothing like other places. I call this hillbilly heaven. We're just plain folk here. If it wasn't for the TV, we wouldn't even know about this woke stuff. In fact, we just started locking our doors a few years ago. I didn't even have a lock for my garage. It's a different world now.

"We don't have to answer to someone else"

Emma and Kara took over the custom furniture store their father started. They both grew up working in the store, and as adults worked elsewhere for a few years for different companies. They've since returned to the family business, and Kara says she and her sister find the experience "way more rewarding," and that they're inspired to uphold the reputation their father worked hard to establish by treating every customer with care.

> We don't have to answer to someone else or be on someone else's timeclock, fulfilling duties as assigned aligned with *their* beliefs and *their* integrity and *their* vision for what they want *their* business to be. That's fine — people can stand for what they want — but it can be a hard pill to swallow if it's not what *you* want. It's nice to be back on our own, with our own control, and to be able to run our own business with our own morals and the things we believe in rather than being tied to someone else.

Emma acknowledges there are pros and cons to being small-business owners. "We all wear a million hats," she says. "Some days it's crazy, and none of us can ever focus on one thing."

Still, the sisters say the relationships they build with customers and the creative liberties they enjoy are more satisfying than "having to punch the clock and be at the mercy of others."

"We get to meet new people, learn their stories," says Kara. "We help fulfill their needs and provide them with something they will cherish a long, long time. I would never trade that for where I worked before."

THE NUTSHELL

Putting your time, talent, and treasure toward a company that hates you is to encourage the evils of wokeness. Be on the lookout for practical ways to avoid feeding the woke machine.

WOKE-PROOF WAYS

+ Choose a few items from the boycott list that you can do without, or seek an alternative brand to buy.
+ Choose a few items from the boycott list that you can make yourself: example: my mother and I have begun making homemade mayonnaise (the French way) each Sunday afternoon. We use eggs given to us from a friend who has a backyard brood, and unless our Italian olive oil is funding "diversity goals," as Kraft is, we're not funding racism with our homemade deliciousness. It's much healthier, and Mama and I bond while we make it, and Dad gives me pointers on how to use my wrist to whisk instead of my entire arm. A real family affair! You can do this with any number of things — learn to make your own candles, laundry detergent, soap, slipcovers. My mother made me a pillowcase for a throw pillow out of a dress whose fabric I adored but which never quite fit me right. (I am full of project ideas for other people to complete!)
+ Write a letter or email to a favorite woke company explaining your opposition to its agenda.
+ Look for local, smaller, family-run businesses to patronize, even if it does cost a little bit more.
+ Take night classes online, at a nearby vocational technical school, or ask someone if you can shadow him or her on the

weekends to work your way into a new career or side-hustle that can get you on an alternative path that leads away from a woke corporation.

Also, consider a part-time gig that could turn into something full-time or could be valuable as a hobby or a service to others in your community. Some ideas:

+ Become a certified personal trainer.
+ Learn to paint interiors or get really good at hanging wallpaper.
+ Offer editing services for people's résumés, speeches, business presentations, and so forth.
+ Give music lessons.
+ Teach beginning gardener classes; help people set up a backyard garden at their own properties, or let them "rent" space at yours, if you have enough.
+ Grow flowers and sell bouquets or fresh arrangements.
+ Chop and deliver firewood. Make it "artisan" if you have to.
+ Work as a pet-sitter or -walker.
+ Become the portable househusband who will help move a couch, mow a lawn, rake leaves, change the smoke detector batteries, etc.
+ Become the person with the truck who can haul scrap or big items across town.
+ Learn to sew and provide seamstress services inside your home; re-upholstery too, maybe?
+ Become a housekeeper.
+ Get really good at rewiring lamps.
+ Certify your home as a commercial kitchen and specialize in something neat (homemade mayonnaise, perhaps?).
+ Custom is key. Make notecards to sell that include scenes and phrases of things Hallmark doesn't sell. (Think pictures of your town, or inside jokes and expressions only people in your region would appreciate.)

- Create custom birdhouses of people's homes.
- Learn to rebind books.
- Learn to frame art and photographs with custom paint colors and materials that are meaningful to your customer, such as wood from an old barn framing, a picture of grandpa painted the same color as his old Ford truck, etc. (While you're at it, explain to me why framing is so expensive.)
- Learn the art of pressing flowers (wooden flower presses are darling!), and preserve people's precious floral memories for them. Etsy is actually a wonderful resource for getting ideas for side-hustles and cottage industries, but look, don't buy! Etsy removes sellers from its pages who express conservative viewpoints.

4

Move!
There's Strength in Numbers

Community is critical and a tax base is powerful. Where you live matters. Many of the people whose perspectives I include in this book live in rural places. I live in the country, too, and encourage everyone to consider moving to a place where losing cell phone coverage is a common occurrence. In the very least, visit these places often and allow the slow pace, natural beauty, and friendliness that generally characterizes less populated locations transform your soul.

The woke playbook is: isolate, alienate, divide, and conquer. Let's not let them do any of these things. Let's band together.

Physical communities are ideal for ending the loneliness epidemic. Yet more people doesn't equal less loneliness: *The Guardian* reported in 2014 on research showing "anxiety and depression rates are higher in urban rather than rural settings."[158] The Roots of Loneliness Project cites six "major factors" for this phenomenon:

1. A transient population
2. Technology that may prevent us from connecting within our own neighborhoods

---

[158] Leo Benedictus, "Sick cities: why urban living can be bad for your mental health," *The Guardian*, February 15, 2014, https://www.theguardian.com/cities/2014/feb/25/city-stress-mental-health-rural-kind.

3. A poor work-life balance
4. Negative politeness, or the tendency people have to ignore social niceties when they are in large crowds
5. City architecture, which tends to be disorienting and depressing
6. Our brains[159]

That last one might be jarring, but it's true. Humans simply haven't evolved to live in this type of artificial environment! We are social creatures who have historically thrived in smaller family-based villages. Constantly being surrounded by thousands of people is more than we were ever meant to process.

A huge happiness study released in 2018 determined that "life is significantly less happy in urban areas." In its report on the research, *The Washington Post*'s headline read: "People who live in small towns and rural areas are happier than everyone else, researchers say."[160] Shorter commute times, less expensive housing, and a more stable population all contributed to people's satisfaction. People in the happiest communities also "are more likely to attend church and ... are significantly more likely to feel a 'sense of belonging' in their communities," reported the *Post*.

> No man is an island, entire of itself. Our lives are involved with one another, through innumerable interactions they are linked together. No one lives alone. No one sins alone. No one is saved alone.
> The lives of others continually spill over into

[159] Chrissy Molzner, "Urban Loneliness & Isolation: The Dark Side of Living in a Big City," *The Roots of Loneliness Project*, https://www.rootsofloneliness.com/urban-loneliness-isolation.

[160] Christopher Ingraham, "People who live in small towns and rural areas are happier than everyone else, researchers say," *The Washington Post*, May 17, 2018, https://www.washingtonpost.com/news/wonk/wp/2018/05/17/people-who-live-in-small-towns-and-rural-areas-are-happier-than-everyone-else-researchers-say/.

mine: in what I think, say, do and achieve. And
conversely, my life spills over into that of others:
for better and for worse. (Pope Benedict XVI)

I've lived in rural Pennsylvania, the Dallas–Fort Worth metroplex, back to "hillbilly heaven" again, Washington, D.C., a town in Idaho with one stoplight, and the "Pennsyltucky" backwoods once again. Every time I visit a city, it's hard for me to believe I ever lived that way. I had stars in my eyes when I went off to college and was freshly graduated, which made the stress and filth of city life more bearable. There's a lot of magic to be found in cities, to be sure — imposing buildings, busy, important people bustling here and there, exotic foods, exciting cultures, a smorgasbord of experiences. But I have to agree with the loneliness experts that constantly processing so much activity and so many people is exhausting, numbing, and unnatural.

Only for the last hundred years has the majority of the American population been located in cities. The year 1920 was the tipping point, when more folks were living in urban places than rural ones.[161] It wasn't until about 2007 that the same could be said of all people, all over the world.[162]

I visited Washington, D.C., recently and felt my blood pressure and tension rise as soon as I was within city limits. Stuck in a stand-still traffic jam in the middle of one of those ludicrous, multi-lane roundabouts, horns honking all around me, police lights flashing up ahead, I surveyed the scene. Everyone was annoyed, in a hurry, and helpless. What a combination! No one even considered letting me merge; they stared straight

---

[161] "America moves to the city," *Khan Academy,* https://www.khanacademy.org/humanities/us-history/the-gilded-age/gilded-age/a/america-moves-to-the-city.

[162] Hannah Ritchie and Max Roser, "Number of people living in urban areas," *Our World in Data,* November 2019, https://ourworldindata.org/urbanization#number-of-people-living-in-urban-areas.

ahead, steering wheel gripped and brow furrowed, intent on making their dinner reservations, or getting to happy hour, or getting home to binge something, or whatever was so urgent.

It struck me that one *must* be selfish in a city, or you'll never get anywhere or get anything done. There are limited resources — only so many parking spaces, so many tables at the restaurant, so many two-bedroom apartments in Logan Circle, so many seats on the subway, so many organic oat milk yogurts at Whole Foods — but *so* many people. You instinctively start viewing everyone not as fellow human beings with whom to share a jolly lollygag, but as competition.

With more people comes more opportunities for things to go wrong, and so more rules must be put in place, too. Keeping track of all the ways you're being micromanaged is exhausting. Waiting in long lines is exhausting. Getting ready early to catch an Uber to stand in a long line is exhausting. Getting ready early to catch an Uber to stand in a long line, only to get stuck in traffic and get to the long line too late is also exhausting. Feeling rushed to finish your dinner because other people are waiting is exhausting. Constantly having to be alert for cars and people and dogs on leashes is exhausting. And not having the energy to look a passerby on the street or fellow subway rider in the eye and share a smile is just sad.

A Rural(esque) Revival

I'm clearly not a city person, and maybe I'm being unduly harsh toward our nation's metropolises. Perhaps I'm just not cut out for the fast-paced, glamorous lifestyle — not energetic enough to handle the incessant stimulation or tough enough to make it in the big city. I'll concede that might be true, with the caveat that the people I know who are happiest in urban places are those who adopt habits of rural living into their routines.

My twin brother and his wife, for instance, have made it a point to get to know their neighbors and invite them over for drinks on the patio. They watch each other's dogs and fetch each other's packages when the other is out of town. They have a handful of spots they frequent where they've become regulars. They're involved in the governance of their ward and partake in community events, like Halloween block parties and Christmas decorating. My brother told me these friendships have blossomed naturally and mainly because he and his wife have a dog they walk frequently. When dogs inevitably approach one another, humans are forced to acknowledge one another's existence. Does dogliness lead to godliness? I think so.

My other friend who lives in D.C., Kat, is the same. When I've hung out with her, I've marveled at how she is on a first-name basis with every bartender, chef, and neighbor we encounter in her part of the city. And yes, I enjoy visiting these people, even if the city itself gives me hives.

Allow me to toss your way a few more morsels to chew upon as you contemplate relocating. Per the Pew Research Center,

> Rural areas tend to have a higher concentration of Republicans and Republican-leaning independents, while a majority of Americans in urban communities identify as Democrats or lean toward the Democratic Party. These patterns have become more pronounced over the past two decades as rural areas have moved in a Republican direction and urban counties have become even more Democratic.[163]

And per the Associated Press:

> By 2030 two-thirds of the world's population will be living in cities, the urban population in developing countries will double, and the area covered by cities could triple, according to a U.N. report.[164]

[163] Kim Parker, et. al, "Urban, suburban and rural residents' views on key social and political issues," *Pew Research Center,* May 22, 2018, https://www.pewresearch.org/social-trends/2018/05/22/urban-suburban-and-rural-residents-views-on-key-social-and-political-issues/.

[164] Edith M. Lederer, "UN report: By 2030 two-thirds of world will live in cities," *AP,* May 18, 2016, https://apnews.com/article/40b530ac84ab4931874e1f7efb4f1a22.

Now, do cities create woke-minded people, or just attract them? It seems to be a mix of both (ever seen *Sweet Home Alabama*?). Various circumstances — family, work, love, vocations — notwithstanding, it seems that left-leaning people likely flock to cities because they *like* rules and/ or are comfortably accustomed to being told what to do. They also value what cities offer — prestige, power, money, fancy food — more than NORMALs do.

NORMALs prefer to rely on themselves rather than government or social services, and so naturally gravitate to places that are free and spacious and offer more opportunities for self-sufficiency. It would also follow that these situations explain why so much woke ideology occurs in urban places: rural people are busy growing gardens, attending church, having backyard BBQs, shooting skeet, and muddin' in the woods, while urban people have two artisan craft cocktails too many and decide to take their self-imposed stress out on the rest of us.

A couple more stats before we get to some delightful storytelling. A 2015 YouGov study conducted in the United Kingdom found that "Only 1 in 4 British people would call their neighbors good friends — but in rural areas the figure is much higher." [165]

Even if you aren't "good friends" with your neighbors, "minimal interactions" with familiar people are incredibly powerful. A pair of researchers found that the regular conversations so common in small-town life — the small talk with the postman and passing chitchat we have at the drycleaners — add up and heighten our health: "even social interactions with the more peripheral members of our social networks contribute to our well-being." [166]

---

[165] Will Dahlgreen, "Love thy neighbour? British people are barely friends with them," *YouGov*, September 10, 2015, https://yougov.co.uk/topics/society/articles-reports/2015/09/10/love-thy-neighbour-british-people-are-barely-frien.

[166] Gillian M. Sandstrom and Elizabeth W. Dunn, "Social Interactions and Well-Being: The Surprising Power of Weak Ties," *Sage Journals*, April 25, 2014, https://journals.sagepub.com/doi/10.1177/0146167214529799.

Living near family is also a plus. You'll have built-in babysitters and a default social/support network right there. Plus, CNN reported on a monumental study that found that "children with the greatest level of family connection were over 49 percent more likely to flourish compared with those with the lowest level of family connection."[167]

Politico reported in 2015 on research by Hazel Markus, a social psychologist and professor in the behavioral sciences at Stanford University, who found:

> We are very much influenced by the places where we live. That's because it shapes who we talk to, the media we encounter. We are influenced a great deal by the people around us, and that can have this persistent psychological change.[168]

Final study, I promise. (Well, at least for now.) From RealClearScience author Ross Pomeroy:

> American conservatives say they are much happier than American liberals. They also report greater meaning and purpose in their lives, and higher overall life satisfaction. These links are so solidly evidenced that, for the most part, modern social scientists simply try to explain them. They've put forth numerous possible explanations.
>
> Marriage tends to make people happier, and conservatives are more likely to be married. Religious belief is also linked to happiness, and conservatives tend to be more religious.
>
> Conservatives are less concerned with equality of outcomes and more with equality of opportunity. While American liberals

---

[167] Megan Marples, "Children are more likely to succeed if they live in this type of environment," *CNN*, May 20, 2022, https://www.cnn.com/2022/05/20/health/family-connections-flourish-parenting-study-wellness/index.html.

[168] David McRaney, "How Your Address Changes Your Politics," *Politico*, August 2, 2015, https://www.politico.com/magazine/story/2015/08/how-your-address-changes-your-politics-120899/.

are depressed by inequalities in society, conservatives are okay with them provided that everyone has roughly the same opportunities to succeed. The latter is a more rosy and empowering view than the deterministic former.[169]

Beware the 'Burbs

As previously noted, the evil themes of wokeness have been gaining ground for decades, and the gloves came off during COVID and the pandemic's devastating aftermath. Yet our attitudes toward one another and how we interact have been shifting for years. Anthony Gigantino, of La Salle University, labeled suburban sprawl "the greatest social change of post-World War II America."[170] Residents of suburbs have more space and must travel for goods and services, as people in rural places do. Essentially, Gigantino observes, suburban dwellers possess a small-town mindset, but rather than look to their neighbors to help fulfill their needs, they still rely on cities and homogenized big business:

> Two reasons why suburban sprawl became a popular inclination after World War II are that housing was cheaper in the satellite neighborhoods due to New Deal legislation (which provided alternatives to high-priced luxury apartments in the city) and that propaganda influenced women to move into new communities, portraying them in a matriarchal position rather than as a member of the work force, of which many women were a part during World War II.

---

[169] Ross Pomeroy, "Why Are Conservatives Happier Than Liberals?," *RealClear-Science,* August 27, 2022, https://www.realclearscience.com/blog/2022/08/27/why_are_conservatives_happier_than_liberals_849615.html.

[170] Anthony Gigantino, "Suburban Sprawl: The Greatest Social Change of Post-World War II America," La Salle University, 2019, https://digitalcommons.lasalle.edu/cgi/viewcontent.cgi?article=1099&context=the_histories.

Sociologists often state that values begin in the household. In the suburbs, a whole new set of values began to emerge in American culture.... Along with the exaltation of status among suburbanites, the values that the suburbs have embraced are arguably detrimental to the foundation of America as a whole. One of the biggest problems with suburban values is the iconization of the individual in society. The assessment of the self has neglected the community because many people who favor the advancement of the individual crave the benefits of a small-town ideology where they feel the state exists for their own personal benefit. Furthermore, while many suburbs try to remain separate from their metropolitan cities, they are in essence dependent upon them.

Reflecting on the habit of Young Urban Professionals — Yuppies, the woke of their day — to gentrify old neighborhoods and rob them of their character, Gigantino offers this astute insight:

Arguably the greatest problem with gentrification is the complete disposal of the neighborhood. Many gentrified neighborhoods are so similar and are home to such a mobile group of people that community has become private and temporary. Being that many of these new neighborhoods are cheaper than living in a major city like New York, people simply spend little time in their residential community because they are either working or commuting. The removal of long-term residents, often of a lower income, and the arrival of new, more affluent residents, is causing another economic and cultural gap that could plague America in a sense of class warfare, which could be similar to the racism difficulty.

A 2018 study on the "social and economic behavior shift in the suburban society" conducted in Indonesia chronicled how in one region, as land use shifted to make way for suburbs, people's livelihoods went from agricultural to non-agricultural.[171] The village entered into the "rapid production and trade of shoes and sandals," and "social interaction between the villagers shifted from social interaction that emphasizes verbal and nonverbal communication directly and face to face to indirect social interaction."

Production activity became "increasingly congested ... causing villagers [not to] have enough time for social interaction." *Silaturahim* — a term Muslimaid.com defines as "the strengthening of relationships with friends, relatives and humanity" — disappeared.[172] Instead of regular, informal contact, villagers only saw each other when they were specifically invited somewhere for an event, such as a wedding. Otherwise, they communicated by using mobile phones. "The characteristics of rural communities that are characterized by their social interactions face to face and [intimately] [are] not found in the rural community," the study concluded.

This criticism of suburban sprawl is a solution-oriented rant, I promise. As people prioritize a generic life centered around modern amenities, ease, and creature-comforts above the rewards of intermingling with a diverse set of neighbors, they become one-dimensional bores intent on satisfying appetites and egos as conveniently as possible.

> The world offers you comfort, but you
> were not made for comfort. You were made
> for greatness. (Pope Benedict XVI)

To thwart the woke objective, we NORMALs need to muster every asset we can. If you're planning to relocate to a small town, the countryside,

-----

[171] S Harianto, et. al., "Social and economic behavior shift in the suburban society," *Journal of Physics,* 2018, https://iopscience.iop.org/article/10.1088/1742-6596/953/1/012187/pdf.

[172] "The Strengthening of Ties," *Muslim Aid,* https://www.muslimaid.org/media-centre/blog/the-strengthening-of-ties/.

or to a different part of the city, seriously consider investing your time and money into older properties. If you take the time to study old homes, you'll understand the psychology of the people who designed, built, and lived in them. They included spaces to gather, visit, read, and pursue hobbies — parlors and sitting rooms and passé things known as *dining rooms* and *porches* — filled with artistic fixtures meant to enchant the dweller.[173] Now, we have ambiguous "open concept" spaces that are as undefined as our morality, and "family rooms" devoid of décor and designed primarily for "bingeing."

"Everything Is Built for Planned Obsolescence"

Christopher Hewett is the founder of Old House Fix, "a library of old house specific resources and a community of old house enthusiasts and experts."[174] Chris and I spoke about common misconceptions about old homes, the challenges and joys they bring, and how they're good for society and the soul.

My wife and I bought our first home in 2005. It was not even four years old yet and the siding started to rot. The door casings were rotted six inches up. I sometimes wonder if that house is still standing.

New houses age more quickly than old ones. Any new house is only new for the first year or two, then it starts settling and you have to start doing things and putting money into it just as you would an old house — maybe not a roof right away, but you still have to do routine things as you would change the oil, rotate the tire, and so on with a car.

---

[173] Adrienne Gaffney, "The Rise and Fall of the Front Porch," *The Wall Street Journal*, September 11, 2019, https://www.wsj.com/articles/the-rise-and-fall-of-the-front-porch-11568206837.
[174] https://myoldhousefix.com/.

Everything is built for planned obsolescence, it seems these days. Appliances, too, you know. They knock down old houses to put up new ones that are disposable.

Our current house is in Ann Arbor's Old West Side historic district and it is the reason I developed a passion for old house restoration and preservation. Old houses are a lot of work sometimes, but if they've been there a hundred years, they'll likely be there for another hundred years if you take care of them. Just think of the materials in many old homes — the old-growth wood that's rot-resistant. The millwork, carved elements in the old houses that you don't get today, because they're too expensive and take up too much time. Everything now is about the most efficient box.

Chris and I discussed how a house and a home used to be such a vital part of a person's life — it's where you experience major family events and enjoy the simple things that sustain you. Family birthday parties, nightly meals together. It's where we share exciting news and exchange priceless pieces of advice. It's life-changing to be able to come home to a place that feels full of character and memories and into which you have personally invested time and love. Chris resumes:

A house or a home?

Is it just a house, or is it a home? Our first house had no history, it had no soul. These old houses have a story from the many people who lived there and raised a family and maybe even hand-crafted it.

Chris says renovating their house helps him bond with his wife. They collaborate — she enjoys researching and choosing period-correct wallpaper, for instance — and "we're so busy doing things with the house, there's no time to go to the casino or the bar or whatever." And when there is a disagreement, "we have to find our way out and compromise," Chris says. "Those are relationship skills you build."

Chris has also built relationships with thousands of old house lovers through his online community. He attended a workshop last year that attracted different tradespeople, undoubtedly from a mix of political backgrounds.

Politics didn't matter; we were there to talk about old houses and windows. [Pursuing a passion] really does allow you to meet different people from different walks of life. I had zero knowledge of old houses fifteen years ago. Now I'm making all these connections and building this directory. There's really no room for politics there, because we're too caught up in, "Should you paint the original trim or not?" Things like that. It's nice to dive back into the house to unwind and almost live like they did before [modern technology]. I enjoy keeping up our house, hanging out outside on our front porch swing.

Chris spends his day at work behind a computer, working as a professional project/program manager specializing in logistics. He has spent years putting back features in his house that were removed or covered up over time, replicating crown molding and adding back trim. The house "looks totally different from the way it used to," he says.

Adding beauty and meaning to your life
Chris says his old house hobby stimulates all his senses — igniting his brain in problem-solving, his hands and muscles in crafting, and his aesthetic sensibilities all at once. He garners great fulfillment not just in completing a project, but in renewing that feeling every time he comes home.

Every time you walk in the room and see the results, and you know what it used to look like and what it looks like now, and the outside, too — you strip your house and paint it and restore the outside. I remember when it was covered in aluminum siding, and still, even though it's been a few years, I get this feeling of satisfaction every time I look at it.

There are so many projects you complete, and every time you drive up to your house or go inside, or just down to your favorite light fixture you've repurposed, you get to see that physically, and it makes you happy. I'm like, "man! I love that lamp." Or "man! that wavy glass is beautiful!" And my wife says, "Yeah, you've said that a hundred times now."

The same thing with antiques. You remember where you were when you bought it, it has a story, it was built to last, it's been through different families, you can pass it on to your kids, and all that adds an element of meaning and beauty to life.

I have this Flemish hall bench I picked up a few years ago. I was in Germany for work and I went into this shop. I saw it when I walked in and said, "I have to have this thing." It's all-oak from the 1890s with hand-carved panels in the back. And I thought, "How am I going to get this thing home?" I happened to have some friends over there who were moving back to the States. I paid them some money to put it in with their goods. It took like six or seven months to get it. That was really an interesting journey for a piece of furniture.

Living in a beautiful home full of history and fine craftsmanship and caring for the property as you would a family member is personally rewarding, but it extends beyond the homeowner to the neighbors who appreciate your work, too. Chris was visited by a ninety-four-year-old man who was born in the house Chris now owns.

We spent the whole afternoon together; it was really neat. He shared some pictures of the front porch, of everyone hanging out on steps during a birthday party, and we took him up to his old bedroom.

A neighborly feel
Chris reflects on the nature of old houses and the places they were built:

Old houses were built around proper city centers, with a court-house and parks and sidewalks. Nowadays, with urban sprawl, people are growing up around strip mall after strip mall. They have to drive everywhere. They don't even have a big town feeling. Here, you know your neighbors a little bit more, you're not spread out so far, and you aren't in that high-rise; it's a more neighborly feel.

With a lot of them, you can get a really good deal. You can buy a fixer-upper at a lower cost, and one thing most people don't think about is locking in that lower tax rate.

Pay the $400 and get the inspection so you know what you're getting yourself into before closing. Do your due diligence. Sketch out a rough estimate of what repairs and upgrades are going to cost.

Buy the house, live in it a year, and get to know the house — what's working, what's not working. Let it tell you what it needs. Don't just come in and gut it. The old trim and doors, they're non-renewable resources too. That old growth, that grain from a two-hundred-year-old tree, you just don't see that in furniture grade wood these days.

Chris adds that another joy of preserving an old house is building new friendships with craftsmen who specialize in restoring windows, refurbishing old stoves, and other traditional trades.

Try a trial time

The Pullmanns live in Indiana. Joy explained that in searching for a place to put down roots, they first considered the church community. Fort Wayne is home to several conservative Lutheran seminaries, and the Pullmanns had friends in the area. Joy's family is from Wisconsin, and she and Nathaniel were in college in Michigan, yet they did not consider either of these to be "well-managed, reliable states."

The strength of the church community was the Pullmanns' first priority, and politics was a consideration. Joy says she doesn't trust Republicans by default, but they do tend to support "less of the craziness."

During a "trial time" in Fort Wayne, the Pullmanns rented for a while, visited churches, and welcomed pastoral visits into their home while they weighed making their move permanent.

THE NUTSHELL

Rural people are happier than urban people. Rural people are more likely to be conservative. Conservatives are happier than liberals. Liberals live in cities. People who live in cities are lonelier and less happy than people who live in the country. People are influenced by the places they live. So... if you want to be happy, live in the country. Where you'll also become a conservative.

Basically, if everyone moved out to the country, or at least had consistent contact with rural places, we'd all be happier and healthier neighbors and friends looking out for one another rather than demonizing each other. Also, wokeness would vanish, and you could use this book to start the campfire for s'mores (an outcome I approve of 100 percent, by the way!).

WOKE-PROOF WAYS

- Leave your house.
- Make an effort to get to know your neighbors.
- Incorporate rural places into your routine, visiting them often.
- Get a dog. You'll make friends with fellow dog owners, you'll be forced to get outside and exercise, and you'll understand how sweet innocent, simplistic love can be.
- Boost your well-being with tiny interactions.
- Make eye contact and say hi to people.
- Go to cash registers with human cashiers instead of the self-checkout.
- Ask for help when you're lost or looking for something instead of wandering around, thereby give others the opportunity to help you.

- Don't overthink giving someone a compliment. Just do it.
- When you're waiting around for something, avoid looking at your phone. Being alert invites others to approach you, and they may need a friend.

I realize not everyone is going to pack up and move to Podunk, but if you're intrigued, World Population Review provides us this list of the most conservative states:[175]

1. Mississippi
2. Alabama
3. Wyoming
4. West Virginia
5. South Dakota
6. Louisiana
7. Oklahoma
8. Tennessee
9. Arkansas
10. Missouri

The most conservative cities (*sigh*, if you must) are these:[176]

1. Lafayette, Louisiana
2. Tyler, Texas
3. The Woodlands, Texas
4. Knoxville, Tennessee
5. Frisco, Texas
6. Carrollton, Texas
7. Murfreesboro, Tennessee
8. Chattanooga, Tennessee
9. Scottsdale, Arizona
10. Plano, Texas

---

[175] "Most Conservative States 2023," *World Population Review,* https://worldpopulationreview.com/state-rankings/most-conservative-states.

[176] "Most Conservative Cities 2023," *World Population Review,* https://worldpopulationreview.com/us-city-rankings/most-conservative-cities.

I can't vouch for this company's work (they didn't answer my interview request), but Conservative Move, an organization of real estate agents, purports to "help you sell your home, organize your move, and find a home in a community where you feel safe, valued, and at home."[177]

---

[177] https://conservativemove.com/.

5

Homefield Advantage
Putting Down Roots

There's No Place Like (a) Home

I feel blessed that I was raised in a rural place and had a home to return to. I didn't appreciate small-town life when I was growing up. In fact, I thought it beneath me, and I couldn't wait to spread my wings. I never considered it as a place I would grow proud of and enjoy, but experiencing other places opened my eyes to how wonderful a little town can be. When I moved back home from Idaho, I planned to hang out in my hometown for a couple months until I decided on my next move. That was five years ago.

I had the advantage of being able to work remotely and live with my parents while I gave my hometown a second chance. A few months of being a typical millennial were enough to make me feel shame, and so I sought an apartment downtown. Through that, I made a friend my own age who convinced me to join the town's revitalization committee. At the gym, I reconnected with a girl I had been friends with while waitressing in high school. I started freelancing for the local newspaper, because I'm nosy and missed local journalism. I also joined the local sportsman's club, because I wanted to learn to shoot trap, and from there, my network really blossomed.

By seeking out woke-proof activities, connections multiply, a network builds, and the wonderful tradition of like-minded people helping one another makes a comeback. I've been part of my local sportsman's club for four years now and have become friends with a diverse set of the most welcoming, kindest people I've ever known. One gentleman keeps bees and has offered to teach me about producing homegrown honey. Another brings pickles to share that his daughter makes from cucumbers grown in their garden.

I ordered a CSA ("community-supported agriculture" — a farm share) last year, because the friend I met while looking at an apartment made me aware of *his* friend who runs a small family farm. Two other women and I shared delivery duties in our town, and through this, I became friends with Paula and her husband Kurt. We have a lot in common, and because we share similar values and interests, they feel inclined to gift me with their garden herbs and berries. To thank them, I've provided resources from the local historical foundation, of which I am the president, because Paula and Kurt love learning about our shared hometown.

Similarly, my parents let a local handyman who has done a lot of work on their home hunt on their property. In return, he gives them venison every winter. Another friend, a woodworker, dries wood in my parents' barn; when their door frame needed to be fixed, he stopped by and did it free of charge. (He also gives us venison — we have an abundance of deer here!)

I fell in love with my hometown and the people who make it tick (okay, not *all* of them). I actually study the old architecture now and appreciate it. I know our riveting town history — an "affair of the heart" and a romantic duel are part of it! — and tell it to anyone who will listen. I volunteer at and attend events, and it's strange for me to go anywhere without running into someone I know.

I am familiar with every alley, street, pothole, and shortcut. I have a friend, human and canine, on every road, and could knock at many doors if I needed help (or a cup of coffee … or a cocktail).

I am comforted by knowing what to expect from the people who surround me — their quirks, their endearing habits, and their irksome ones, too. I know people's cars, and we honk and wave and pull over to talk on sleepy side streets. I like being held accountable by the older ladies at church and the old guys who go to the gym at dawn, both of whom give me a hard time when I'm a no-show. Running into people I know at random is a nice surprise, like hearing your favorite song on the radio as opposed to firing it up on Spotify.

Done right, small-town life is much like a sitcom. There are times it can feel suffocating, and there are certainly annoying characters, some shysters and bad eggs, but "better the devil you know," and all that. It's fun to be able to talk about town landmarks and happenings and fellow townsfolk and not have to explain yourself. It's like sharing an inside joke with three thousand people. The local eateries at lunchtime feel more like a school cafeteria full of familiar faces than a restaurant open to the public. When the elderly regulars don't come in for a few days, the proprietress notices and calls to make sure they're alright. She sends them meals if they need them. When my lawnmower was in the shop recently and my neighbor saw me struggling with a manual (non-motorized = *grueling*) lawnmower, he insisted I use his gas-powered machine, partly because he knows my friendly mother from her frequent trips to the grocery store where he works.

That said, you have to try. You have to *want* to like the place you live and look for reasons to enjoy it. You may have to adjust your notions of "success" or "entertainment" and nurture an appreciation for the simple and the absurd. You'll have to get comfortable with some kooky characters, head-scratching nicknames, and a slower pace. The more you look for ways to contribute to the community, the easier assimilation will be.

Social Pollination

I like to think of what I've been blessed with not as a small-town web, because spiders are creepy and kill the things that come into their homes, but as the process of pollination. Small-town worker bees gather kindness, knowledge, skills, favors, grace, and love from one person and feed it to another, as a bee collects pollen from flowers when he goes about making honey. Social pollinating is just as sweet.

I now feel ashamed of my former attitude toward my hometown and regretful of the years I took it for granted. I'm doing my best now to make up for lost time.

> To be rooted is perhaps the most
> important and least recognized need
> of the human soul. (Simone Weil)

Author Bill Kauffman is a kindred spirit in this way. He details his own repatriation in *Dispatches from the Muckdog Gazette: A Mostly Affectionate Account of a Small Town's Fight to Survive,* and writes frequently (in a way that makes my soul shout, "me too, me too!") about the disastrous effects of "urban renewal" and his small town's struggle to "maintain a distinct identity, a character, rather than becoming just another formless wattle on the continental blob."

Bill delivered a talk in 2017 on how "Loyalty to Place Can Renew American Towns."[178] He granted me permission to cite from it freely. It deserves to be printed here in full, but so does everything Bill writes. For now, enjoy this an *amuse bouche*:

"Our hometowns deserve our love"
> I recall my family grousing about urban renewal. They understood that every building carries within a fund of meaning and memory that can never be duplicated or replaced, and I think they sensed

---

[178] Bill Kauffman, "Loyalty to Place Can Renew American Towns," *The American Conservative,* October 10, 2017, https://www.theamericanconservative.com/loyalty-to-place-can-renew-american-towns/.

that when these buildings were gone, the memories might remain but the corporeal evidence of a life lived disappears, and we would become as ghosts, strangers flitting through a strange land. The children would leave, because their anchorage was no longer visible. When the signposts of your life vanish, it doesn't make much difference where you live. Or work. Or shop. One place is pretty much the same as the next — not hostile to our residence therein, but merely indifferent.

And if we are disloyal to our place, to the place our ancestors made, then why should our children show any loyalty to us? If the city in which they grow up is stripped clean of its landmarks — and I don't mean just the homes of great men, of presidents and thieves — I mean the corner groceries and baseball fields and the front-porched homes that make a neighborhood — well, why should young people choose to stay in such a self-disrespecting place? Why not just move to a manicured suburb with high average SAT scores — say, Columbine, Colorado, where all your dreams can come true?

Our hometowns — or the places we make our hometowns — deserve our love. We can treat them with love and care and solicitude, or we can treat them as carelessly as we would a used Big Mac wrapper.

[Our hometowns] reveal to us at the most unexpected moments the alternative to the insanity that's going on out there, in TV land, in the unreal America. In Batavia [New York] it's the heavenly grease at the Pok-a-dot diner, the chestnut trees on the campus of the New York State School for the Blind; it's the novels of John Gardner and a crowd chanting "BHS! BHS!" at a Batavia High basketball game. That's what's real. That's what keeps our town alive. [We all have] our own analogues of these things. Protect them. Preserve them. Sing them. Enhance them. Share them.

"It makes life richer and more meaningful"
I asked Bill how he managed to convince his wife Lucine, a Los Angeles native, to move to his small hometown in upstate New York, and how she coped with assimilating. He told me:

> Way back in 1988, Lucine and I had been married for just over a year, and I convinced her to move from D.C. (where we lived in an apartment) to my hometown of Batavia, NY. I told her it would be a one-year experiment. (That year has been measured in Old Testament terms, a la Methuselah.) I had always been homesick for Batavia, a working-class town in the rural Rust Belt of western New York. It might not look like much to someone just passing through, but to me it was a wondrous and mysterious repository of memories and myths and stories and lore and legends and all the drama and comedy in the world. Lucine assimilated so well that she ended up serving two terms as town supervisor of Elba, the town five miles north of Batavia where we bought a house in 1992. She was also the long-time president of the Landmark Society of Genesee County and she hosts a weekly half-hour interview show about the arts and culture of our county on Batavia's radio station.
>
> It's hard to idealize a place when you actually live there. Very easy for makers of truck commercials or political campaign ads to do so, but those of us who live in small towns know that they also contain hurt and corruption, fentanyl, and sadness. But life on the human scale is just more real. There is a substantiality, a depth of connection that you cannot get in the upwardly mobile suburbs or the transient professional enclaves in cities. (You can find it in city neighborhoods.) To know the people at the coffee shop, in church, on the community theater stage, in the baseball stadium grandstand, and to know their backstories, their triumphs and heartaches, their illnesses and foibles — to me, it makes life

richer and more meaningful. I have a strong libertarian streak and I hate telling people what to do, so I don't hold myself out as an example of How to Live Life, but I can't imagine a better life I might have lived.

"Make yourself native to your place"

I would add that one needn't return to one's hometown to find what you and I have found and are finding. After all, many people grow up in multiple places, or — like Lucine — their cities undergo such wrenching change that they are unrecognizable to native sons and daughters. So I like the advice of Booker T. Washington: "Cast down your bucket where you are." Or to paraphrase Wendell Berry, make yourself native to your place. Put down roots. Get involved. Reach out. Connect. Our country — our beloved country — is in lousy shape, and it can only be revived at the grass roots, by people making the decision to commit themselves to a place, a community. The only patriotism that makes sense to me is the patriotism of small places — anything bigger is just jingoism and noise.

Challenges and Limitations

Brenden Boudreau and his wife Elizabeth repatriated to rural Michigan from the Denver metroplex a few years ago. Brenden says:

Living in a rural/non-city atmosphere certainly has its blessings and challenges. It's nice to live out in the country with a little elbow room around you and your neighbors; however, with young children that may make it more difficult to make nearby friends. There is a young family who just moved next door with kids about the same age as ours, so there is hope there for friendship. Most of our children's friends were through our church, which sadly just shut down recently, but we're in the midst of visiting new churches with hopes to get settled in one soon.

We live right next to a farm field, and it has been really fun for the kids to see the various crops that the owner of the land grows on it. This fall the farmer gave my two oldest kids and me a ride in his combine as he was harvesting soybeans. It was an awesome experience for the kids (and my daughter actually fell asleep in my lap during the hour-long ride, ha!). The farmer loves seeing kids who have an interest in farming. My oldest son loves tractors, so who knows, that could be a future career opportunity for him.

We do have a garden, which the kids love to help out in, as well as just eat the vegetables right off the plants as they begin to ripen, so that's fun for them and a good learning opportunity.

They generally love being outside, which is just great. That's how I was when I was younger, too, until new technology started coming in and drawing me and my generation back inside. We're hoping to encourage that desire for outside play and limit their use of technology. The studies are out there of the benefits of outside play and the harm that new technology causes to young children.

The Great Escape

Brian and Lauren Spicher were living in the crowded and growing Lancaster/Harrisburg, Pennsylvania, area, and Brian's roofing/contracting business was in high demand. Both Brian and Lauren get emotional when they talk about the toll it was taking on him. Lauren recalls:

> Brian was getting really, really stressed with work. And it was causing some health issues. And I knew how much he wanted to break away from that.

Lauren is from Long Island originally. Brian is from the rural, mountainous part of Pennsylvania, and the family had bought a cabin in the woods near Brian's family. At the time, Lauren told her husband, "Don't ask me to move here. I can't live here."

During the height of the COVID pandemic, though, Lauren home-schooled their four children, and the family made frequent trips to the cabin.

Every time we'd pack up, we didn't want to go back to Lancaster. It started to remind me of Long Island and why I wanted to move [from there]. I wasn't very gung-ho at first — no, we're not doing it. But my heart was softened. Brian's parents are right down the road. The kids can live outside. I knew it would be the right environment for our children to grow up in. Their cute little charter school is down the street. Being here, it started to really grow on me. Just being on the porch with our coffee and listening to the birds.

Having family nearby and a built-in support network certainly helped the Spichers move, but still, it involved an enormous change and a big leap of faith. Says Lauren:

The hardest thing for me, I think, was leaving behind what I've already accomplished — home, but also my friends, and a church community, which was really big for us. So one of my fears was that I would have to kind of start all over again. It definitely was a hard decision for me to make — to say yes to that and be okay with not having friends right away.

I also had a fear for my children. We lived in a place where everything was at our fingertips. Schools are great. I had a fear for my kiddos, and it's still a little bit of a fear, as they get older in a place that's very rural like this, what are they going to do? Limited opportunities for them was another worry.

The sacrifice for the kiddos is that there are not as many children around. We lived in a spot in Lancaster where there was a community pool in our backyard and the park right there. They miss the interaction — it was more fast-paced when it came to being around other children. They see their friends from school when they're in school, but everybody lives further away. They do have their cousins to play with here.

The sacrifice for me was leaving my friends, and also I moved further away from family. Instead of an easier three-and-a-half-hour drive from Long Island, it's now five-plus hours. Knowing that I would be further away from my family was hard, and it still is a little hard, but, you know, we have to make the effort to travel. It's not like I'm across the world.

"My faith played a huge role"

I had to get over those fears and just be okay with starting new. And I don't regret it. My faith played a huge role. It's important for people of faith to find a church community where they can really connect with the community they're going to be settling in. I think if it wasn't for our church here, it would be a lot harder, because a lot of my friends are from our church.

Just trusting God, too. I really feel like everything — from the moment I said, okay, let's do this, let's sell your business, let's sell the house — everything just fell into place and it was, I say it's God. It really was God.

I would say getting over that fear involved trust that this was our calling, our next journey. There will always be those fears, but I feel those fears are more about us, and are selfish.

"I was really tired — mentally, physically, everything"

Brian chokes up when he reflects on his condition before he and his family changed course and how much joy the transition has brought them:

My business was growing and I didn't know how to keep up with it. That was my biggest struggle. And then I would try to work harder and get my guys to work harder to keep up with it. And then my demand was higher, and it was just burning me out. I was just really tired — mentally, physically, everything. It was making me sour. I didn't even really enjoy it. I had this dream to just get out, to escape it. I would come up here [to the woods] and think, "I want to live up here."

I'm at a point now where I feel like — for my kids' sakes, I feel like I have to go after my dreams. I don't think back much. I'm always forward thinking, but yeah, when you think back and you think of how everything lined up, it's kind of amazing how we got this place.

I think some of my fears came from living in a very tightly condensed, townhouse community. We would go on walks through the neighborhood, and I would just see kids out in the playground and I would see needles on the ground. I'd be like, man, my kids are gonna be teenagers. I'm gonna have to teach them about this. I would rather be out hiking with them in the woods and going fishing with them and having more opportunities outside.

"Our oldest son is thriving here"
Lauren says,

Our oldest son is thriving here when it comes to the outdoors. He has every opportunity when it comes to hunting and fishing. The kid went fishing so much this summer, which he wouldn't have gotten that opportunity before, because first of all, Brian would've been working all day every day with the roofing company. And then there's really not many places [around the city]. We now have a little creek in our backyard. We're friends with the tree farm that has a massive pond over there that we fish at a lot. Now, on Sundays after church, we go to Brian's mom's house and have lunch together. I feel like our kids will continue to thrive here, but we have to put time and effort into being aware of their interests and cultivating them.

Brian had intended to go into the wood business, producing mulch and landscaping materials; but Lauren was fascinated by the tiny home movement, and now, Brian is putting his contracting know-how to use and learning from local Amish craftsman to build true mortise-and-tenon tiny homes with trees felled on the Spichers' land. They hope to create a tiny home community someday, where like-minded people seeking a simple, outdoor-centric life can live as neighbors. According to Brian:

> It's neat to challenge yourself to learn new things. You can get stuck and there is something to be said for doing one thing your whole life and doing it really well. But there's also something about being teachable your whole life and being willing to learn. That's where I've been for the past year-and-a-half: learning about tiny houses, about cows, about sawing lumber. It just seems like every day I'm having to learn something new, which is exciting. I did a lot better financially in Lancaster, and that's kind of what enabled us to do this [lifestyle].
>
> When I think of young couples, I would tell them — you have to work and limit yourself. We worked really hard to make this an opportunity. I think if we were just starting out, if we could go back, I think we would try to minimize our expenses the best we could, whether that meant living with my parents and making connections — getting involved in my community more instead of just thinking, "oh, I gotta get outta [this rural place]." I would've looked for something small and thought about land more than about a house.

"Putting yourself out there to your neighbors is important"
"If somebody moved somewhere fresh," says Lauren, "I would say a church community, for those who have faith, is the best way to make friends and assimilate. I found being involved in my kids' school has helped too."

Brian agrees:

Putting yourself out there to your neighbors is important. Go around and introduce yourself. Just saying, "Hey, can you help me with this?" We have an older couple right over the hill here. They never had kids. They have a 160-acre farm. They don't know what to do with it. They can't keep up with it. And I offered to help him one day and he just took me on a ride around his farm with his four-wheeler. He didn't really want the help. He just wanted to talk. He wanted somebody to talk to and show his farm to. There are people out there who I think, especially in a more rural setting, it seems like people will just stay to themselves if you don't go to them. Being willing to put yourself out there, ask for help, being willing to help, if you have a skill or talent, it's good to be able to share that with another person.

"It's a small community," Lauren goes on:

People tend to keep a little bit to themselves. But once you make that step — like our neighbors, once I made the point to go to their house and speak with them in their home, then they opened up and now it's great. When I'm at the driveway picking up the kids, the neighbor will stop and he'll talk with me. Which he wouldn't have done before. I feel like it's not necessarily hard making friends, you just have to make the initiation, to speak with them first.

Taking that step to make things happen

Last year we wanted to get the community involved, and we did a live nativity. My family, Brian's sister and her children and his mom and dad, created a live nativity scene. It was a drive-through in front of his sister's house. And I thought that was just really neat. It's just thinking out of the box and taking that step forward to make things happen. Sometimes that's what it takes, you know?

And then once people see it, they think, "Oh, they can do it. Let's, do this thing I had in my mind, but I was too scared to do it, or didn't think people would be interested in it." So we did the live nativity and we had like 30 some odd cars come through. And then we're going to do Christmas caroling.

Brian's sister's is an organic farmer, and that's really great to have. We get a lot of our fresh produce from her; we're spoiled that way. We do hunt, too. I do find myself supporting local here now. We have one little store. When I was living in Lancaster and I had everything at my fingertips, I would just hop in the car and go wherever — Hobby Lobby, this place, that place. Here, it takes more time to travel, and we have to think about gas prices and things like that. There's a lady, Nancy, down the road, who makes her own sourdough bread in the brick oven. It's a really cool spot.

"This is my dream"
Brian says,

> We used to go out a lot more when we were in Lancaster and spend more money on fast food or just eating out. Now we barely do it. And to be honest with you, I really don't miss it at all. There has not been that much sacrifice. I'm trying to think. I was done with work. I was done with the business, anyway. I was just done. This is where I wanted to be. This is my dream.
>
> You can watch all the YouTube videos you want, you can talk about it, and you can read every book there is, but you have to just go for it. Because if you don't, you'll just continue to let that fear and let those what-ifs control you. You gotta take a chance, and that's what we did and we're happy.

Lauren feels the same way:

> When I sit in the back of the house, next to the fire, and I see the kids thriving, I think it was a really good move for our family.

Especially with the times we are living in, I just know the way the world is going. It is not how I want my children to grow up.

THE NUTSHELL

God's creation enlivens our senses and deepens our relationship with Him; seek beauty in your life, in the wilds of nature and in traditions that glorify Him.

WOKE-PROOF WAYS

+ Evaluate if moving is an option; if you aren't moving to a familiar place, research conservative places, read the local newspapers, visit, rent for a while, visit local municipal meetings, talk to townsfolk.
+ Consider preserving an older property.
+ If you're committed to city living, visit rural conservative places often and adopt their habits.
+ Patronize things when you don't really feel like it – keep the summer firefighter's festival going; patronize local theater; attend benefit dinners; be a part of music in the park.

6

Cultivating Community
Branching Out with Clubs and Comradery

Remote work is making it easier than ever for folks to "vote with their feet," as the saying goes. But for some, moving just isn't an option. It may take a little more effort, but you can build a woke-proof friendship circle and supportive community regardless of where you live. The woke playbook is isolate, alienate, divide, and conquer. This is how we don't let them.

Historically, the workplace — where you'd spend most of your waking hours, five days a week — was where you'd make friends and sometimes meet future spouses. These days, nearly 30 percent of work happens at home,[179] and the number of virtual workers is predicted to increase.[180]

As someone who has worked remotely for many years, I know the advantages well. Being able to run an errand on your lunchbreak or take care of some emails between sets at the gym is awesome. And yet the many other hours I spend working away, alone and in silence, can make

[179] Daniel de Visé, "Nearly 30 percent of work remains remote as workers dig in," *The Hill,* February 20, 2023, https://thehill.com/policy/technology/3862069-nearly-30-percent-of-work-remains-remote-as-workers-dig-in/.

[180] Bryan Robinson, "Remote Work Is Here To Stay And Will Increase Into 2023, Experts Say," *Forbes,* February 1, 2022, https://www.forbes.com/sites/bryan-robinson/2022/02/01/remote-work-is-here-to-stay-and-will-increase-into-2023-experts-say/?sh=19a78c9520a6.

me weary. I'm not alone (at least in one sense): a 2021 "Post-Lockdown Friends & Happiness in the Workplace Survey" found that for many people, having a "work best friend" makes work more enjoyable and makes workers more productive, more creative, and more likely to stay at their place of employment.[181]

Obviously, you can have a *remote*-work best friend, but another post-COVID survey by JobSage found "84 percent of Americans have a harder time making friends when working remotely," "fully remote workers report 33 percent fewer friends at work," and "66 percent of remote workers have not made a work friend."[182]

In an examination of the new era of remote and hybrid-office work, *The Washington Post* reported, "Research shows time and again there's simply no substitute for meeting face to face."[183] In fact, studies show that requests made in-person "are 34 times more effective than those sent by email," and "a physical handshake promotes cooperation and influences negotiation outcomes for the better."

Such findings further demonstrate what we observe in the tech age — how social media and automatic everything keeps human beings from bonding with one another and realizing the many benefits of human contact. Being able to call and text at any time is great, but compared to physical communication and socialization, there's so much that's lost.

If you're spending nine hours a day on social media, you're not inventing the cure for cancer,

----

181 Paris Stevens, "The 2021 Post-Lockdown Friends & Happiness in the Workplace Survey," *Wildgoose,* June 9, 2021, https://wearewildgoose.com/uk/news/friends-happiness-in-the-workplace-survey/.

182 Kelli Mason, "Study: Fully Remote Workers Report 33% Fewer Friends at Work," *Job Sage,* July 5, 2022, https://www.jobsage.com/blog/coworker-friendships-survey/.

183 "The science of being there: Why face-to-face meetings are so important," *The Washington Post,* https://www.washingtonpost.com/sf/brand-connect/hilton/the-science-of-being-there/.

> and you're not going to learn how to read, you're
> not going to learn how to make friends or talk
> to other humans. I think wokeness is maybe a
> symptom of that disease. (Dr. Andrew Mullalley)

Life is better lived with a tribe and frequent friendly interactions. According to the Mayo Clinic, "Socializing not only staves off feelings of loneliness, but also it helps sharpen memory and cognitive skills, increases your sense of happiness and well-being, and may even help you live longer. In-person is best, but connecting via technology also works."[184]

Susan Pinker, a psychologist, drives the point further, comparing face-to-face contact to a vaccine and to morphine because of the stress-reducing and feel-good (dopamine) chemicals such contact releases.[185]

Harvard Health asserts strong relationships are "every bit as powerful as adequate sleep, a good diet, and not smoking. Dozens of studies have shown that people who have social support from family, friends, and their community are happier, have fewer health problems, and live longer."[186]

Research from The Family Dinner Project has found that "regular family meals offer a wide variety of physical, social-emotional and academic benefits," including a "greater sense of resilience," and a lower risk of substance abuse, teen pregnancy, depression, and rates of obesity.[187]

---

[184] Vivien Williams, "The benefits of being socially connected," *The Mayo Clinic,* April 19, 2019, https://newsnetwork.mayoclinic.org/discussion/mayo-clinic-minute-the-benefits-of-being-socially-connected/.

[185] Maria Cohut, Ph.D., "What are the health benefits of being social?" *Medical News Today,* February 23, 2018, https://www.medicalnewstoday.com/articles/321019.

[186] "The health benefits of strong relationships," *Harvard Health Publishing,* December 1, 2010, https://www.health.harvard.edu/staying-healthy/the-health-benefits-of-strong-relationships.

[187] "Benefits of Family Dinners," *The Family Dinner Project,* https://thefamilydinnerproject.org/about-us/benefits-of-family-dinners/.

It goes without saying, but I'll say it anyway: the better the company you keep, the more beneficial your social interactions will be, and the better person you are, the better your friends will be. A 2017 *New York Times* report cited research that found that "social interactions can enhance good health through a positive influence on people's living habits. For example, if none of your friends smoke, you'll be less likely to smoke."[188]

Therefore be imitators of God, as beloved children. And walk in love, as Christ loved us and gave himself up for us, a fragrant offering and sacrifice to God. But immorality and all impurity or covetousness must not even be named among you, as is fitting among saints. Let there be no filthiness, nor silly talk, nor levity, which are not fitting; but instead let there be thanksgiving. Be sure of this, that no immoral or impure man, or one who is covetous (that is, an idolater), has any inheritance in the kingdom of Christ and of God. (Ephesians 5:1–5)

Mingling with virtuous people is key to mental, physical, emotional, and spiritual health, yet the number of people going out and doing stuff together is dwindling. Teenagers aren't even very eager to drive anymore. Reports *The Washington Post*: "60 percent of American 18-year-olds had a driver's license in 2021, down from 80 percent in 1983, according to data from the Federal Highway Administration."[189]

Robert D. Putnam chronicled the decline of what he calls "social capital," or "the very fabric of our connections with each other," way

---

[188] Jane E. Brody, "Social Interaction Is Critical for Mental and Physical Health," *The New York Times*, June 12, 2017, https://www.nytimes.com/2017/06/12/well/live/having-friends-is-good-for-you.html.

[189] Caitlin Gibson, "Why aren't teenagers driving anymore?," *The Washington Post*, February 21, 2023, https://www.washingtonpost.com/parenting/2023/02/21/teens-not-driving/.

back in 2000, with *Bowling Alone: The Collapse and Revival of American Community*. The "about the book" release explained:

> Putnam draws on evidence including nearly 500,000 interviews over the last quarter century to show that we sign fewer petitions, belong to fewer organizations that meet, know our neighbors less, meet with friends less frequently, and even socialize with our families less often. We're even bowling alone. More Americans are bowling than ever before, but they are not bowling in leagues. Putnam shows how changes in work, family structure, age, suburban life, television, computers, women's roles and other factors have contributed to this decline.[190]

Most of the organizations I am aware of and belong to in my small town are made up of retirees. Sure, they have more time to dedicate to such things, but they've all been members of the Kiwanis, the Elks, their parish council, sportsman's club, fire department, and so forth for decades, since they went to work their first jobs (they were likely recruited by a friend from work). Yet volunteerism and civic involvement for younger generations have been on a steep decline for some time.[191]

Why? Well, I hate to sound like a broken record, but when you're spending an average of eight hours and five minutes looking at a screen every day, how *would* you have time to give away to the Knights of Columbus or develop an interest in polka dancing? The COVID pandemic brought this ugly reality to light in a *big, fat* way: while we all had more leisure time, set free from commuting, and in some cases, working, how many of us set our minds to learning a second language, revisiting the "Classics Everyone Should Read at Least Once," or mastering the harmonica? A

---

[190] Bowlingalone.com.
[191] Linda Poon, "Why Americans Stopped Volunteering," *Bloomberg*, September 11, 2019, https://www.bloomberg.com/news/articles/2019-09-12/america-has-a-post-9-11-volunteerism-slump.

lot of us coped with the stress by eating loads of homemade bread and getting drunk.[192]

Most Americans don't have hobbies or interests or something tangible to show for their work. Whereas our identity used to be tied to what we produced, now, "over 80 percent of all US jobs are predominantly sedentary, placing full-time office workers at increased risk for cardiovascular and metabolic morbidity and mortality."[193] So we attempt to add meaning to our lives and value to society by grasping at some other identity.

As someone whom *Psychology Today* would describe as an "omnivert" (the personality version of non-binary, I guess?), I understand not wanting to leave the house and be sociable. But ninety-nine times out of a hundred, I'm glad that I did. Plus, once again, God seems to be telling us through our design that it's good for us to get out and interact with our fellow man. And the U.S. Department of Health and Human Services actually agrees with the Church for once:

> Civic participation encompasses a wide range of formal and informal activities, such as voting, volunteering, participating in group activities, and community gardening. Some are individual activities that benefit society (e.g., voting) or group activities that benefit either the group members (e.g., recreational soccer teams) or society (e.g., volunteer organizations). In addition to the direct benefit that civic participation provides to the community, it also produces secondary health benefits for participants.
>
> Volunteering is a common form of civic participation that can yield health benefits. Studies show that volunteers enjoy better

[192] "One year on: Unhealthy weight gains, increased drinking reported by Americans coping with pandemic stress," *American Psychological Association*, March 11, 2021, https://www.apa.org/news/press/releases/2021/03/one-year-pandemic-stress.

[193] Allene L. Gremaud, MS, et. al., "Gamifying Accelerometer Use Increases Physical Activity Levels of Sedentary Office Workers," *American Heart Association*, https://www.ahajournals.org/doi/pdf/10.1161/JAHA.117.007735.

psychological well-being and more positive emotional health. Volunteering can increase social resources like having friends to call, which may help explain the association between volunteering and reduced levels of anxiety and depressive symptoms. Additionally, one study found volunteering can relieve stress as measured by cortisol (a hormone released when feeling stressed). Volunteering might be especially beneficial for older adults; a study of adults age 60 and older found that volunteers had a lower risk of cognitive impairment.

Simply belonging to groups can improve health as well. Membership in formal groups (e.g., Girl Scouts, Kiwanis, Rotary, PTA) or informal groups (e.g., book clubs, bird watching clubs) has been shown to increase social capital and decrease social isolation among members. As a result, these groups may indirectly improve the physical and mental health of their members. For example, a women's group, the Red Hat Society, has been shown to provide emotional support and a sense of community to its members. Many formal and informal groups also engage in charitable activities that directly benefit health research.

Individuals who are involved in community gardening may form a sense of neighborhood pride, experience an increased appreciation for their neighborhood, and be more motivated to get involved in community life. Community gardens also increase access to healthy foods. A thematic review of the effects of community gardens notes that 13 studies have found higher levels of fruit and vegetable consumption in areas with community gardens.[194]

The beauty of most clubs and organizations, unless they're based on some explicitly partisan cause, is that they're typically apolitical. If

---

[194] "Civic Participation," *Healthy People 2030*, https://health.gov/healthypeople/priority-areas/social-determinants-health/literature-summaries/civic-participation.

you're there for the purpose of indoor rock climbing, quilting, bird-watching, hot-rodding, playing chess, making pottery, learning local history, hiking, speaking Spanish, practicing calligraphy, foraging for wild mushrooms, or fundraising for the church roof, conversations generally revolve around these things and not the Woke Word of the Day. Let me tell you, when my town's Kiwanis Club is cooking a thousand chickens over a firepit and getting all those dinners packed up and out the door while lines of cars snake around the building, there's no time to debate "how white supremacy culture narratives function to center whiteness across the food system, effectively reinforcing systemic racial inequality and by extension disadvantaging BIPOC people" (as they do at Duke University).[195] Fostering community service and healthy hobbies is vital to a thriving society, and the failure to do so has left a lot of people with a lot of free time on their handheld devices and a lot of once-robust communities floundering.

It is therefore of supreme importance that we consent to live not for ourselves but for others. When we do this we will be able first of all to face and accept our own limitations. As long as we secretly adore ourselves, our own deficiencies will remain to torture us with an apparent defilement. But if we live for others, we will gradually discover that no one expects us to be "as gods." We will see that we are human, like everyone else, that we all have weaknesses and deficiencies, and that these limitations of ours play a most important part in all our lives. It is because of them that we need others and others need us. We are

---

[195] Alison Conrad, "Identifying and Countering White Supremacy Culture in Food Systems," *Duke Sanford World Food Policy Center*, September 2020, https://wfpc.sanford.duke.edu/reports/identifying-and-countering-white-supremacy-culture-in-food-systems/.

> not all weak in the same spots, and so we supplement
> and complete one another, each one making up in
> himself for the lack in another. (Thomas Merton)

So how do you find a club or organization to join? Church is an excellent place to start; has anyone ever been to a church that *wasn't* in need of volunteers? Another way of finding a club to join is to find a hobby. Virtually every hobby has a group associated with it, if only an informal one. How do you find a hobby? Almost anything can be a hobby. There's probably a skill you always wanted to learn how to do, a sport or activity you've wanted to try, a game or pastime you enjoy. Hobbies that are hands-on and involve physical exertion are best. I reported recently on a survey that found people whose work involves physical labor, pain, and being outdoors are the most satisfied. Allow me to reiterate some of my own brilliance here for your edification:

> The results are in and nature (i.e., God) wins again. A Bureau of Labor Statistics survey has found that lumberjacks and farmers are the happiest, least stressed, and most fulfilled workers, further evidencing that everything we need to be joyful and satisfied in this life is not manmade. Nor does it have much if anything in common with the prevailing culture.
>
> A *Washington* Post analysis of the survey noted, "The most meaningful and happiness-inducing activities were religious and spiritual," followed by "the second-happiest activity — sports, exercise and recreation."
>
> As society becomes softer and more entitled and as we slog further from our ancestral roots, we're more inclined to dismiss the simple, unchanging truths about mankind: that the earth was made for us, and we were made to be in and of the earth.
>
> Technology isn't all bad (though I lean more toward Luddism with each passing day), but it's meant to *enhance* our existence,

not consume it. What I find most intriguing about the *Post*'s reporting on the Labor Statistics study is that lumberjacks and those working in agriculture also reported the highest levels of pain on the job.

In a day and age in which much of life's pursuits are aimed at keeping suffering to a minimum — you needn't ever risk hunger pangs again with DoorDash, or endure a dull moment with social media — we are also more depressed, anxious, and unhappy than we've been in decades. Our life expectancy rates are down and dropping, too.

The thing is, you can't improve on God's design. The answers to all our human problems have existed for eternity, and no number of apps, "breakthrough" shortcut weight loss pills, Netflix binges, or instant gratification "likes" will ever replace the simple reality that the lumberjacks and farmers know better than anyone: that pain and suffering, hard work and sacrifice are necessary and fruitful when applied to a noble end.

And now to sound like an old grandpa: nothing beats fresh air and good old-fashioned manual labor. Gen Z might view trade jobs as icky (NPR reports the "application rate for young people seeking technical jobs — like plumbing, building and electrical work — dropped by 49 percent in 2022 compared to 2020"), but the benefits of this type of work abound. Besides paying well generally, job satisfaction among tradespeople is extremely high (83 percent, per SCI Texas). There are obviously downsides to a physically demanding job, but to be so disconnected from the straightforward, hard outdoor work inherent in our heritage for too long has devastating effects on our nation, which is easy to see.

Of course, this is not to say that everyone needs to toss their keyboards out the window and go all George Washington on their nearest forest. But we ought to be incorporating much more outdoor manual labor in our daily lives. Walking in the woods — what the Japanese call *shinrin-yoku*, or "forest bathing" — mowing your own damn lawn, splitting some firewood, hunting, fishing, camping, growing vegetables in a garden, any sort of pioneer work that produces callouses — does wonders for the mind, body, and soul.

Mastering a task like one of these, particularly one that could further one's survival, is the best feeling in the world. As the Center for Growth points out, physical labor provides an extra shot of endorphins that "feels like a natural high."[196]

Speaking of saving society, Piedmont Healthcare tells us that it also just so happens that lifting heavy things is "the best exercise to boost testosterone." And who could argue we need a little more of that?[197]

That's food for thought regarding hobbies. But back to clubs and organizations. How to find them? Start by attending some local events and learning what the organization that puts them on is all about. Talk to people giving away literature at booths. Take flyers and read newspapers and check out those boards with papers pinned to them at the back of coffee shops and grocery stores and the YMCA to see what's happening in your neighborhood. When you're at the local sporting goods store, ask the manager if there's a group that meets every week to tie fly-fishing flies. At the greenhouse, there may be a beginners' gardening class.

> Don't get so busy making a living that you
> forget to make a life. (Dolly Parton)

---

[196] "Physical Labor and Mental Health," *The Center for Growth,* https://www.the-centerforgrowth.com/tips/physical-labor-and-mental-health.

[197] https://www.spectator.co.uk/article/lumberjacks-know-the-secret-of-happiness/.

If you're feeling apprehensive about joining a new club, I offer you three pieces of encouragement:

1. No one is thinking about you as much as you are thinking about you. "What if my outfit is inappropriate? What if I get there too late and there's nowhere to sit? What if I'm bad at [shooting trap, line-dancing, pickleball, crocheting] and look like a fool?" This is one instance where people's inclination toward self-absorption is helpful.

2. These clubs and organizations are desperate for new members. They will be happy to have you and will welcome you enthusiastically. The people who join clubs and organizations do so because they're outgoing, sociable people themselves. Or else they're lonely people looking for connection. Either way, they'll be glad to be your friend. What's more, people love sharing their knowledge and passions with others. If you are the worst trap shooter east of the Mississippi, all the members of gun club will be happy to give you pointers, lend you their gun, and share their tips, their yellow shooting glasses, and their special reloaded shells to help you (yes, I'm speaking from experience). Everyone was a beginner once, and people in clubs remember what it was like when they were in your shoes. Don't you love sharing knowledge about something you're an expert on? Allowing others to do so is doing them a favor.

3. What's the worst that could happen? Someone will scream, "YOU'RE SO DUMB!" and dump cheesy potato casserole on your lap? Doubtful. And if they do, it's a great story to tell at your Banned Books tea party.

Making friends and building high-quality networks of like-minded NORMALs gets easier the more you do it. Sometimes it seems our society has forgotten how to interact with one another. We walk everywhere with Apple AirPods deafening us to the sounds of humanity.

We fulfill a sense of safe sociability through our phones — interactions that, even when they're with real people, are hollow, because they can be curated, deleted, blocked, and turned off and on ("throwaway culture" extends to humans). We can take our time in reacting and responding, as if we're living in a scripted novel and not real life, where words have consequences. Once you start making the effort though — making eye contact with people, smiling, saying hello, commiserating cheerfully on a shared experience, offering a joke, asking questions, offering help, being generally open to others — you know, treating people like humans, rather than closed-off, self-centered, suspicious, and combative, as the woke warriors would have us be — a whole new enriching world is yours for the taking.

That said, clubs and organizations are a straightforward way to take ownership of a community and build a network of pollinators. They're not necessary, of course, for pursuing a new interest, and virtually any avocation that stimulates the mind and safeguards the soul from woke contagion is worthwhile. The *Harvard Business Review* reports:

> One study from the Society of Behavioral Medicine suggests that people who take part in leisure activities have fewer negative emotions and are less stressed. The study even found that our heart rates are literally lower when we engage in our hobbies.[198]

The Australian government agrees:

> Research shows that people with hobbies are less likely to suffer from stress, low mood, and depression. Activities that get you out and about can make you feel happier and more relaxed. Group

---

[198] Kelsey Alpaio, "Can Hobbies Actually Make You a Better Person?," *Ascend*, October 29, 2021, https://hbr.org/2021/10/can-hobbies-actually-make-you -a-better-person.

activities like team sports can improve your communication skills and relationships with others.[199]

And *Psychology Today* reminds us, "Working with Your Hands Does Wonders for Your Brain":

> Activities that use your hands relieve stress and help you solve problems. Using our hands may actually be key to maintaining a healthy mood, and the lack of this type of activity may contribute to feelings of irritability, apathy, and depression.[200]

THE NUTSHELL

Social interaction benefits your mental, physical, and spiritual health. Hobbies do, too, and they're also a great way to escape woke influences and build self-sufficiency.

WOKE-PROOF WAYS

- Join a club or volunteer organization, or start one yourself!
- Get a hobby; a chimneysweep once told me he loved his work because it's the perfect combination of being "intellectual and leaving me physically exhausted and a little dirty."
- Establish traditions, especially if you have kids. Give yourself and them things to look forward to. Punctuate your life with simple, reliable, joy-filled goalposts. Growing up, my mother always took us to a special breakfast place after pediatrician appointments. Since we don't eat meat on Fridays, we have

[199] Kelsey Alpaio, "Purposeful activity - hobbies," *Australian Government Department of Health and Aged Care*, July 11, 2019, https://www.headtohealth.gov.au/meaningful-life/purposeful-activity/hobbies.

[200] Susan Biali Haas M.D., "Working With Your Hands Does Wonders for Your Brain," *Psychology Today*, June 21, 2019, https://www.psychologytoday.com/us/blog/prescriptions-life/201906/working-your-hands-does-wonders-your-brain.

"Bacon and Egg Day" every Thursday, and it's a family treat. Try going to the same diner every Saturday morning, stopping at the same ice cream stand when going to visit Grandma — these things are more important than we might think, especially as memories that sustain us.

+ Use the evening downtime when you would typically scroll through your phone or watch TV to strum the guitar, practice jewelry-making, stroll through the neighborhood, conduct a self-guided study of the classical composers while cooking dinner, call a friend, putter in the garden.
+ Stop wearing earbuds everywhere. Make yourself open to conversation.
+ Use social media only as a last resort for social interaction. Instead of texting, call. Instead of calling, go over to the person's house and knock on the door.
+ Reduce your social media usage to a set amount of time per day.
+ Keep your eyes off your phone as much as possible: instead of a digital list, write down your to-do list. In addition to keeping your eyes up and away from the screen, writing things by hand increases brain activity and makes it more likely you'll remember the milk, too![201] There's a reason high-tech Silicon Valley parents send their kids to tech-free schools.[202]
+ Try going without social media altogether for one day a week, then two, then only use it on the weekends, etc. If you can delete it altogether, or limit your usage to one app, do so!

[201] University of Tokyo, "Study shows stronger brain activity after writing on paper than on tablet or smartphone," *Science Daily*, March 19, 2021, https://www.sciencedaily.com/releases/2021/03/210319080820.htm.
[202] Matt Richtel, "A Silicon Valley School That Doesn't Compute," *The New York Times*, October 22, 2011, https://www.nytimes.com/2011/10/23/technology/at-waldorf-school-in-silicon-valley-technology-can-wait.html.

◆ Mail Christmas cards. Give the gift of tangible love. Texts, emails, and whatever "the cloud" is are "out of sight, out of mind." There's nothing quite like receiving a handwritten letter in the mail, especially when it's a surprise! As John Donne said, "Sir, more than kisses, letters mingle souls."

7

Creating a
Wholesome Home
A Refuge for the World-Weary

Small towns lend themselves naturally to familiarity and coziness, but the charming parts we love about settings for Hallmark Christmas movies (the original, pre-woke ones) can be replicated almost anywhere. I'm still cautious of suburbs surrounded by strip malls, but where there's a will, there's a way!

Old city neighborhoods were constructed in a time when community was still a priority. Think of the way the characters in *A Streetcar Named Desire* basically live in a New Orleans commune. Or how the alleys, roofs, and pubs in *On the Waterfront* serve as public property. (Yes, I like young Marlon Brando.) The common theme of rural, small towns and old cities is that the same people interact often with one another in familiar spaces.

Thus, regardless of where you live, you can make your own home a familiar space in which to gather friends and nourish one another with familiarity and coziness.

I was trying to wind down one night recently while staying at my parents' house and turned on the tube. A nick@nite advertisement for "Family Movie Night" came on that showed a family of Shrek ogres burping and breaking wind on one another. The Addams Family, in turn, blew something up and threw axes at each other. It was shocking and repulsive and meant to be comical family entertainment. Compare that to a Beatrix Potter book. If this is a snapshot of what family life consists of in average America, it's no wonder we're all depressed.

We can do better. It starts with revisiting visiting. I interviewed a local woman recently ahead of her one-hundredth birthday. She reflected on experiencing "the horse and buggy days to a man on the moon!" When asked what she missed most about the old days, she said, "Nobody visits anymore. People used to stop by. Not anymore."

Doesn't this old woman know we're all in a hurry? We have Important Things to do! Visiting our friends and neighbors and relatives is not one of them.

Why not? What are we in such a hurry to do, if not to visit with a sweet, cheeky, hundred-year-old woman who has seen more of the world than anyone else we know and who has more fascinating memories and wisdom to share than nick@nite has crass?

> The ordinary acts we practice every day at home
> are of more importance to the soul than their
> simplicity might suggest. (St. Thomas More)

Strive to make your home a woke-proof refuge from the socio-political madness raging in the outside world. Think of it as a retreat *to* reality — meaning a place where truth and wisdom live and are fortified through the free expression of ideas and edifying conversation; a place where virtue blossoms and flourishes through noble behavior and worthwhile activity. Create a stronghold for your own soul and those of everyone who enters your home, wherein all are nourished, refreshed, and strengthened in their pursuit of a woke-proof life.

"Surround yourself." It's a phrase used by self-help guru Tony Robbins, farmhouse décor sign designers, and the Ad Council (probably) to encourage people to get rid of the deadweight in their lives. Let's say you've moved to a woke-proof place where NORMALs live in greater abundance, and you're avoiding woke influences found in digital realms. Or perhaps you're stuck in a woke city. You've joined a club and have started volunteering, you have a handful of NORMAL acquaintances, but now what?

"Surround yourself" is right. Not just with NORMAL companionship, but with influences that inspire an appreciation for creation and the beauty of life. What we see, hear, and touch every day affects us. I call it the "Favorite Mug Phenomenon." My mother and I often have coffee together in the morning. There are two mugs in her cupboard that are just *better* than the rest. The shape of them, their size, the way they fit your hand, the smoothness of the part that touches your lips, the handles. We both acknowledge this fact and will sometimes fetch the preferred vessels out of the dishwasher and clean them by hand because they're just that superior. We have two spoons in rotation, too, that are more finely made — properly weighted and graciously formed. Rummaging happens a lot for them in the cutlery drawer. Having a few Favorite Mugs instead of a vast collection of Other Mugs (and spoons) is the way to go for kitchenware as well as most things in life — including companions.

Judging from the popularity of "griege" paint colors and ultra-popular and depressing industrial design, it seems modern people don't exert as much effort into considering their environments or the things that affect them. Part of this, I'm sure, is due to the fact (here I go again) that people spend much more time looking at screens than at walls and out windows.

In your journey to woke-proof your life, though, you'll barely ever be looking at a screen, and you'll be spending a lot more time aware of your surroundings and engaged in the company of people you love. You'll want them to have a comfortable, charming place to gather and for your home to reflect your values.

> If the world had a front porch like we did back then /
> We'd still have our problems but we'd all be friends /
> Treating your neighbor like he's your next of kin /
> Wouldn't be gone with the wind / If the world had a
> front porch, like we did back then (Tracy Lawrence)

Numerous studies have affirmed that décor — lighting, layout, color, and such — affects mental and physical health.[203] Something I find more telling is a study released by the IKEA Life at Home Report. CNBC reported that it found, "Having elements in your home that reflect your identity could boost your mental health." Many of the people — nearly one in three — who "believe their place is reflective of who they are" reported "it's their possessions that bring back memories and experiences — including family pictures and collectable items — that make their home a reflection of their identity." Yet of the thirty-seven thousand people surveyed across 37 countries, "just 58 percent believe their homes reflect their identity."[204] (Perhaps because they were IKEA customers?)

That leaves a lot of people living in bleak dwellings and being negatively affected by it. You needn't be Martha Stewart to add warmth and whimsy to your home. You don't need a lot of money, either. The first step is to get out of the "buy everything online" rut. Go exploring. Take your time and let pieces of art and furniture find you. Borrow something to hold you over (I can attest to the beachy, chill vibe that a pair of plastic chaise lounges lend to a living room) while you make trips to antique

[203] Joseph Lamour, "How the Decor in Your Home Can Actually Impact Your Mental Health," *Lonny*, December 21, 2020, https://www.lonny.com/How+The+Decor+In+Your+Home+Can+Actually+Impact+Your+Mental+Health.

[204] Renée Onque, "Having elements in your home that reflect your identity could boost your mental health," *CNBC*, February 7, 2023, https://www.cnbc.com/2023/02/07/youre-more-likely-to-enjoy-your-home-when-it-reflects-your-identity.html.

shops, thrift stores, flea markets, your church's rummage sale, your grand-mother's garage, the side of the road, and elsewhere.

Antiquing is a wonderful woke-proof pastime for myriad reasons. When you buy something old, you're not funding a woke corporation. Antiques remind us of a time before woke forces permeated society and smothered humor, patriotism, traditional values, and communal activities. It's fun to collect items with old-timey illustrations and quaint language from a time when advertising was a real artform. It's also helpful to bolster one's sanity with imagery and other connections to the past that remind us the world wasn't always so crazy and chaotic. There was a time, not so long ago, when neighbors would gather for picnics, cocktail parties, and card games. Incidentally, the Library of Congress refers to the 1950s as the era of "The Hobby Boom," when "home life was glorified, [and] the art of crafting at home became an obsession for many."[205]

Antique collecting also reduces waste and is good for the planet! "Made from natural materials and with artisanal techniques, antiques were sustainable before sustainability was even a thing," notes Jute Home.[206]

But wait, there's more . . .

Nostalgia isn't a bad thing. "Can't repeat the past"? No, you can't, Jay Gatsby. But you can cherry-pick the best parts and replicate them for the good of the world in the here and now. *Everyday Health* reports nostalgia can, of course, make a person sad, but it can also "boost mood, promote a sense of self [by helping] you feel connected to who you were in the past, who you are in the present, and who you will be in the future," strengthen bonds with family and friends, and "make you more optimistic" as you recall good times and use them as motivation.[207]

[205] https://blogs.loc.gov/headlinesandheroes/2021/02/the-hobby-boom-of-the-1950s/.

[206] "Why Choose Antiques," *Jute*, https://jutehome.com/why-choose-antiques/.

[207] Moira Lawler, "5 Ways Nostalgia Is Good for Your Health (and When It's Not)," *Everyday Health*, October 20, 2022, https://www.everydayhealth.com/emotional-health/ways-nostalgia-is-good-for-your-health-and-when-its-not/.

"It's an investment in time"
Steve owns a vinyl record shop near where I live. During a recent visit there, we discussed how listening to music on records offers a type of magic you don't experience on a digital streaming service:

> You can hold records in your hand. They're tangible, something real. The artwork is bigger. It becomes yours, like a book you've dog-eared. It'll get pops and skips that are unique to your record.
>
> There's movement on the turntable, which connects you to the music more, and the crackle, which reminds you the record is moving — I like jukebox machines for the same reason. Listening to music is a more involved process. You're more invested in the music, especially if it's something like a jazz record. You can hear all the instruments and what's going on, whereas on your phone, you might be doing more than one thing and then within two seconds you're not into it and you're onto the next thing. With a record, you'll listen to the whole album. It sets the tone for the evening or whenever you're hanging out. It makes people slow down and really listen to music. To take a record off, choose a different one, take it out of its sleeve, and put it on the turntable — it's a ritual. It's an investment in time, instead of just having some music on as background noise.

"Vinyl records are a way to disconnect from the political aspects of the day"
Records also help you learn more about the music itself. What the styles were like when the album was made. I'll sit down, look at the liner notes, read the back of the album, look at the big pictures.

You'll come across weird stuff you didn't know existed when you're looking for certain records. I have a fifteen-year-old girl who comes in here once a week looking for certain things on her list. She might be able to go online and get it, but she wants to *find* it, to stumble upon it. It's like a treasure hunt. And she makes an event out of it — she'll come in and pet my dog, and if I see something come in that I think she'll like, I'll set it aside for her and make suggestions.

My shop is a judgement-free zone. Politics and culture definitely intersect in music, but we don't talk about it in here. It's about discovery. Music brings out different things in people and is a great unifier. As the world gets more complicated, vinyl records are a way to disconnect from the political aspects of the day. All I talk about with customers is what we found music-wise. It's a great hobby for people.

"We live in a throwaway society"

Items that invoke wholesome thoughts and fond feelings ought to stick around to do the same for our descendants. Owning something of value that you worked hard to purchase and that you care for and cherish is an outdated ideal in the age of "fast-fashion" and mercurial home design trends. But it shouldn't be. Kara, from the family furniture store, explains:

> We live in a fast-paced world with short attentions spans — a throwaway society. It's always on to the next trend, and everything moves so quickly with social media. We try to educate people that if you invest in something timeless, it's a one-time purchase, and you'll save money in the long run. A lot of people learn that lesson the hard way. We try to help them understand that there are certain core things that are never going to go out of style that you can have your whole life and cherish and pass down through generations and serve as reminders of loved ones.

In his study of "The Role of Possessions in Constructing and Maintaining a Sense of Past," University of Utah researcher Russell W. Belk concluded poignantly:

> Previous studies of time in consumer research have ignored the role of possessions in creating and maintaining a sense of past. A sense of past is essential to a sense of self. The self extends

not only into the present material environment, but extends forward and backward in time. Possessions can be a rich repository of our past and act as stimuli for intentional as well as unintentional recollections. While few of us undertake as comprehensive a life history review as Proust, our memories constitute our lives; they are us. We fervently believe that our past is accumulated somewhere among the material artifacts our lives have touched — in our homes, our museums, and our cities. And we hope that if these objects can only be made to reveal their secrets, they will reveal the meanings and mystery of ourselves and our lives.[208]

Surround yourself with sights, sounds, and sensations that capture the America we NORMALs are fighting to regain. Remind yourself as much as possible in your home environment and through your activities what that life was like before wokeness and why it's worth preserving. Show your friends, family, and neighbors, too.

We've been so busy keepin' up with the Jones
Four car garage and we're still building on
Maybe it's time we got back to the basics of love
("Luckenbach, Texas," Waylon Jennings)

THE NUTSHELL

Most people don't live in homes that reflect their identities; cultivating a space that evokes woke-proof values provides a refuge for you and those you love where you can relax and be nourished and refreshed.

[208] Russell W. Belk, "The Role of Possessions in Constructing and Maintaining a Sense of Past," *The Association for Consumer Research*, 1990, https://www.acrwebsite.org/volumes/7083.

WOKE-PROOF WAYS

♦ Instead of storing them in your phone for years, print out photos. Put them in frames where you'll see them often.

♦ Have books that have influenced you positively around where you can easily pick them up and re-read them.

♦ Create occasions for your loved ones that are too good to resist. Host tea parties, potlucks, cocktail parties, dinner parties, taco night, black-and-white movie night, a friend brunch after church, cookouts, and so forth.

♦ Get known for something and share your talents: Bake the best pies on the block. Take on the role of cocktail connoisseur (you'll be the hit of every party!). Get really into canning things and develop a spaghetti sauce recipe (using your own homegrown tomatoes, of course) that everyone raves about. Learn a few magic tricks and put on a show after dinner. Make the front of your house a floral masterpiece for passersby to enjoy. Learn to knit and gift your community with hats in their favorite colors.

8

Self-Sufficiency
No More Coercion

Self-sufficiency means not being subject to the ideological dictums and constant threat of cancelation at the hands of the woke judge and jury. Self-sufficiency also involves incorporating health-giving hobbies and satisfying skills into your life that can lead to alternative career paths, side hustles, and closet industries that can move you out from under the man's thumb and insulate you from monetary coercion. It's also nice to be able to offer something to your small-town friends who share with you their old-time skills and know-how.

Being independent is exactly what the woke masterminds don't want you to do. You're either a victim, and owed things, or else a bigot of some kind who must pay for the crimes of being NORMAL by giving everything you have to the victim class.

Before the madness let loose, though, humans lived a naturally healthy life. We got fresh air and exercise by completing chores. We ate food from the farm and garden. We lived in small, neighborly places that satisfied our social natures and our need for nature-nature. Whereas time outside used to be a regular and virtually unavoidable part of life, doctors now prescribe nature walks to treat stress and the myriad diseases it causes.[209]

---

[209] Jillian Mock, "Why Doctors Are Prescribing Nature Walks," *Time*, April 27, 2022, https://time.com/6171174/nature-stress-benefits-doctors/.

Now, reports *Fast Company*, "studies have found that in North America and Europe, we spend 90 percent of our time indoors." Which is probably why so many home décor blogs suggest incorporating elements from the out-of-doors — natural light, wood grain materials,[210] plants, and fresh flowers — in creating indoor spaces that improve mental health.[211] God went to all that work to create a beautiful world for us to enjoy, and we can't even be bothered to give it the time of day. What's more, reports *Healthline*, "More than half the world's population is predicted to be overweight or obese by 2035."[212]

Like everything wokeness tries to destroy, self-sufficiency is healthy, life-giving, and brings us closer to God. The Australian & New Zealand Mental Health Association, reporting on the link between self-sufficiency and mental health, reported that "a deep-rooted sense of inner completeness and stability" supplies people with an "inner sense of well-being [that] equips them to be more resilient to negative life events."[213] In fact, such an attitude explains in part why conservatives are healthier than liberals. *Psychology Today* reported on a study that found "people with conservative political attitudes tend to have better health than their liberal counterparts because the former place greater value on personal responsibility."[214]

210 Elizabeth Yuko, "12 Home Decor Tips for a Mental Health Boost (That Have Nothing to Do With Decluttering)," *Real Simple*, January 24, 2023, https://www.realsimple.com/home-decor-for-mental-health-7098644.

211 Sarah Haley, "Home Décor That Will Help Your Physical & Mental Health," *Real Simple*, September 14, 2021, https://www.truedispensers.com/blogs/news/home-decor-that-will-help-your-physical-mental-health.

212 Christopher Curley, "Obesity: Report Predicts Half the World Will Be Overweight by 2035," *Healthline*, March 6, 2023, https://www.healthline.com/health-news/obesity-report-predicts-half-the-world-will-be-overweight-by-2035.

213 "The Link Between Self-Sufficiency & Mental Health, *Australian and New Zealand Mental Health Association*, December 22, 2020, https://anzmh.asn.au/blog/mental-health/link-self-sufficiency-mental-health.

214 Scott A. McGreal, "Are Conservatives Healthier Than Liberals?" *Psychology Today*, February 28, 2019, https://www.psychologytoday.com/us/blog/unique-everybody-else/201902/are-conservatives-healthier-liberals.

> The world is full of magic things, patiently waiting
> for our senses to grow sharper. (W.B. Yeats)

Rather than absorb vitamins and minerals naturally from fresh food and sunshine, we swallow pills wrapped in plastic. Instead of building up our bones and muscles and strengthening our cardiovascular systems through carrying hay bales and shoveling manure, after a long day of sitting in front of a computer, we drive across town to a stinky gym and pay money to elliptical under the glow of fluorescent lights while watching *Mike & Molly* reruns. We've run out of time to make dinner, so on the drive home we grab a plastic tub of some preservative-laden food-product with 382 ingredients and plop down on the couch in front of a screen to eat it.

What if you could put an end to this very sad, woke trend by doing something active outside that produces healthy food with all the benefits of a hobby and the woke-proofing power of self-sufficiency? You can, cheaply and easily, with one "life hack."

Care for a garden. I'm convinced that if everyone in America were involved in gardening, wokeness would go *poof*! We'd have fewer mentally ill and obese people, and time spent in nature, which reduces stress in itself, means less time spent absorbing and supporting destructive woke causes.

Yale University reported in 2020 on a study that found:

> People who spent two hours a week in green spaces — local parks or other natural environments, either all at once or spaced over several visits — were substantially more likely to report good health and psychological well-being than those who don't.
>
> The effects were robust, cutting across different occupations, ethnic groups, people from rich and poor areas, and people with chronic illnesses and disabilities.[215]

---

[215] Jim Robbins, "Ecopsychology: How Immersion in Nature Benefits Your Health," *Yale Environment*, January 9, 2020, https://e360.yale.edu/features/ecopsychology-how-immersion-in-nature-benefits-your-health.

The Yale article goes on to quote Richard Louv, an author, journalist, and coiner of the phrase "Nature Deficit Disorder," who summed up the findings this way: "Nature is not only nice to have, but it's a have-to-have for physical health and cognitive functioning."

Time outside boosts mood, reduces stress and loneliness, and accomplishes all the things all woke-proof-approved activities do! Gardening is especially beneficial, and the U.K.'s National Health Service actually issued a statement in 2018 urging health professionals to encourage their patients to garden "to reduce the pressure on NHS services."

> There is anxiety that the NHS cannot cope now and in the future with the health needs of an increasing and ageing population. It is also realized that pharmaceutical drugs, transformative though they have been, are increasingly expensive and are not always as effective as they appear in the results of early, enthusiastically reported, clinical trials. Drugs are also prescribed at the cost of side effects, which are a leading cause of admissions to hospital, particularly for the elderly.
>
> Why does gardening seem to be so beneficial to health? It combines physical activity with social interaction and exposure to nature and sunlight. Sunlight lowers blood pressure as well as increasing vitamin D levels in the summer, and the fruit and vegetables that are produced have a positive impact on the diet. Working in the garden restores dexterity and strength, and the aerobic exercise that is involved can easily use the same number of calories as might be expended in a gym. Digging, raking, and mowing are particularly calorie intense; there is a gym outside many a window. The social interaction provided by communal and therapeutic garden projects for those with learning disabilities and poor mental health can counteract social isolation. Furthermore, it has also been reported that the social benefits of such projects

can delay the symptoms of dementia (an effect that might be partly due to the beneficial effects of exercise).[216]

Being around animals, as I noted earlier, improves health, and it's not just true for indoor pets. Keeping farm animals "can significantly boost your immunity," and the food they produce is much more nutritious. Eggs from backyard or family farm-raised chickens "have approximately 25 percent more vitamin E, 75 percent more beta carotene, and as much as 20 times the amount of omega-3 fatty acids as do factory farmed eggs,"[217] reports *Mother Earth News*. Similar statistics hold true for milk and dairy products and home-grown meat.[218]

"Nature bathing," as it's sometimes called, can also bring us closer to our creator. Or so say St. Augustine of Hippo and St. Josephine Bakhita, whom I trust. They are saints, after all! St. Augustine said,

Some people, in order to discover God, read books. But there is a great book: the very appearance of created things. Look above you! Look below you! Read it. God, whom you want to discover, never wrote that book with ink. Instead, He set before your eyes the things that He had made. Can you ask for a louder voice than that?

Likewise, St. Josephine: "Seeing the sun, the moon and the stars, I said to myself, 'Who could be the Master of these beautiful things?' I felt a great desire to see him, to know him and to pay him homage."

[216] Richard Thompson, "Gardening for health: a regular dose of gardening," *Yale Environment*, June 18, 2018, *National Library of Medicine*, https://www.ncbi.nlm.nih.gov/pmc/articles/PMC6334070/.

[217] Nicole Caldwell, "Benefits of Backyard Eggs," *Yale Environment*, March 14 2013, *Mother Earth News*, https://www.motherearthnews.com/homesteading-and-livestock/benefits-of-backyard-eggs/.

[218] Kristen Boye, "How keeping farm animals keeps you happier and healthier," *Yale Environment*, October 10, 2019, *Rethink Rural*, https://rethinkrural.raydientplaces.com/blog/how-keeping-farm-animals-keeps-you-happier-and-healthier.

So gardening is basically the best thing you can do to woke-proof your life. Why didn't I mention it first? Well, first I had to convince you how bad the woke agenda really is. Then I had to make sure you were solidly rooted in wisdom, that you weren't bankrolling too many woke companies, and that you and any children in your life were safe from woke influences, too. Then I had to ensure your home life was woke-proof and that you were spreading your NORMALcy to your friends and family and neighbors. So now, finally, here is your reward. Go play in the garden!

What's that? You don't know where to start? Meet Ashley Colby, an environmental sociologist from Chicago who now runs the Rizoma Field School in Uruguay, where she and her family "strive to be a living example of living sustainably while not sacrificing quality of life." At the school, they are exploring "how to find a way for humans to live well while making the Earth healthier and more habitable, both socially and ecologically."[219]

Ashley's book, *Subsistence Agriculture in the U.S. (Routledge-SCORAI Studies in Sustainable Consumption)*, examines "the somewhat hidden, unorganized population of household food producers ... who are hunting, fishing, gardening, keeping livestock and gathering and looks in depth at the way in which these practical actions have transformed their relationship to labor and land."

Ashley's work provides fascinating and surprising ways anyone can take more control of one of life's most basic tenants: food. According to Ashley, the United States is "the anomaly relative to most of the world" when it comes to locally produced food. In her extensive world travels, Ashely encountered little food markets everywhere, but in America, she considered that there is "maybe too much bias toward cool young hipsters doing community gardens," and perhaps "there are people who have always [produced much of their own food] who are left out of the conversation a little bit."

[219] https://rizomafieldschool.com/about/.

Ashley decided to find out and confirmed, "Urban people aren't inventing this.... Some of the people who are doing the most pro-environmental actions in the world are people who are conservationists, hunters, fishermen, small-scale gardeners, regenerative agriculture farmers, who are also very conservative, and very skeptical of climate change narratives."

That said, agricultural pursuits anywhere are transformative. Studies on the influence of urban community gardens have found that they help to improve people's knowledge of nutrition, increase their intake of fresh produce, beautify neighborhoods and foster "social connections, reciprocity, mutual trust, collective decision-making, civic engagement, and community building."[220]

"It was crazily easy to find subsistence food producers"
In her research, Ashely talked to people from all sorts of demographics who produced at least half of the food they consume themselves. Here's some of what she's learned along the way:

The process for my book involved identifying a population of what I called "subsistence food producers," which are people who are producing at least 50 percent of their own food. At first wasn't sure I'd be able to find enough people doing that in Chicago. I quickly found that it was possible, amazingly. I first found a few people through different email listservs — Advocates for Urban Agriculture, Chicago Chicken Enthusiasts. There were also urban agriculture activist groups who did things like a Chicago chicken coop tour, so they had their places listed, and I was able to find people that way. And I was able to do snowball sampling, where I'd ask people, "Do you know anyone else who does this?"

It was crazily easy to find people; And this was in 2015. I couldn't believe how easy it was to find people, and I'm sure it's

---

[220] "Research & Benefits of Community Gardens," *NC State*, https://nccommunitygardens.ces.ncsu.edu/resources-3/nccommunitygardens-research/.

grown since then. I had three groups in my interviews — urban, rural, and suburban — which was really good.

"You can be a subsistence food producer anywhere"

You can be a subsistence food producer anywhere. Obviously, the city people had space limitations. I wondered if people would be able to get to subsistence level in the city, and basically, they got to that level through some sort of combination of backyard gardening, community gardening, and then they did a lot of bartering and trading with people in rural areas. A lot of the urban people I interviewed had some kind of understanding or informal economic exchange with actual organic farmers, where they would trade eggs for vegetables, or something like that, because having chickens in your backyard takes less space than growing a vegetable garden in terms of yield. So the urban people would overproduce on something and exchange it for a CSA [Community Supported Agriculture] box or something like that, and that got them to subsistence level.

I make the argument that basically, early on in the Industrial Revolution, we were separated from our more traditional style of community where people work in the home, their work is more under their own control, they have more control over their means of production and their own subsistence. During the Industrial Revolution, work and community and connection to nature and control over what you do with your own work became alienated from the source. What I found was the rural people, a lot of them, have been doing this and never really lost that connection. They kept that through time — it was common to hunt, to fish, to provide for yourself to some extent.

"They became re-enchanted with nature"

But the urban people were coming to it for the first time and didn't necessarily go into it thinking, "I want to re-embrace nature," or anything like that. A lot of them didn't even do it for environmental reasons. They just thought, "I don't trust the food in the store," or, "It's not healthy enough for my family."

A lot of people got radicalized by becoming a parent and wondering *what's in this food, I don't know what's in this, I don't want to feed it to my family, and I don't trust labeling.* Then they got into it and started self-producing, and there's this process by which they became re-enchanted with nature fundamentally, but nature in a cultivated garden.

Caring a lot about the interaction between how you produce food and not introducing negative externalities like pouring a bunch of chemicals on it, because that's what you were trying to avoid from the beginning. And then getting a better sense of how nature works by working with it to produce food for yourself.

"Networks started to form"

And then a weird thing happened which I was totally not expecting to find.

People who are relatively new to this kind of thing of course were seeking help. I just assumed they would read books or something and kind of figure it out on their own, but they were forming friendships with other people who were either newbies or people who had done it before.

There's an anecdote in the book where someone told me they had started a compost pile in a chicken coop in their city lot, and their neighbors could see it through their three-foot chainlike fence.

The neighbors were recent immigrants from the Caribbean, and they said, "This is all the stuff we used to do where I'm from," and they started talking shop about how the compost pile works, and how do you over-winter them, and all this stuff, and the guy I was interviewing said, "Without this garden, we never would have met this neighbor, and now we're sharing tips and exchanging things."

Networks started to form. I call them "practitioner networks," but basically it's people who are just talking shop about chickens or gardening or whatever, and they start to form friendships, and then they start to exchange things — do you have extra this? I have extra that, let's exchange informally — and it all works out in the end, this non-formal bartering, like a gift economy almost. It blossoms from there.

"They are able to lean on those networks"

One event that happens every year, it's pretty interesting, is called the Advocates for Urban Agriculture Livestock Expo. It's a free event put on by this organization, and people bring their different livestock to tell other people how well keeping livestock works in the city.

People come and they try to wrap their heads around chickens versus ducks versus rabbits. You can keep all these things. There are different regulations for different animals and ways to process them to keep it legal. People are just talking shop, and it was just so cool, because in Chicago especially, there is just so much strife on different parameters, even before the pandemic — political, race, so many different ways in which people separate themselves — and it was so cool to walk into a place to see people being able to connect over something simple and practical.

Then I saw those connections develop over time into friendships and networks that were practical, informal economies, and during the pandemic, some people reported back to me that they were exchanging things and they knew who had what in the middle of any kind of supply-chain crisis; they were like, "at least I know Barb has eggs, and I'll be able to exchange with her for cheese," or whatever. They are able to lean on those networks whenever any sort of disruption happens.

My sense in Chicago especially, though, is that it has to be one-on-one, building trust relationships. I don't trust you necessarily because you're on the Chicken Enthusiast list or whatever, but if I met you in person and I had a good exchange with you, then now you're an asset. You can do a minimum, viable relationship building by just having one exchange and see how it goes and build from there.

"There are multiple benefits of doing any amount of self-production"
You don't have to get to even subsistence level of food production. There are multiple benefits of doing some small amount, of not food even. It could be craft production. Even just learning to do things with your hands. Sewing things or fixing things or crafting things or doing home repairs. Any amount of self-production gives you more sovereignty, gives you a sense of meaning and connection to the material world, and fundamentally a better understanding of nature, and then, sometimes, it also connects you to a community of people who are interested in doing that same kind of thing.

People who are more resilient and more sovereign — I don't think there's any real downside to self-sufficiency.

A lot of people will say, "It's so unrealistic. You expect people to all become farmers." No, I'm saying something like just have a few chickens in your backyard in the city. Even to go to a local orchard after they've done their main harvest and get their secondary harvest that isn't as pretty and turn that into applesauce is a process that is fun for you, it's fun for kids, it helps you become more sovereign, it connects you to the local farmer.

There's just a lot of ways to participate in small-scale production or home production, craft production, whatever you want to call it, and there are so many stacked benefits of doing that kind of thing.

"Humans cannot be separated from their environment"

I argue this a lot — humans cannot be separated from their environment if we want to have a robust environmentalism. A lot of the environmentalist movement now basically thinks humans are necessarily destructive, they need to be separated from nature, they need to be put in cities, and then what ends up happening is you externalize all the environmental problems, and people don't see them, and they just think they go away, but they don't.

Whereas people who are actively managing their landscapes, in the book I called this "ecological embeddedness," if they're involved in their landscape, they're not going to do these externalized practices as much, like using excess chemicals or overhunting or overfishing, if it's their environment that they rely on to live. The ones who are embedded in their environment are the ones who are going to be making the best environmental choices, of course.

A lot of people have it in their head that the only way change can happen is from the top down and that they have to pull on the levers of power, but I do think people have power, the masses of people, we all do have massive amounts of sovereignty. That will make an impact, not only in your daily life, but in the aggregate too.

Some people critique that and say, "Protect yourself," but what else are you going to do? Things are really bad. You can try to do politics, but in the meantime, I have kids to feed. I want them to eat healthy food. If I don't know where to get that, I'm going to make it. And that's a lot of people in my networks. "At least I can control this" is the mindset.

You don't have to agree politically to exchange some eggs and vegetables with your neighbor. When we come together, we realize, we all just want our children to eat well, we all just want to connect with nature and have meaning in our lives and meaningful work, and I think deep down everybody knows that and realizes the power of these virtues, more or less.

Let me introduce you to Brett Markham, author of *Mini Farming: Self-Sufficiency on ¼ Acre* and several other books.[221] Brett seems to be about the most woke-proof person there is, and he's been that way since long before "woke" was a concept.

Brett asserts on his website that "self-sufficiency is freedom — it is choice. The more of your own needs that you can meet independent of a volatile employment market or fluctuating food prices, the more choices you have."

"More time with those who matter most to you"
Following Brett's method, mini-farming is undertaken with "conscientious efforts ... to adopt methods and materials that minimize costs and labor while maximizing productivity." In answering the question "Why self-sufficiency?" Brett writes,

> If you are able to produce a substantial amount of your own food, and stop paying others for your bread, beer and wine, that can make a difference in the need to work a second job or allow a spouse to stay home and homeschool children. It can increase the quality of your life by giving you time with those who matter the most to you.

Fortunately for us, Brett is generous with his time and wisdom. Inspired by his wonderful books and other writings, I interviewed him and gained much more than knowledge about growing my own food.

As we've said over and over, it seems you can't do much in modern life without politics being infused in it. Most people don't want to live with a radical agenda being forced on them and all the ensuing distress. The way Brett lives, it seems as though he can insulate and safeguard himself from the fighting. He uses the Serenity Prayer on his blog, noting, especially during the COVID-19 pandemic, how if you rely on yourself,

---

[221] Brett L. Markham, *Mini Farming: Self-Sufficiency on ¼ Acre* (Skyhorse Publishing, 2010).

then you can choose to participate in the world or not. I asked him for his thoughts on all this, and what his experience has been like living this way in New Hampshire. He told me this:

> To a large extent, we have a choice in what we expose ourselves to and how we evaluate what we see. There's a famous set of books called *Dune* by a guy named Frank Herbert, and he said something that I think is really profound in that book, and the idea is that fear is the mind-killer. If you think about fear, how it was used during the COVID pandemic, fear was used to inspire compliance, even with things that didn't necessarily make a lot of sense. It was also used as a basis for creating in-groups and out-groups. People would feel fully justified on the basis of fear treating other people in a less-than-human way. You have the dual situation where fear takes away your critical factor, much like hypnosis does. That's how hypnosis works, by bypassing the critical factor. Fear, therefore, can be used to justify almost any action, no matter how outrageous; it completely removes morality from the equation.
>
> The first thing my wife and I do is, we don't watch news. We don't even have TV. We still can get news over the Internet or what have you, but we even make a practice of limiting that. Because most "news" is really not news. I got rid of the TV way back in 1996 because it was upsetting me so much. They would report something I'd seen with my own eyes, and what they would report was not what I saw. Even the choice of what is or is not reported, even the words used to describe it are all a way to try to bypass the critical factor or to limit your range of thinking.

"The credibility is always on the side of the left, because they control everything"
Most of what would be considered traditional news agencies today are what would be called "left-wing," but you can see the

same thing on the right. For example, when it came to the COVID vaccinations — and I have a background in micro and molecular biology, so I have a good background to judge the truth of these things — *anybody who didn't want to get vaccinated was trying to kill grandma. These are evil people, it would be okay to kill them, right?* You even saw an open wish that anybody who didn't get the vaccine would just die. On the other hand, if you were to go to a lot of right-wing sites, you would have seen a belief that this thing was meant to be a depopulation shot. That it was intended to kill people. I'm sure it did kill some people, but I don't think that was its intent or that it was *designed* to kill.

The problem you run into is that credibility is always on the side of the left, because they own everything, and they can control what most people see. If you're on the right, you have to be beyond perfectly accurate, or else anything that you say that can be debunked will completely ruin what you have to say.

Address things at a level of the things people are concerned about
Obviously, people who purchase Brett's books and read his blogs and watch YouTube videos already are, like myself, intrigued by his lifestyle and have likely been exposed to it in some form. They know how good and rewarding and fulfilling and delicious and nutritious and good it can be. But if he's talking to someone in a center city or a suburb, where they go past a Walmart and a Home Depot and a this and a that, and they consume media on their phone and their TV, and they never have a moment's silence — how does he get through to someone like that? They'd probably say, "I don't want to garden. That's dirty and gross. I'll just go to the store." How does he get somebody to take that first step, who's never even considered it and is perhaps turned off by the concept?

Everybody has something that concerns them, and most people will reveal what's important to them within sixty seconds of talking to them. Some people are concerned about insecticides, "forever chemicals," things of that nature. And that's not really based on one's political status; it's mostly just based on one's awareness. And this is a real issue. Some people are aware, for example, that testosterone rates are falling so quickly in the Western world, that by 2050, we won't be able to reproduce without assistance. That's basically an extinction-level event here. Joe the Bodybuilder, for instance, is concerned about his testosterone for no other reason than helping his muscles get bigger. And you've got people who are having difficulty with conception now. They want to have babies, but their husband's swimmers don't swim the way they should. You have practical, real-life issues, and a lot of people are concerned about these things, and you can talk to them and say, "Look, one way you can address this is by taking control of this yourself." Because you can trust yourself not to lie about what's in your food. And so, you can address it at the level of the things that people are concerned about.

A far less strenuous method of small-scale farming
Some people just don't care. There's a class of people that their food purchases are based on calories per dollar. They're always going to be buying lots of Little Debbie cakes, because those are a good calorie-dollar deal. But increasingly, and I think especially as people get a little older, they become aware of the importance of what they put in their bodies and what it means for them. I think it's easy to talk to people about it, but there's a hurdle. And the hurdle is effort. What they imagine when they think of a garden is grandma's garden, where grandpa went out there, and for three days straight did nothing but manhandle a rototiller. And it looks like an insane amount of work. So what you do instead is tell them, "I know this looks and sounds like something that's a lot of work, but, as you know, I've developed methods that allow you to do it part-time." I explain why you use a raised bed,

why you plant things close together. I talk to people about how you can do this in a way that is far more efficient of your time, far less strenuous in the long run, and therefore, it's not going to take a lot away from Netflix binges or whatever else is important.

It sounds funny when he says it like that, but it's true. That's a big theme of this book. People are so "busy" these days, they "don't have time" for a garden. Look at the things you're doing — the things we're all doing! We're on our phones, watching Netflix, sitting in traffic, standing in line. No wonder we "don't have time." Well, we do, of course. We're just using it poorly. Brett agrees:

I think the average person spends something like fifty-six hours a week on visual entertainment. That's more time than they spend at work. That's enough time to have an entire second life. I don't mean to establish a new identity in Brazil or something. I have a bunch of different degrees in a bunch of different things. And part of that is not because I'm particularly smart. A lot of that is just, instead of watching TV, I'll learn something. If you take that five hours a day or more that the average person is spending being visually entertained, and you invest that instead into learning a new thing, you add that up over time and you do that for twenty or thirty years, and you've gained the equivalent of who knows how much education.

My next book is probably going to be on solar things. And I needed to build a rack that would hold heavy batteries. So I learned how to weld! Right? You go to Harbor Freight and spend 120 bucks on a welder, buy some welding rods, look up a couple of books and a couple of videos on how to weld, and you teach yourself how to weld. But you can't do that if you're stuck in front of the tube.

Now, every time Brett needs something welded (which is probably fairly often), he can do it himself.

"Extended family gives you an insane amount of resilience"
I also like to emphasize how once you have a skill, you can, not quite barter with your neighbors and friends, but exchange mutually beneficial skills and knowledge. "If Brett knows how to weld, I'll ask him to weld something for me, and the next time he needs a wooden bench, I can provide him that, because I have woodworking skills." Things like that. Whenever you have a community of skilled, smart, generous, kind people, it really makes life a lot easier, simpler, and (I'd say) better.

It totally does. For me, my community is centered around a church in town. What will happen is, one of my fellow elders in the church, every year he does two batches of meat birds. My wife and I go over and we help him process those birds. We go over in the morning, and by the time lunchtime has arrived, we've got them all bagged. Because we've gotten good at it. So I go over with my table and my killing cone and my tabletop chicken plucker that I put in one of my books — the thing works great — and we get it done.

I help him out with that, and then last summer, I needed help with my roofing, and he helped me with my roofing. So being able to exchange skills and create a network, partly this is a substitute for the nuclear family, which people tend to think of as a basic family, but that's actually only been the case since the Industrial Revolution. The nuclear family was about creating mobile labor. Prior to that, most people grew up, lived, and died within five miles of the same spot; extended family was the thing. Extended family gives you an insane amount of resilience.

"The message of religion is timeless"
What a lot of people are doing, for example, where I live, and people belong to a church and exchange all this, is we build our own extended family through church. People could do that through other institutions, radio-controlled airplane hobbies

or things like that, but church is probably a better ideal for that simply because it has an intrinsic sort of value system that favors mutual aid. It also has a focus that is beyond politics. That's really important, because politics is so temporal and so focused on the news cycle. The message of religion is timeless. We're all mortal; we're all going to die. And when we are looking at the things we regret in our lives, it's really almost never anything having to do with the material world or politics or things we use to show off status to each other — any of that. It's all about our relationships. Religion, along with helping people form new relationships, also provides guidance for their current relationships. A lot of the religious points-of-view that are timeless and not politically focused are things that when you follow them give you a much more natural life.

A big part of a sane mindset is being able to identify things in ourselves like envy and to eradicate them to the best of our ability. A lot of politics is about taking other people's stuff. Waging war against your neighbor by another means [that's not "war" in the sense of firing guns]. If you are no longer envious of your neighbor, you don't resort to politics to take his stuff.

"A muskrat lives as a muskrat is intended to live"

You also won't be envious if you follow the lifestyle you advocate for, in which you take care of yourself and your family, you mind your own business, and when the need arises, you go help your neighbor pluck chickens, and he helps you with your roof. You're not in competition, you're all helping one another, and it's all very convivial and loving and caring and sharing, and that's how humans are supposed to live. It turns out that following the tenants of most religions results in biological advantages, too. If you treat others as you want to be treated, if you don't cheat on your wife, you're less likely to be stressed, you're less likely to have diseases. Science follows religion and vice versa. And the lifestyle you promote is good for you. Being outside gets you Vitamin D. Vegetables you grow yourself and eggs you raise in your own yard have much higher nutrient levels. All these beautiful things point to a Creator who laid out how to live as a human through obvious, self-evident, simple truths.

Once again, Brett and I are on the same page:

I wrote a book about that called *Modern Caveman*, because people grow disabled too early. If you look at animals in the wild, they don't have a period of decrepitude prior to death to any great degree. They will lose vitality for maybe the last year of their life. Until then they are very capable, and a lot of this is because a muskrat lives as a muskrat is intended to live. Humans are intended to get a certain amount of exercise and so forth.

Doing things like mini-farming modulates your labor. During certain times of the year, you're investing a lot of labor in it. Other times of year, you're not investing much labor at all. When you're putting in a new bed, you're double digging it, that can be kind of strenuous. But you're doing that for two hours, and the next day, you're not doing that. Instead, you're using a garden hoe. So you're having a natural ebb and flow of the strenuousness of your activity that allows you to use your body in the way it was intended.

Loneliness is a huge, huge problem. Our work environments are very artificial. You have to be careful with every word you say, not just in the political sense of contemporary politics and wokeness and things like that, but you have to be careful in terms of basically who's brown-nosing who and so forth, and it can be pretty complicated to navigate. And most of these jobs, you're sitting down for eight hours a day playing with a spreadsheet or writing software or something like that. At one point, I had a job writing medical billing software for a place and I was getting pretty rotund. It was a long drive there, right around a ninety-mile commute in a major metro area. I was getting up in the morning at 5:30, hitting the road, getting there at 8-ish or so, and then leaving there at 5, getting home at 7:30, and there's no way that that can be healthy, right? So of course I had to join a gym. But to counteract that much sitting, I found that I had to spend maybe three hours a day doing the gym. And obviously this was not very good for my home life. It was like, "Hey babe, I just got home, and I'm going to leave you now, and I'll be back after you're in bed, because I have to hit the gym." That's not conducive to a good home life.

"You can have a foot in both camps"
A lot of people can't, practically speaking, quit their job and go be a farmer overnight. They can usually do a lot more than they think, but there are understandable fears of the unknown, fear of being uncomfortable and uncertain, and our world has gotten to the point that most people rely on jobs and a lifestyle like the one you just described. So, what would Brett recommend for someone who is intrigued by this alternative lifestyle but is worried about making what they perceive to be "extreme" changes, or who want to take baby steps toward this way of life? What are smaller, immediate things people can do to get them on the path to a healthier, happier, more natural life?

I designed the whole *Self-Sufficiency on a ¼ Acre* system while I was working as a network engineer for an ISD [Information System Development company] eighty-nine miles away from where I lived. I had that exact circumstance, and so I designed that whole mini-farming system with the idea in mind that you would have a full-time job, so that you could do mini-farming in the evenings after you got home from work. You can have a foot in both camps; I designed it that way because that's how I had to do it.

The first thing you do, when you get home, instead of turning on whatever you're going to watch or typing on Facebook or whatever — designed to hijack our dopamine system — go outside for just one hour and start building your raised bed. The best time to start a garden is in the fall. If you go outside for just one hour a day, that's it. If you have to, set a timer on yourself. Start with: I'm going to double-dig this bed. Then, I'm going to lay this out, I'm going to put some concrete blocks around it, and so forth. Just that one hour of various exercise is going to be just as valuable to you as going to the gym. And, every hour you invest is going to bring you closer to being self-sufficient. You can get a lot of work done in that one hour. At the end of fall, after you've finished your last raised bed, you'll put in garlic and you'll spread carrot seeds. Everybody has trouble with carrots, but if you wait until the ground is just frozen, and you cast your carrot seeds where you want them, nature will bring them up exactly at the perfect time to outrun the weeds.

Nature is so smart!

Right! You can harness Mother Nature to work on your behalf. It's much easier. My advice to people is get out there, invest that one hour. And you only have to do it in the fall. Then, around Christmas time, order your seeds. A huge problem people run into is that you plant out your stuff that is susceptible to frost after Memorial Day, but the whole spring is rainy and wet and not suitable for working outside in a lot of cases. You may have two weeks between the time the rain stops and it's time to put in your garden. But if you've got it done in the fall, what happens is, you start things inside in February, and that way, you can plant many things that aren't susceptible to frost out in April. You don't have to knock yourself out, because the beds are already ready.

Another thing to be focused on when a person starts out is what I'll call just plain calories. Personally, I'm a low-carb guy. I don't do sugar, but for the average person to have peace of mind right now, maybe focus on growing things like potatoes, onions, carrots, parsnips — things that have a fair amount of caloric punch. Vegetables are only going to provide 10 percent of your calories. Things like Swiss chard are critical because of the vitamins, but you can't live on them. There's not enough energy content there. So I would tell somebody concerned about the future, as they're initially getting started, to focus on crops with high caloric intake.

Making a go of it

I ask Brett how practical would he say it is for somebody just starting out to be able to limit trips to the store to supplement their produce by doing what he describes on a quarter acre. Here's what he says:

It's extremely practical. It's very easy to do. The big thing that gets you is being able to put things away, i.e., freeze it — that's the biggest thing for most vegetables. What I do is set up an assembly line with my wife. It's just the two of us doing this. We have a big steamer that fits on the stove, and she has a timer. She'll put the vegetables in the steamer and steam it however long it needs to be steamed for, for blanching purposes. Right next to that we have a five-gallon bucket with a colander in it and that's got ice water in it. She dumps it straight into the ice water. That'll only stay in the ice water for between 30 and 60 seconds. I'll take it out of the ice water, I put it on clean towels and get the excess water off. Then I put another clean towel over the top of it to get the rest of the water off, and then I put it in bags I've already made for the vacuum sealer, and I pop it straight in those bags and vacuum-seal it. By the time I'm done vacuum-sealing, my wife has already dumped the next batch into the bucket with the ice water. By assembling-lining it like that, we have a system going where, in no time flat, in just a couple of hours, we can process a gargantuan number of vegetables.

Say you make yourself a couple of four-foot-by-sixteen-foot beds. In one of those beds you can plant half of it with, say, chard. You're going to grow a ton of chard. Chard shrinks down when you blanch it, but it doesn't shrink that much. You can easily put away fifty packages of chard. And we weigh them when we do them, so we know how many servings we have. So you can easily put away fifty servings of chard. Well, how many days a week are you eating chard? Maybe once a week, right? So I've literally gotten a year's supply of chard just from a four-foot-by-sixteen-foot raised bed. In the other half of that bed, I can grow some other vegetable like zucchini. You can put three zucchini plants. Out of those three zucchini plants, you can get fifty bags of servings for two. Then you've got your other bed. You can put broccoli in it, and get a fair amount of broccoli out of that bed. You'll get probably half-a-year's supply of broccoli. In the second half of that bed you'll plant tomatoes, and you'll grow the kind that climbs up a pole. On the backside of one of the other beds, you'll grow pole beans. If you plant just eight feet of pole beans — which takes just six inches of a bed — you'll have probably a hundred servings for two of pole beans.

You can basically have all the vegetables you need from two beds that are four-foot-by-sixteen foot. That's the whole secret with close planting. I'm just using the example of two beds to give you the idea of what the yields are like. If you're going out and spending an hour at the end of the day, after you've come home from your 9-to-5 job making TPS reports, and you've commuted home and just invest that one hour and do that every day or almost every day between the start of September and the middle of October, you're going to have more than just two raised beds.

You're going to have four or five, and so just from the investment of the first year and that first fall, you are easily going to have all the vegetables you need, plus extra. You're not going to have your core calories, but you are going to have all the vegetables you need.

"It puts the family within part of the rhythm of nature"
What I've done over time is planted raspberries, grapes, apples, pears. I don't eat a lot of those things because I restrict my carbs to fifty a day, but I can sell those. People want those. That gives me something that I can bring over to my church friend's place when I help slaughter chickens, and I can bring home some chickens that I didn't have to raise myself. You can do a lot with just those four beds. And there's no reason not to put in two more beds the next fall. Or maybe the next fall you build a chicken coop, so in the spring you can get yourself some egg-laying chickens. Every fall, you add to your garden.

An important thing too is that it adds to the dynamic of family life. It puts the family life within part of the rhythm of nature.

I told Brett how struck I was by the beauty of what he said. "Well, I'm glad," he replied:

My wife and I complement each other and help each other. She's not going to be dragging concrete blocks. She's five feet tall and weighs 115 pounds. She's not going to be doing that. She's also not going to be digging the beds. She's not heavy enough to get the fork in if she jumps on it. Some things are going to be my job. On the other hand, she is going to be perfect at other things. She's going to be doing her part, and I'm going to be doing my part, and we're going to work together to achieve a common goal that's outside of all of the stuff that would happen at a job, all of the stuff that's on the radio, and that's powerful.

Engaging kids, saving money
It's also such a positive thing for kids, too. Instead of plopping them down in front of an iPad to watch obnoxious cartoons or porn on TikTok, then

take them to the McDonald's drive-thru to eat garbage, they're outside, bonding with their parents, learning to work with their siblings and share, hearing stories from grandpa, and so forth. Brett concurs:

> People are lazy. It's natural for us to wish to accomplish something with the least possible effort. But that laziness of having a screen keep a kid out of our hair doesn't pay off in the long run. We really have to keep in mind that we have to engage kids. My father always kept me engaged — letting me help him fix cars, helping him with chickens, helping him with the garden, with some home-improvement project, whatever it was. All along, every step of the way, as I was helping him, I was learning things. I didn't necessarily always appreciate it, but later on, when I moved to my current house, I learned that it was missing foundation. They had poured some cement around the ground to make it look as if it had a foundation, but it was really rotten boards sitting on dirt. A lot of the foundation was located near the well, so I didn't bring in heavy equipment to do it, but because of what I had learned from my dad, I actually had the confidence to be able to put a foundation under it myself. I did call my dad a couple times to ask his advice, but I had the confidence to go get a cement mixer and be able to do all the things I needed to do to fix the problem. I had a car that sat for a while that needed new brakes. I had to replace the calipers and rotors on it. I was able to do it myself because I had helped my dad do that type of stuff a hundred times. And of course that saves a lot of money.
>
> When you feel effective, it makes you feel more fully like a person. That's a key advantage of doing anything like that, including raising your own food. You bust out that bag in January that you put away the previous July, and you feel something cool about that. The thing is, too, that relieves stress from you personally. That's something you don't have to worry about. The fewer things

you have to worry about, the less of an impact the fearmongering and woke madness will have on you.

"It's something a person can start while they're working the day job"
It's something a person can start while they're working the day job. And they never have to quit the day job, but over time, what happens is your attitude about the day job changes, as you add to your facilities. A lot of times people are spending a lot of their money on things they don't need anyway, but when your focus is on different things, like growing your own food and cooperating with your husband or wife, or you're going back and forth to your friend's house from church to do things with them, you find you need a lot less stuff. You might need tools, but these things are durable. They last a long time, so you don't have to buy them every year.

You find your actual needs become far fewer than they were before, and as your needs become less, and more and more of your needs are being supplied by you, you find that you have fewer monetary requirements. So maybe rather than taking that job that's two hours away, you can take a job that pays a little bit less that's closer. You need to have U.S. dollars, right, to pay your property taxes and stuff. You can't come in with a couple of chickens. They won't accept them. You have to go work for the man, but your attitude about working for the man is very different when your needs are fewer, and therefore, you aren't going to work those sixty hours a week to make partner, because you don't need to make partner. Your self-esteem is no longer tied up in your job title. That's a problem for a lot of people. If you live life in which your home is not just a hotel, but a cooperative enterprise, titles don't matter. A big part of the stress people face is completely artificial and induced by a system that didn't even exist two hundred years ago. We treat it as if it's existential, and permanent, and important, but it's not. What's important is our relationships with each other, because that is the forever stuff.

The Nutshell

Self-sufficiency offers a person a choice in how much he is subject to outside forces that may be contrary to his beliefs. Self-sufficiency is freedom; it's also satisfying and a way by which humans are able to become fully alive. It's also, of course, been linked to improving emotional health and physical well-being (notice a trend yet?), in addition to benefiting the earth.

Woke-Proof Ways

+ Start a garden; if not a garden, then grow *something*, one thing at least — tomatoes, a few peppers, even just a single mint plant on your windowsill — and cook with it.
+ Choose one thing in your life at a time that you pay someone else to do and learn to do it yourself. The next time your faucet turns leaky, determine to figure out how to fix it. Don't be afraid to ask for help!
+ Fix stuff and refurbish items instead of throwing them away. Story time: My mother discovered an old vanity in the attic that had been my grandmother's in the 1940s. We enjoyed sprucing it back up and involving friends in the project. We took paint chips to the local hardware store — a social hub in our town — where we were amazed by the skill of the paint technician who was able to match the antique colors to a T. We bought other supplies there, sought advice from the employees we know well (and got to know even better), and saw familiar faces with each trip. We went to a custom mirror-cutter in the next town to replace the broken one. My mother

relayed stories about my grandmother — who died when I was a baby — throughout the project. In the end, we had built something together that I will cherish forever, and which brings me joy and a flood of happy memories every time I see it.

Conclusion
Pray, Do Your Duty, and Win the Race

As you endeavor to put the knowledge I pray you've gained from this book into practice, I urge you to embrace woke-proofness first and foremost as a mindset of peace. Since wokeness is fundamentally a rejection of God, the primary objective of woke-proofing your life is to seal out the forces that seek to separate you from God and to fill your life with practices that bring you closer to Him.

Evil, woke forces are powerful and relentless, and so to woke-proof, you must pray always. St. Francis de Sales advises us, "The essence of prayer is not to be found in always being on our knees but in keeping our wills clearly united to God's will in all events. The soul which holds itself ready and open to yield itself obediently on any occasion, and which receives these occasions lovingly as sent by God, can do this even while sweeping the floor."

Pray to the Holy Spirit for understanding, that you remain alert to the things that weaken your relationship with God. Pray for the strength to heed the inspirations of the Spirit. Pray for fortitude when you'd really rather *not* do without some neat thing made by a woke corporation, and when you'd really rather *not* volunteer at the church picnic. Pray for patience as you explain the woke-proof lifestyle to a scoffing skeptic. (A useful quip from Flannery O'Connor to keep in your brainpocket: "The truth does not change according to our ability to stomach it emotionally.") And pray thanking God for the grace to do your duty and for the reward of peace and joy that He grants you and your loved ones for doing His will.

Woke-proofing our lives, we know, is a challenge, but it does get easier, especially as we lean on and learn from one another. And the tranquility thing is real. I sometimes explain the woke-proofing concept to people as a clip from a Looney Tunes cartoon that made a big impression on me as a kid: two characters get into a scrap. A fight cloud of dust and arms and legs and stars denoting *ouch!* commences. Then one of the characters — Bugs Bunny, if I had to guess — takes a big step outside of the scuffle and tiptoes away. The other character continues to fight with himself inside the fight cloud. We woke-proofers are Bugs Bunny in this scenario, and he's always the hero, isn't he?

When we step outside of the pointless woke fight cloud, we can see clearly. Unburdened by manufactured conflict, we are free to focus our lives on the things God has ordained, and not the distractions and turmoil perpetuated by man. We are able to anchor our lives in truth, beauty, and goodness that begets *more* truth, beauty, and goodness. I've witnessed, particularly in writing this book, how the more we seek virtue, the more God provides us opportunities to perform good works, the more we appreciate creation, the more virtuous people He puts in our lives, and so forth. Many of the people I interviewed throughout this book were connected through one another, and some revealed themselves through just the right, unbelievably timed circumstances. To map them all out would be to draw the most beautiful, intricate, miraculous tapestry!

As you journey along the woke-proof path, keep in mind that there are *always* alternatives to woke ways and that an entire army of NORMAL, woke-proof Americans is standing by to help you pursue them.

Godspeed.

For the time is coming when people will not endure sound teaching, but having itching ears they will accumulate for themselves teachers to suit their own likings, and will turn away from listening to the truth and wander into myths. As for you, always be steady, endure suffering, do the work of an evangelist, fulfil your ministry. For I am already on the point of being sacrificed; the time of my departure has come. I have fought the good fight, I have finished the race, I have kept the faith. Henceforth there is laid up for me the crown of righteousness, which the Lord, the righteous judge, will award to me on that Day, and not only to me but also to all who have loved his appearing. (2 Timothy 4:3–8)

Appendix 1

Following is a list of companies that publicly opposed Georgia's election integrity law or Florida's Parental Rights in Education Act (the "Don't Say Gay" bill) or support radical LGBTQIA+ and BLM campaigns, abortion, climate change, and other woke causes.

APPAREL

Abercrombie & Fitch
Adidas
Aritzia
Balenciaga
Banana Republic
Collina Strada
Converse
Deckers Brands (UGG, HOKA,
    Teva, Sanuk, and Koolaburra by
    UGG)
Dr. Martens
Everlane
Fabletics
Fashion Nova
Fossil
For Love and Lemons
Ganni

Gap
H&M
Hummel
Kate Spade
Kenneth Cole
Kohl's
Levi Strauss & Co.
Lululemon
Macy's
Madewell
Marc Jacobs
Nike
Nordstrom
Old Navy
Ovis
Pacsun
Patagonia
Popflex Active

Prabal Gurung
Puma
QVC
Ralph Lauren
Reebok
REI Co-Op
Richer Poorer
Saks Fifth Avenue/Off Fifth
Savage x Fenty, founded by
   Rihanna
SHEIN
Spanx
Stitch Fix
Tiffany & Co.
Tory Burch LLC
UnderArmour
Vans
Victoria's Secret
Warby Parker

BEAUTY
Anastasia Beverly Hills
Axe
Bath & Body Works
Billie
Biossance
Bliss
Body Shop
Boy Smells
ColourPop
Estee Lauder
Glossier
Harry's Inc.
Lipslut

Lush Cosmetics
Morphe
Olay (Oil of Olay)
Pacifica Beauty
Procter & Gamble/Pantene
Sephora
Unilever (Dove, Caress, Degree)

ENERGY
Duke Energy
Eaton (electrical and industrial
   power management company)
Equinor
GE
Hess Corporation

ENTERTAINMENT
Bravado (music and fashion
   merchandising)
Civic Entertainment Group (mar-
   keting and PR)
Comcast NBC Universal
Creative Artists Agency (talent and
   sports agency)
Disney
Eventbrite (ticketing website)
ESPN (Disney)
Hulu
Jazz Lincoln Center
Live Nation Entertainment
Major League Baseball
Major League Soccer
NASCAR
NCAA

NBA
NFL
NHL
Netflix
Paramount
Sonos (sound systems)
Sony Interactive Entertainment
Toms
Viacom
Warner Media
Ubisoft (video games)

BUSINESS AND FINANCIAL
Amalgamated Bank
Bain & Company (consulting
    firm)
Bank of America
Bank of New York Mellon
Berkshire Partners
Blackrock (financial services
    company notorious for ESG
    investing)
Boston Consulting Group (con-
    sulting firm)
Broadridge Financial Solutions
Cambridge Associates (global
    investment)
Capital One
Citigroup
Credit Karma
Climb Credit (lender)
Cowboy Ventures (investor)
Deutsche Bank
Deloitte

Discover Financial Services
    (Discover Card)
EY (consulting firm)
FirstMark Capital
General Catalyst (venture capital
    firm)
Goldman Sachs
H&R Block
IBM
JPMorgan Chase
Khosla Ventures (venture capital
    firm)
Loop Capital Markets (investment
    bank)
M&T Bank
Mastercard
Merrill Lynch
PwC (PricewaterhouseCoopers,
    consulting services)
Prudential Financial
Raymond James
ScotiaBank
Slow Ventures (investment firm)
Smith & Company (advisory firm)
Sound Ventures (technology
    investor)
Spark Capital (venture capital firm)
Synchrony (credit cards)
That Game Company
Trillium Asset Management
T. Rowe Price (global investment)
Truist Financial
Vanguard (investment advisor)
Wells Fargo

FOOD AND DRINK
Absolut Vodka
Anheuser-Busch/Budweiser
Ben & Jerry's
Bloomin Brands (Outback Steakhouse, Carrabba's Italian Grill, Bonefish Grill, etc.)
BrewDog
Burger King
Chick-Fil-A
Chipotle
Chobani
Coca-Cola Company
Door Dash
Ferrara Candy Company (Nutella, Tic Tac, and Kinder brands)
Gatorade
General Mills
Giant Eagle
Grubhub
Harris Teeter
Impossible Foods
Intelligentsia Coffee
Jeni's Ice Cream
Just Eat Takeaway
Kellogg Company
KIND
Kraft Heinz
Kroger
La Colombe
Mars North America
McDonald's
Miller Brewing Company
Misfits Market

Molson Coors Beverage Company
Mondelez International
Nabisco
Pepsi/Frito-Lay/Cracker Jack/ Cracker Jill
Quaker Oats
Sodexo Magic (food and facilities management)
Starbucks
Sweetgreen
Tito's Vodka
Thrive Market
Whole Foods
Wrigley

HEALTH CARE AND FITNESS
Amerisource Bergen (drug company)
Bayer
Biogen (biotechnology company)
Blue Cross Blue Shield
Bristol Myers Squibb (pharmaceuticals)
Cardinal Health
Cigna
CVS Health
Fitbit
Gilead Sciences
Johnson & Johnson
McKesson Corporation
Merck
Ohio Health
Peloton
Planet Fitness

Pfizer
PreDxion
United Health Group

HOME, PETS, GEAR, AND TOYS
Burton Snowboards
CODAworx
    (commissioned art hub)
Etsy
Hasbro (toys and games: Nerf,
    Transformers, Play-Doh, Peppa
    Pig)
Lego
Legoland (home of the world's
    largest Lego Pride parade)
Lucozade
Mattel (Barbie and American Girl
    Doll)
Mattress Firm
Michaels (crafts)
Newell Brands (consumer goods:
    Elmer's Glue, Yankee Candle,
    Rubbermaid, Coleman, Sharpie)
Paper Source
Petsmart
Seventh Generation (laundry/
    cleaning/baby products)
Stanley Black & Decker
Steelcase (furniture)
Williams Sonoma

INSURANCE
American International Group, Inc.
    (AIG)
Erie Insurance

Geico
Metlife
Mutual of Omaha
Progressive Insurance
State Farm
USAA

MEDIA
Condé Nast
Hachette
Harper Collins
Macmillan
New York Times (and almost every
    other news outlet in Western
    countries)
Penguin Random House
Simon & Schuster
Vice Media Group
Vox Media

ONLINE SERVICES
Asana
Bumble
Buzzfeed
Constant Contact
Discord
Docusign
Dropbox
Duolingo
Ebay
Evite
Facebook
GoDaddy
Goodreads

Google
Indeed
Instacart
LinkedIn
Mailchimp
Match Group (Match.com, Tinder, OkCupid, etc.)
Momentive/Survey Monkey
Nextdoor (app)
PayPal
Pinterest
Reddit
Shopify
Slack
Skillshare
Snap (Snapchat, Spectacles, Bitmoji)
Softbank
Strava (running app)
Stripe (payment processing)
Square (mobile payment)
TikTok
Vistaprint
Yahoo Inc.
Yelp
Zola (online wedding sites)
Zoom Video Communications
Zynga Games
23andMe (DNA testing)

REAL ESTATE
CBRE
Cushman & Wakefield
JLL
Newmark
Redfin
Zillow

TECH
Adobe
Accenture (IT services and consulting)
Alphabet, Inc. (technology conglomerate and holding company of Google)
Apple
AT&T
Best Buy
BMC Software
Box Inc. (content cloud)
Cisco (technology company)
Dell Technologies
HP
Intel
Insight Partners (global software investor)
Intuit
Leidos (energy technology)
Lockheed Martin
McKinsey & Company (consulting firm)
Microsoft Corporation
Oracle (software products, including Java)
Plaid (financial services app)
Salesforce, Inc. (software company)
SAP (software)

ServiceNow (software company)
T-Mobile
Twilio (communication technology company)
Verizon
VMWare (cloud computing company)
Warburg Pincus (private equity investment firm)
Zendesk (software company)

TRAVEL
Airbnb
Alaska Airline
American Airlines
Boeing
Delta Airlines
Expedia
Chevron
Four Seasons Hotels & Resorts
Hilton
Hyatt Group Hotels & Resorts
IHG Hotels & Resorts
JetBlue
Lyft
Marriott
TripAdvisor
Uber

United Airlines
Virgin Atlantic

VEHICLES
Advance Auto Parts
American Honda Motor Company
Audi/Volkswagen
Ford
General Motors
Jeep
Rivian

OTHER
Amazon
Dollar Tree
Emerson Collective (for-profit charity that funds the *Atlantic* and other properties)
Office Depot
Otherwise Incorporated (branding, graphic design, marketing)
Family Dollar
Lowe's
Target
Trout Unlimited
Walmart
WeWork (coworking space)
YouTube

Appendix 2

Following is a list of companies with conservative values and companies that keep out of culture wars altogether. This list was compiled by Dave Seminara, and added to it is a list that the Concerned Women for America Legislative Action Committee granted me permission to include.

APPAREL
Academy Sports
Alexo Athletica
Altar'd State (Pro-Life Apparel)
Carly Jean Los Angeles
Culture of Life 1972
Dillard's
Jockey
These Three Boutique
Wrangler

BEAUTY
Elevate Beauty
EverBe
Hope Beauty
Jeremy's Razors
Makeup America

BUSINESS AND FINANCIAL
Berkshire Hathaway
Lending Tree
Strive Asset Management

ENERGY
Shell Oil

ENTERTAINMENT
CBN
Dollywood
UFC
WWE
DailyWire+
Great American Family
PureFlix
Six Flags

FOOD AND DRINK
Albertson's
Black Rifle Coffee
Bubba Gump Shrimp
Caribou Coffee
Food City
Good Ranchers
Goya Foods
In-N-Out
Nathan's Famous hot dogs
Safeway
Sheetz
Seven Weeks Coffee
The Holy Roast Coffee
Waffle House

HEALTH CARE AND FITNESS
Equinox Fitness/SoulCycle
On Running

HOME, PETS, GEAR, AND TOYS
Ashley Furniture
Bass Pro Shops
Hobby Lobby
Home Depot
Menards
MyPillow

INSURANCE
Buffer Insurance

REAL ESTATE
Berkshire Hathaway

TECH
CharityMobile
Patriot Mobile

About the Author

Teresa Mull's writing has appeared in the *New York Times*, the *Baltimore Sun*, the *Miami Herald*, the *New York Post*, the *American Conservative*, and many other publications. Teresa is currently an assistant editor of the *Spectator World*, a policy adviser for education at the Heartland Institute, and part-time editor of the *Philipsburg Journal*, where her beloved terrier, Pitkin, has a weekly advice column. Her pastimes include country drives, trap shooting, outdoor exercise, and befriending off-beat characters. She collects her writings at TheAmericanFrontPorch.com.

CRISIS Publications

Sophia Institute Press awards the privileged title "CRISIS Publications" to a select few of our books that address contemporary issues at the intersection of politics, culture, and the Church with clarity, cogency, and force and that are also destined to become all-time classics.

CRISIS Publications are direct, explaining their principles briefly, simply, and clearly to Catholics in the pews, on whom the future of the Church depends. The time for ambiguity or confusion is long past.

CRISIS Publications are contemporary, born of our own time and circumstances and intended to become significant statements in current debates, statements that serious Catholics cannot ignore, regardless of their prior views.

CRISIS Publications are classical, addressing themes and enunciating principles that are valid for all ages and cultures. Readers will turn to them time and again for guidance in other days and different circumstances.

CRISIS Publications are spirited, entering contemporary debates with gusto to clarify issues and demonstrate how those issues can be resolved in a way that enlivens souls and the Church.

We welcome engagement with our readers on current and future CRISIS Publications. Please pray that this imprint may help to resolve the crises embroiling our Church and society today.

•